Canon EOS R5 Mark II

Photography Handbook

The Concise Guide to Capturing Stunning Photos and Videos with Precision and Creativity

Hector Nickie

Copyright © 2024 **Hector Nickie**

All Rights Reserved

This book or parts thereof may not be reproduced in any form, stored in any retrieval system, or transmitted in any form by any means—electronic, mechanical, photocopy, recording, or otherwise—without prior written permission of the publisher, except as provided by United States of America copyright law and fair use.

Disclaimer and Terms of Use

The author and publisher of this book and the accompanying materials have used their best efforts in preparing this book. The author and publisher make no representation or warranties with respect to the accuracy, applicability, fitness, or completeness of the contents of this book. The information contained in this book is strictly for informational purposes. Therefore, if you wish to apply the ideas contained in this book, you are taking full responsibility for your actions.

Printed in the United States of America

TABLE OF CONTENTS

TABLE OF CONTENTS III
FIRST THING FIRST 14
CHAPTER 1 15
INTRODUCTION 15
    OVERVIEW OF CANON EOS R5 MARK II AND ITS ACCESSORIES 15
    HANDLING 16
    THE CANON EOS R5 MARK II'S AUTOFOCUS 18
    EYE CONTROL 18
    FRAME RATE 19
    PRE-CONTINUOUS SHOOTING 20
    DUAL SHOOTING (STILLS AND VIDEOS) 20
    HIGH ISO 21
    PROCESSING IN THE CAMERA 22
    IMAGE STABILIZATION 23
    ACCESSORIES 23
        Best All-in-one Lens for Canon EOS R5 Mark II 23
        Why does this Lens Stand Out? Why does it Work Well with the Canon EOS R5 Mark II? 24
    WHAT ARE THE BEST PRIME TELEPHOTO LENSES FOR THE CANON EOS R5 MARK II? 26
        Key Features: 26
        What's Great About It? 27
        Next Up: 27
        Key Features: 27
        What's Great About It? 28
        Next Up: 28
        Key Features: 28
        What's Great About It? 29
        Key Features: 30
        What's Great About It? 30
    BEST TELEPHOTO ZOOM LENSES FOR CANON EOS R5 MARK II 30
        Key Features: 31
        What's Great About It? 31
        Ideal for: 32
        Key Features: 32
        What's Great About It? 33
        Ideal For: 33
    THE BEST STANDARD PRIME LENSES FOR THE CANON EOS R5 MARK II 36
    COMPARISON: CANON RF 50MM F/1.2 L USM VS CANON RF 50MM F/1.8 STM 38
    BEST STANDARD ZOOM LENSES FOR CANON EOS R5 MARK II 39
        Canon RF 24-70mm f/2.8 L IS USM Lens 39

    Canon RF 28-70mm f/2 L USM Lens 40
  COMPARISON: CANON RF 24-70MM F/2.8 L IS USM VS CANON RF 28-70MM F/2 L USM 41
    Aperture: 41
    Focal Range: 41
    Portability: 41
    Final Thoughts: 41
  BEST WIDE-ANGLE ZOOM LENSES FOR CANON EOS R5 MARK II 42
    1. Canon RF 15-35mm f/2.8 L IS USM 42
    2. Canon RF 14-35mm f/4 L IS USM 42
    3. Canon RF 10-20mm f/4 L IS STM (Hypothetical) 43
    Conclusion 44
  BEST WIDE-ANGLE PRIME LENSES FOR CANON EOS R5 MARK II 44
    Canon RF 16mm f/2.8 STM Lens 44
    Canon RF 35mm f/1.8 Macro IS STM Lens 45
    Canon RF 24mm f/1.8 Macro IS STM Lens 46
  BEST PORTRAIT LENSES FOR CANON EOS R5 MARK II 47
    Canon RF 85mm f/1.2 L USM Lens 47
    Canon RF 135mm f/1.8 L IS USM Lens 48
  BEST MACRO LENSES FOR CANON EOS R5 MARK II 49
    Canon RF 100mm f/2.8 L Macro IS USM Lens 49
    Canon RF 85mm f/2 Macro IS STM Lens 50

CHAPTER 2 52

INITIAL SETUP: CHARGING THE BATTERY AND ATTACHING THE LENS 52

  CHARGING THE BATTERY 52
  CHARGE TIME AND CONDITIONS 54
  PRE-CHARGING REQUIREMENTS 54
  SAFETY AND BATTERY MAINTENANCE TIPS 54
  PUTTING IN THE BATTERY 55
  REMOVING THE BATTERY 56

CHAPTER 3 57

CAMERA SETUP 57

    Step 1: Inserting the Battery and Memory Card 57
    Step 2: Charging the Battery 57
    Step 3: Attaching the Lens 57
    Step 4: Turning on the Camera 57
    Step 5: Choosing Language and Time Zone 57
    Step 6: Setting the Time and Date 57
    Step 7: Configuring the Camera's Settings 58
    Step 8: Customizing the Quick Control Screen 58
  THE SET-UP MENU 58
    Set-up Menu Overview for the Canon EOS R5 II 58

Goals of the Set-up Menu	59
SET-UP MENU OPTIONS	59
Amber-Coded Set-up Menu Options for Canon EOS R5 II	59
Important Note	60
Record Functions+Card/Folder Sel.	60
Set-up 1 Menu: Card and Folder Management for Canon EOS R5 II	60
Storage and Playback Separation	61
Handling Still Photos on the Canon EOS R5 II	62
Conclusion	63
Managing Movie Clips on the Canon EOS R5 II	63
Conclusion	64
Default Settings	64
Customization Options	64
Customization Tips	65
Card Priority Settings for Video Recording	65
Tips for Effective Use	66
Creating and Managing Folders on Your Canon EOS R5 II	66
Tips for Folder Management	67
Viewing Available Folders on Your Canon EOS R5 II	67
Tips for Folder Management	68
Selecting or Creating a Folder on Your Canon EOS R5 II	68
Tips for Effective Folder Management	69
Changing a Folder Name on Your Canon EOS R5 II	69
Tips for Naming Folders	70
Exiting the Folder Management	70
Tips for Creative Folder Naming	70
Benefits of Organizing Folders	71
File Numbering	71
File Numbering System on the Canon EOS R5 II	71
Conclusion	72
Movie Clip Numbering	73
Format Card	77
Auto Rotate	78
Add Movie Rotate Information	78
Language	80
System Frequency	80
Help Text Size	81
Beep	82
Volume	82
Screen Brightness/Viewfinder Brightness	83
Screen/Viewfinder Color Tone	83
Fine-Tune Viewfinder Color Tone	84
Screen and Viewfinder Display	84

UI Magnification	*85*
HDMI Resolution	*85*
Cooling Fan Settings	*86*
Shutter at Shutdown	*86*
Sensor Cleaning	*87*
Power Saving	*87*
Reset Camera	*88*
Custom Shooting Mode (C1–C3)	*88*
Save/Load Camera Settings On Card (R5 II only)	*90*
Battery Information	*90*
Registering Your Battery Packs	*91*
Copyright Information	*92*
Manual/Software URL	*92*
Certification Logo Display	*93*
Firmware	*93*

CHAPTER 4 .... **94**

WORKING WITH THE AF SYSTEM **94**

AF OPERATION	94
ONE-SHOT AF	94
SERVO AF	95
MANUAL FOCUS	95
AF METHOD	96
FACE+TRACKING AF	96
1. Pick a Subject to Detect	*97*
2. Enable/Disable Eye Detection	*97*
3. Faces Detected	*97*
4. Set Initial Focus Point	*98*
SPOT AF	98
Moving the Focus Point	*99*
Resetting the Focus Point	*99*
Alternative AF Modes	*99*
Recommendations	*100*
1-POINT AF	100
Expanded AF Area Benefits	*100*
Tips for Using Expanded AF Area	*100*
EXPAND AF AREA	101
Expanded AF Area Details	*101*
Tips for Using Expanded AF Area	*101*
Benefits of a Larger Focus Area	*102*
How to Use a Larger Focus Area	*102*
Tips for Success	*102*
Key Features of Expand AF Area	*103*

    How to Use Expand AF Area Effectively *103*
    Tips for Optimal Performance *103*
  EXPAND AF AREA: AROUND 104
    Key Features of Expand AF Area: Around *104*
    When to Use This Mode *104*
    Tips for Using Expand AF Area: Around *104*
  ZONE AF 105
    Key Features of Zone AF *105*
    When to Use Zone AF *105*
    Tips for Using Zone AF *105*
  LARGE ZONE AF (VERTICAL)/(HORIZONTAL) 105
    Key Features of Large Zone AF *106*
    When to Use Large Zone AF *106*
    Tips for Using Large Zone AF *106*
    Key Features of Expand AF Area *107*
    When to Use Expand AF Area *107*
    Tips for Using Expand AF Area *107*
    Key Features of Zone AF *108*
    When to Use Zone AF *108*
    Tips for Using Zone AF *108*
  MAGNIFIED VIEW 109

CHAPTER 5 111

AUTOFOCUS MENU 111

  AF MENU OPTIONS 111
  AF OPERATION 111
    Subject to Detect *111*
    Eye Detection *112*
    Action Priority *112*
  MF PEAKING SETTINGS 112
    Focus Guide *113*
    AF-Assisted Beam Firing *113*
    Lens Electronic MF *114*

CHAPTER 6 115

EXPLORING CANON EOS R5 MARK II'S VIDEO CAPABILITIES 115

  INTRODUCTION TO THE R5 MARK II'S 8K VIDEO RECORDING 115
  THE MOVIE SHOOTING MENU 116
    Movie Recording Size *116*
  HIGH FRAME RATE 117
    Main Recording Format: *117*
    RAW Movies *118*
  RECORDING PROXY MOVIES 118

MOVIE CROPPING 118
DUAL SHOOTING (STILL PHOTOS AND MOVIES) 119
SOUND RECORDING 119
   Four-Channel Recording *119*
AUDIO FORMAT: 120
   Audio Settings: *120*
RECORDING LEVEL 121
WIND FILTER 121
ATTENUATOR 122
MICROPHONE DIRECTIONALITY 122
AUDIO STATUS 122
HDR MOVIE MODE 122
SHADOW COMPENSATION 122
SATURATION 123
LIMITING THE MAXIMUM BRIGHTNESS. 123
TIME-LAPSE MOVIE 124
SELECT [MAIN REC.]. FORMAT]. 126
MOVIE SELF-TIMER 127
TALLY LAMP 128
PRE-RECORDING SETTINGS 128
SELECT [RECORDING TIME] 129
RECORD THE MOVIE. 129
IS (IMAGE STABILIZER MODE) 129
   IS Mode *129*
   Movie Digital IS *130*
FALSE COLOR SETTINGS 130
   False Color Overview *130*
   Functionality *130*
   Limitations *131*
   Important Note *131*
FALSE COLOR DISPLAY 131
   Fake Color Index Overview *131*
   Typical Color Mappings *131*
   Usage *132*
ZEBRA SETTINGS 132
   Zebra Pattern Warnings Overview *132*
   How to Use *132*
   Adjusting Exposure *133*
SHOOTING INFORMATION DISPLAY 133
   Customizing Display Information *133*
   Benefits *134*
STANDBY: LOW RESOLUTION 134
   Low-Quality Preview Mode *134*

Benefits	*134*
Limitations	*135*
Customization	*135*
CANON LOG HDMI OUTPUT RANGE	135
TIME CODE	135
Count Up	*136*
Start Time Setting	*136*
Movie Rec. Count	*136*
Movie Play Count	*137*
HDMI	*137*
Drop Frame	*137*
OTHER MENU FUNCTIONS	137
HDMI Display	*137*
Camera + External	*137*
External Only	*137*
HDMI RAW Output	*138*
MANUAL EXPOSURE SETTINGS FOR VIDEO	138
1. Aperture	*138*
2. Shutter Speed	*138*
3. ISO	*139*
4. Exposure Compensation	*139*
5. Manual Focus	*139*
6. Zebra Pattern	*139*
7. Histogram	*139*
8. Peaking	*139*
MOVIE PLAYBACK AND EDITING	139
1. Movie Playback Modes	*140*
2. Movie Editing	*140*
3. In-Camera Raw Processing	*140*
4. HDMI Output	*140*
5. Wi-Fi and Bluetooth Connectivity	*140*
6. Canon Image Transfer Utility	*140*
7. Canon Digital Photo Professional	*140*
8. Third-Party Editing Software	*141*
CHAPTER 7	**142**
THE PHOTO SHOOTING MENU	**142**
IMAGE QUALITY	142
PICTURE SIZE	142
PICTURE STYLE	142
WHITE BALANCE	142
AUTO LIGHTING OPTIMIZER	143
HIGH ISO NR	143

Lens Aberration Correction	143
Long Exposure Noise Reduction	143
High ISO Speed Noise Reduction	143
Multiple Exposure	143
HDR Mode	144
Interval Timer	144
Time-Lapse Movie	144
Image Quality	144
Cropping/Aspect Ratio	145
Expo.comp./AEB: 0 –	146
ISO speed settings	146
Anti-Flicker Shooting	147
Anti-flicker shoot: Disable	147
High-Frequency Anti-Flicker Shooting	148
Recommended Tv Setting	148
For Manual Setting:	149
Flash Function Settings	150
Flash Firing	*150*
E-TTL Balance	*151*
E-TTL II Metering	151
Continuous Flash Control	*152*
Sync Speed Priority	*153*
Slow Synchro	154
Flash Function Settings	155
Shutter Sync	157
Flash Exposure Compensation	158
Flash Exposure Bracketing	158
Flash Custom Function Settings	159
Clear Settings	159
Metering Mode	159
Evaluative Metering	160
Partial Metering	160
Spot Metering	160
Center-Weighted Average Metering	161
Practical Tips for Using Metering Modes:	161
AE for Priority Subjects During AF	161
Metering for Detected Individuals	*161*
How to Use This Feature	*162*
Metering Options for Detected Subjects	*162*
How to Set This Up	*163*
Picture Style	163
Picture Styles Overview	*163*
Available Picture Styles	*163*

- *Customizing Your Style* 164
- SYMBOLS 166
- SETTINGS AND EFFECTS 167
- MONOCHROME ADJUSTMENT 168
- SELECTING PICTURE STYLES 168
- DEFINING PICTURE STYLES 168
- ADJUSTING STYLES WITH THE PICTURE STYLE EDITOR 169
- UPLOADING A PICTURE STYLE TO THE CAMERA 170
- COLOR SPACE 171
- CLARITY 172
- HIGHLIGHT TONE PRIORITY 173
- WHITE BALANCE 173
- WHITE BALANCE SHIFT/BRACKETING 175
- LENS ABERRATION CORRECTION 176
  - *Peripheral Illumination Correction* 177
  - *Distortion Correction* 177
  - *Focus Breathing Correction* 177
  - *Digital Lens Optimizer* 177
  - *Chromatic Aberration Correction* 178
  - *Diffraction Correction* 178
  - *Cautions* 178
- LONG EXPOSURE NOISE REDUCTION 178
  - *Noise Reduction Settings* 178
  - *Key Considerations* 179
  - *Noise Reduction Settings for Long Exposures* 179
  - *Key Tips:* 180
- HIGH ISO SPEED NOISE REDUCTION 180
  - *ISO Noise Reduction Settings* 180
  - *Considerations:* 181
  - *Noise Reduction Options* 181
  - *Tips for Use:* 182
- DUST DELETE DATA 182
- DUST DELETE DATA APPENDING 184
- MULTIPLE EXPOSURE 184
  - *Multiple Exposure Options* 185
- MULTIPLE EXPOSURE CONTROL 186
- NUMBER OF EXPOSURES 187
- SAVE SOURCE IMAGES 187
- CONTINUE MULTIPLE EXPOSURE 188
- FOCUS BRACKETING 188
- SET [DEPTH COMPOSITE] 189
- SET [CROP DEPTH COMP.] 190
- SET [FLASH INTERVAL] 190

TAKE THE PICTURE	191
INTERVAL TIMER	191
SILENT SHUTTER FUNCTION	191
SHUTTER MODE	192
Mechanical Shutter	*192*
Electronic 1st-Curtain Shutter	*192*
Electronic Shutter	*193*
RELEASE SHUTTER WITHOUT CARD	193
TOUCH SHUTTER	194
HIGH-SPEED DISPLAY	194
METERING TIMER	194
DISPLAY SIMULATION	194
OPTICAL VIEWFINDER SIMULATED VIEW ASSIST	195
BLACKOUT-FREE DISPLAY	196
SHOOTING INFORMATION DISPLAY	196
Screen Information Settings	*197*
Viewfinder Information/Toggle Settings	*197*
VF Vertical Display	*197*
Grid Display	*197*
Histogram Display	*197*
Display Size	*197*
Lens Information Display	*197*
Reset	*198*
REVERSE DISPLAY	198
VIEWFINDER DISPLAY FORMAT	198
DISPLAY PERFORMANCE	198

CHAPTER 8 199

EOS R5 MARK II CUSTOM SETTINGS 199

TAB MENUS: CUSTOM FUNCTIONS	199
Restrict Shooting Modes	*199*
Exposure Level Increments	*199*
ISO Speed Setting Increments	*200*
Speed from Metering/ISO Auto	*200*
Bracketing Auto Cancel	*200*
Bracketing Sequence	*200*
Number of Bracketed Shots	*201*
Safety Shift	*201*
SAME EXPO. FOR NEW APERTURE	201
AE Lock Meter. Mode after Focus	*202*
Set Shutter Speed Range	*202*
Mech Shutter/Elec 1st-curtain	*202*
Electronic	*203*

Set Aperture Range	203
Ae Microadjustment	203
FE Micro Adjustment	203
Limit Continuous Shot Count	204
Add Cropping Information	204
Av Setting Without Lens	204
Default Erase Option	205
Release Shutter w/o Lens	205
Retract Lens On Power Off	205
Add IPTC Information	205
Custom Function C. Fn 5	206

CHAPTER 9 207

Image Review and Playback	207
Playback Menu	207
Protect Images	207
Erase Images	208
Select and Erase Images	209
Select Range	209
All Images in Folder	209
All Images on Card	209
Additional Options after Setting Image Search Conditions in Playback 5 Menu	210
Rotate Stills	210
Change Movie Rotate Info	210
Rating	211
Image Copy	213
Print Order	215
RAW Processing	216
In-Camera Upscaling	218
Upscaling Process:	218
Important Considerations:	218
Quality Considerations:	219
Resize	219
Resizing Images	219
Cropping	220
Slide Show	221
VR Preview	222
Setting Image Search Conditions	222
Resuming from Previous Playback	222
View from Last Seen	223
Magnification (Approximate)	223
Blur/Out-of-Focus Image Detection	223
Displaying the Highlight Alert	224

PLAYBACK INFORMATION DISPLAY	224
AF POINT DISP.	225
PLAYBACK GRID	225
MOVIE PLAY COUNT	225
CONCLUSION	**226**

First Thing First

The Canon EOS R5 Mark II is a game-changer in the world of photography—a powerhouse that redefines what's possible with a mirrorless camera. Whether you're a seasoned pro or an ambitious enthusiast, this extraordinary camera is packed with cutting-edge features that will transform your approach to both photography and videography. With blazing-fast autofocus, unmatched image stabilization, and innovative pre-capture shooting, the R5 Mark II is designed to help you capture every moment with incredible precision and clarity. From the heart-pounding action of sports photography to the fine details of a portrait shoot, this camera delivers exceptional performance in any scenario.

In this book, we'll unlock the full potential of the EOS R5 Mark II, guiding you step-by-step through its powerful features and hidden gems. You'll learn how to harness its advanced capabilities to streamline your workflow, enhance your creativity, and take your photography to the next level. Whether you're looking to capture breathtaking landscapes, create cinematic video content, or simply improve your everyday shots, the R5 Mark II has the tools you need to push the boundaries of what's possible. Get ready to dive in, because with the Canon EOS R5 Mark II, your creative journey is about to reach new heights.

Chapter 1

Introduction

Overview of Canon EOS R5 Mark II and its Accessories

The R5 Mark II represents a significant enhancement over its predecessor, the R5, offering not just the expected upgrades typical of a Mark II version but also some exciting new features. Creative photographers now have expanded options, making this camera appealing to both professionals and enthusiasts alike, thanks to its impressive usability and image quality that Canon is known for.

Here's a brief overview of the key innovations in the Canon EOS R5 Mark II:

- **Revolutionary Pre-Capture Shooting Tool**: This game-changing feature ensures you won't miss important moments. It's also found in the new Canon EOS R1, which makes it even more exciting!
- **Eye Control AF**: This technology allows you to focus on subjects simply by looking at them. Previously available on the R1 and R3, it's fantastic to see it included in the R5 Mark II.
- **Enhanced Autofocus Features**: New options like People Priority AF, Action Priority AF, and improved focus tracking enable creative shooting while letting the camera handle the technical details.
- **New Stacked CMOS Sensor**: This sensor enhances frame rates, autofocus capabilities, dynamic range, and accuracy in white balance and metering.
- **Advanced Electronic Shutter**: Experience frame rates of up to 30fps without blackout, and shutter speeds reaching 1/32,000. This allows for wide-open lens use even in bright conditions without needing an ND filter. You can also use flash with the electronic shutter, and rolling shutter blur has been minimized.
- **Improved Video Capabilities**: While my focus is primarily on still photography, the R5 Mark II offers impressive video features, allowing you to capture stills and video simultaneously. These capabilities make it an ideal choice for hybrid photographers, and they might even encourage me to explore video on my trips.

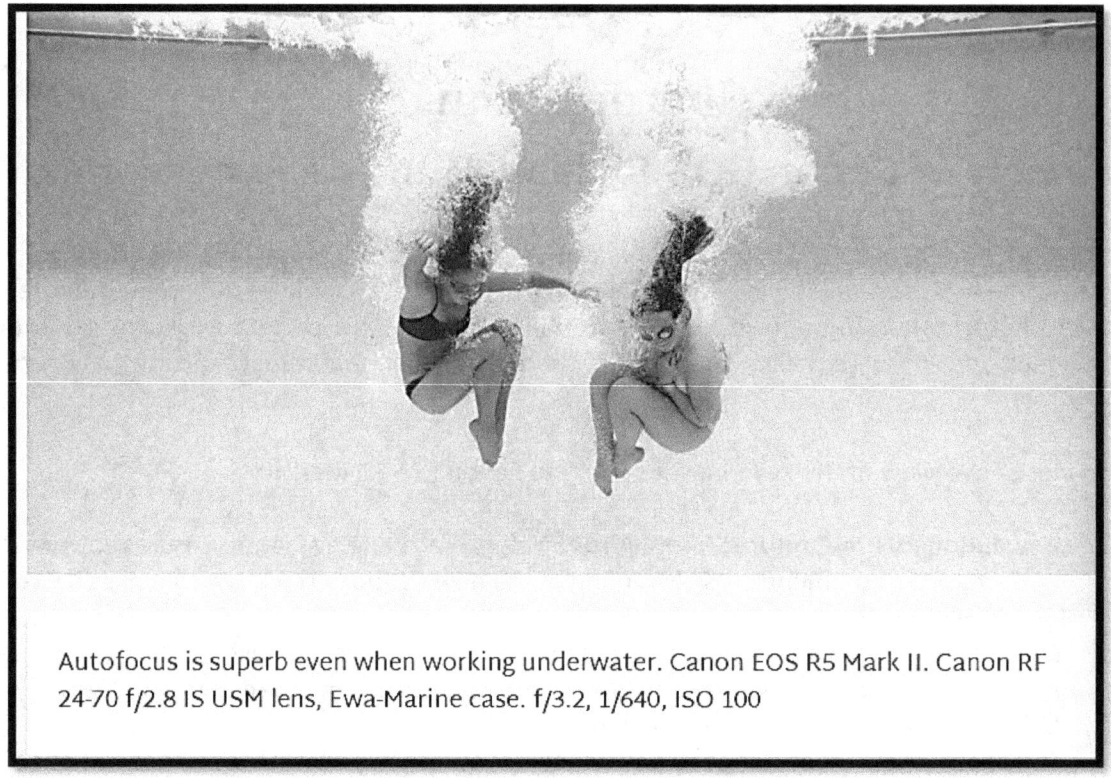

Autofocus is superb even when working underwater. Canon EOS R5 Mark II. Canon RF 24-70 f/2.8 IS USM lens, Ewa-Marine case. f/3.2, 1/640, ISO 100

Handling

Photographers familiar with the Canon EOS R5 will find the R5 Mark II quite user-friendly. Weighing in at 746g with the battery and card, it's slightly heavier than the 738g R5. Most button placements remain consistent, though there's a notable change on the top left: the old on/off switch has been replaced by a convenient stills/video switch, making it easy for hybrid photographers to toggle between modes quickly.

As a portrait photographer, I appreciate that the maximum file size remains at 45MP. This allows for large prints suitable for wall art, and you can crop images significantly without sacrificing quality. Canon has also introduced a handy in-camera upscaling feature that enables you to enlarge a JPEG image to four times its original size with just a button press.

The R5 Mark II retains the dual card slots of its predecessor—one for CF Express cards and the other for SD cards. This setup works well for my workflow, as I back up my RAW files to the faster CF Express card while saving JPEGs on the SD card.

The new LP-E6P battery comes with the R5 Mark II, and while the LP-E6-NH batteries from the original R5 are compatible, certain features, such as pre-continuous shooting, require the new battery. It's wise to keep the older batteries handy for emergencies, but using the new ones is recommended for optimal performance.

Battery life is solid; a single charge lasted through an extensive morning session photographing my family. While there hasn't been a comprehensive side-by-side comparison, it appears the battery life is improved over the R5.

Like its predecessor, the R5 Mark II is weather-sealed, making it suitable for light rain, although it shouldn't be submerged. The new, durable hot-shoe cover provides added protection when a flash isn't in use.

Customization options abound with the R5 Mark II, allowing you to assign various settings to buttons and dials for easy access to frequently used features. I found customizing the Quick menu and assigning drive modes to buttons significantly enhanced my experience. This allowed me to swiftly switch between lower frame rates for quieter scenes and 30fps for fast-paced action.

With the extensive customization options available, I believe using custom modes is ideal for different shooting scenarios. For example, I added my underwater settings to C3 before a recent pool lesson, making it simple to prepare the camera and its underwater housing while the kids got ready. There's also a dedicated mode I created for casual shooting. If you haven't explored custom modes yet, they can save you valuable time.

Finally, once you've fine-tuned your settings, you can save them to a card. This feature allows for easy transfers to a second camera body and provides a backup on your computer for peace of mind.

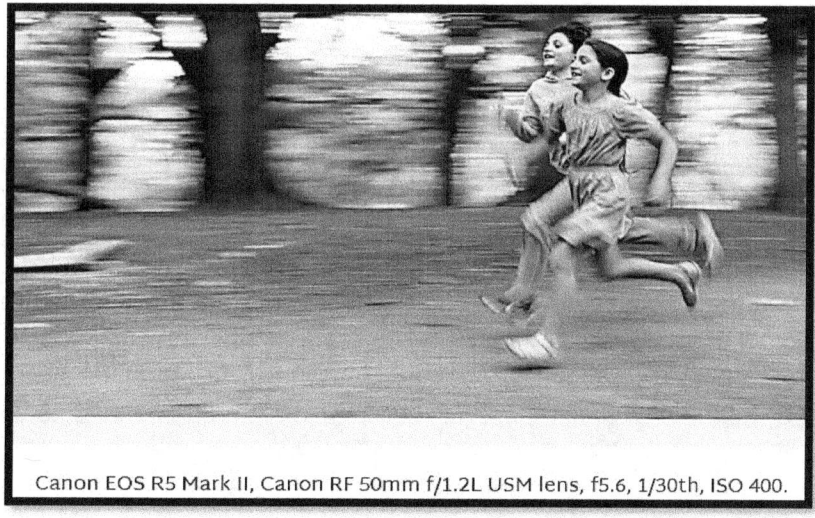

Canon EOS R5 Mark II, Canon RF 50mm f/1.2L USM lens, f5.6, 1/30th, ISO 400.

The Canon EOS R5 Mark II's Autofocus

The EOS R5 Mark II boasts significant enhancements to its autofocus system, thanks to its new back-illuminated and stacked CMOS sensor, as well as an improved image processing system. This upgrade results in faster focus locking and more accurate tracking, even in fast-paced scenarios. During my tests, the autofocus performance felt superior to that of the R3, although I haven't done a direct comparison.

When using the R5 Mark II, I can confidently expect sharp images, allowing me to concentrate on composition while the camera manages focus. This opens up exciting creative possibilities for my photography.

Among its standout features, the constant focus tracking capabilities are particularly impressive. The camera quickly and accurately locks onto faces and navigates obstacles effectively, even in challenging situations, such as kids running through trees or playing amidst bubbles. Compared to the R5, this is a significant improvement.

For those familiar with the R5 and the 1-series DSLRs, the previous Servo AF modes (Case 1 for general use, Case 2 for tennis, Case 3 for cycling, and Case 4 for sports like football or gymnastics) have been revamped. The new system includes an automatic mode and a manual mode where you can customize parameters to adjust the sensitivity of autofocus tracking. In my test shoots, I set it up to mimic Case 2 from the R5, which worked exceptionally well.

While it's fantastic that the R5 Mark II excels at tracking focus, the next question is: how do we instruct it on what to track?

Eye Control

I was thrilled to discover that the Canon EOS R5 Mark II includes eye control autofocus, a feature I previously experienced with the Canon EOS R3. With eye control, you can simply look at your subject, and when you press the AF-ON button, tracking begins. This functionality is incredible, allowing for quick transitions between subjects.

To set it up, you just point your camera at a small circle in different areas of the frame and focus on it while the camera tracks your eye movements. It's a straightforward process, and you can create multiple calibrations. For instance, you could have one calibration for wearing glasses and another for contacts, or even different settings for various photographers using the same studio equipment.

Unfortunately, I recently had to get new glasses, and the eye control feature on my old varifocals doesn't work as effectively with my new Canon EOS R3, which I was excited to try out. As a result, I've temporarily disabled this feature.

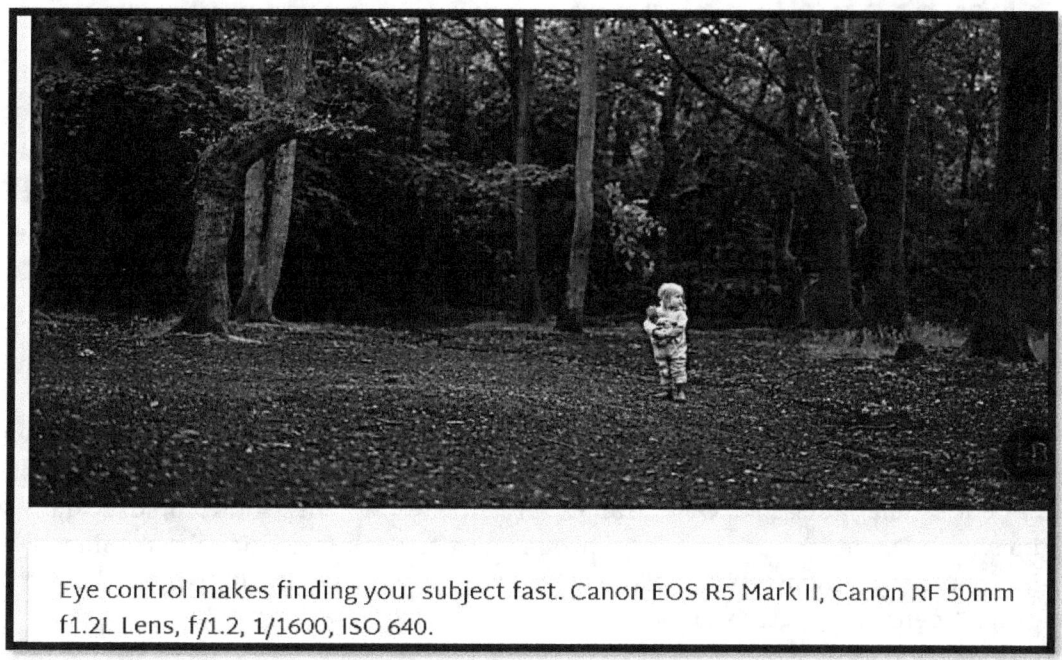

Eye control makes finding your subject fast. Canon EOS R5 Mark II, Canon RF 50mm f1.2L Lens, f/1.2, 1/1600, ISO 640.

Frame Rate

The Canon EOS R5 Mark II features an increased frame rate, which is beneficial for capturing fast-moving subjects. The mechanical shutter can shoot at approximately 12 fps, while the electronic shutter can reach up to 30 fps.

You have the flexibility to set different frame rates for each mode. For instance, you can choose high-speed continuous shooting on the electronic shutter at either 30 or 20 fps, with additional options for high-speed settings at 20, 15, 12, 10, and 7.5 fps, and lower speeds at 1, 2, 3, 5, 7.5, 10, 12, and 15 fps. This variety allows for tailored shooting according to your specific needs.

As a photographer, I appreciate the audible sound of the shutter; it helps me gauge my shooting speed and alerts my subjects when a photo is taken. It can be easy to inadvertently take multiple shots at a high frame rate when intending to capture just one, especially if I forgot to adjust the shutter speed after panning shots. While the R5's electronic shutter is very quiet, which is great for situations like photographing a sleeping baby, many people find it challenging to know when a picture is being taken with a silent shutter. Fortunately, the R5 Mark II allows me to enable a realistic shutter sound when using the electronic shutter, which is a thoughtful feature for ensuring everyone knows when a photo is being captured.

Pre-Continuous Shooting

One of my favorite features of the new Canon EOS R5 Mark II is the pre-continuous shooting mode, which pairs perfectly with its fast frame rate and enhanced autofocus. When activated, the camera starts capturing images as soon as you half-press the shutter button, storing them in its buffer until you fully press it. This allows you to capture up to 15 RAW photos before taking the shot, significantly increasing your chances of catching that fleeting magical moment.

Initially, I wasn't sure how pre-continuous shooting would benefit me as a family photographer. I could see its advantages in sports photography, where timing is critical for capturing a goal or a key moment. However, I was uncertain about its utility in family settings.

As it turns out, this feature is fantastic for working with teens, who can be unpredictable! It allows me to capture those fleeting expressions—like a shy glance or the instant a child leaps from the bottom of a pool, sending a splash of water everywhere. Many times, the action unfolds so quickly or builds up so subtly that it's easy to miss. Since learning to use pre-continuous shooting, I've been able to photograph moments I would have otherwise overlooked. I'm excited about the possibilities this opens up for future shoots.

That said, I wouldn't want to use this setting all the time, as it can quickly fill up memory cards. However, it's incredibly valuable in the right situations. Like all Canon R-series cameras, the R5 Mark II offers extensive customization options, so I added the pre-shoot setting to my Quick menu for easier access.

Dual Shooting (stills and videos)

The Canon EOS R5 Mark II includes video capabilities, although I haven't explored them yet since I'm not particularly experienced in that area. However, one feature that immediately caught my attention is dual shooting, which allows you to capture both still images and videos simultaneously at 6 fps in a 16:9 JPEG format.

In the past, I hesitated to shoot video during family sessions, as it often distracted me from my primary goal of delivering excellent still photos for my clients. But with this new feature, I can now record high-quality JPEGs while shooting video at the same time. This is a fascinating development, and I'm eager to delve deeper into it once I have the R5 Mark II in hand.

From my brief experience with this feature, I can see the potential for capturing great clips for my clients or for social media, all without sacrificing my focus on still photography. I believe that both social and professional photographers who want to incorporate short video clips into their still image portfolios will find this feature incredibly valuable.

High ISO

For family photographers like me, who often shoot in clients' homes without full control over lighting, low-light performance is crucial—often even more so than the latest flashy features. I frequently have to make the most of the available light, which isn't always abundant. While flash or LED panels can be helpful at times, they aren't always feasible.

With each new camera, I like to see how far I can push its capabilities. With my R5, I usually shoot at ISO 5,000, occasionally needing to go up to ISO 10,000. So, how does the R5 Mark II perform?

It turns out I can push the limits even further than I expected, especially when utilizing the new noise reduction tool in the camera. During my test shots, I tried ISO 10,000 indoors, and the quality was impressive enough for a 24" double-page spread in an album. I captured a shot of a child being tossed in the air at 1/160th of a second—a relatively slow shutter speed due to low light—and the child's eyes were very sharp.

In comparison, the R5 doesn't perform as well at ISO 5,000. The smoother tones and reduced noise from the R5 Mark II make it ideal for indoor photography.

I even pushed it further outside, shooting under a dark tree in the woods at ISO 51,200. While the JPEG straight out of the camera was noisy, the results after applying the camera's noise reduction were surprisingly good. An A2 test print demonstrated that this ISO setting is usable for shooting when necessary, and the results are capable of being printed large.

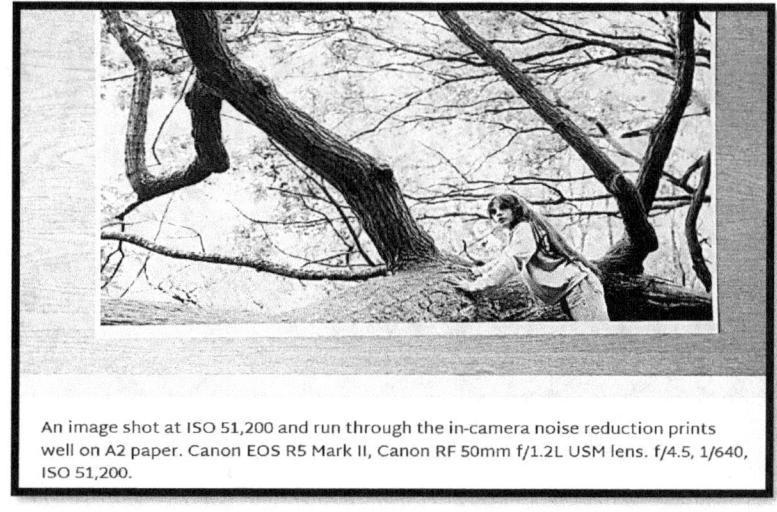

An image shot at ISO 51,200 and run through the in-camera noise reduction prints well on A2 paper. Canon EOS R5 Mark II, Canon RF 50mm f/1.2L USM lens. f/4.5, 1/640, ISO 51,200.

Processing in the Camera

With just the press of a button, the Canon EOS R5 Mark II can capture images at resolutions ranging from 8,192 x 5,464 pixels to 16,384 x 10,928 pixels and save them as JPEGs. It also features built-in noise reduction, which is beneficial when processing images for agencies, especially alongside the RAW processing capabilities of the R5.

Additionally, you can shrink the image size directly in the camera for easier sharing, with options for a standard JPEG at 24 megapixels, S1 JPEG at 12 megapixels, or S2 JPEG at 3.8 megapixels. The camera allows for cropping and straightening images, as well as adjusting the aspect ratio to 4:3, 9:16, 3:4, or 16:9.

RAW files can be processed in-camera and converted into JPEG or HEIF formats, allowing you to modify picture styles, color space, clarity, brightness, noise reduction, white balance, and apply the lighting optimizer before saving the new file. This feature is particularly handy for quickly sending edited images when time is of the essence.

The R5 Mark II also includes a Blur/Out-of-Focus image detection setting, which should assist in selecting the best shots, although I haven't had the chance to test it yet. Its primary aim appears to be facilitating photojournalists in quickly editing and transmitting images from the field. However, I can see myself utilizing this feature to edit photos and send them to my phone via the Canon Connect app for social media posts. It would also be useful for wedding photographers wanting to share a few images with the couple on their wedding day.

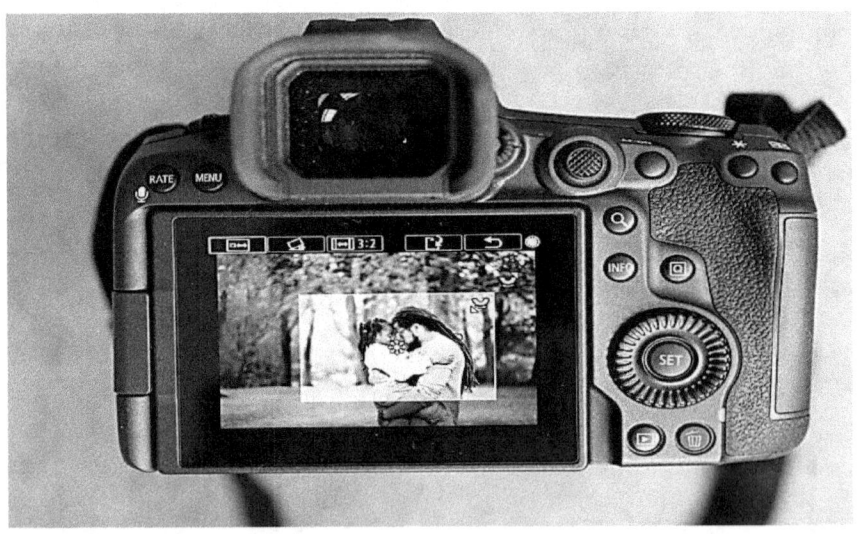

Image Stabilization

The in-body image stabilization on the Canon EOS R5 Mark II surpasses the already impressive stabilization of the R5. When combined with in-lens stabilization, it offers up to 8.5 stops of total stabilization. In practical terms, if you were to photograph a little girl standing still while she moved an umbrella at 1/15th of a second using the Canon EOS RF 50mm f1.2L lens, her image would be sharp, while the umbrella would show motion blur.

This feature is particularly beneficial for those with unsteady hands who prefer not to use a tripod. I can envision using it creatively during landscape photography trips, and I'm excited to experiment with slow shutter speeds during portrait sessions. Adding intentional blur can introduce a unique artistic element to my images, and this stabilization capability will help me achieve that more effectively.

ACCESSORIES

Best All-in-one Lens for Canon EOS R5 Mark II

Canon RF 24-240mm f/4-6.3 IS USM Lens

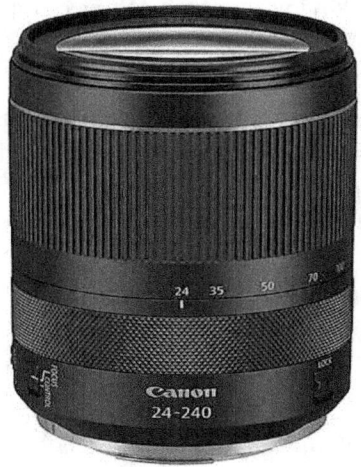

The Canon RF 24-240mm f/4-6.3 IS USM lens is a standout all-in-one option for the Canon EOS R5 Mark II, offering a wide range of features. Many consider it an ideal choice for photographers and filmmakers who need versatility without the hassle of constantly switching lenses. Its extensive focal length range makes it perfect for those on the go or for anyone looking to avoid lugging around a heavy bag filled with multiple lenses.

Why does this Lens Stand Out? Why does it Work Well with the Canon EOS R5 Mark II?

Versatile Focal Range

One of the standout features of the RF 24-240mm lens is its versatile focal range. Starting at 24mm, it allows for wide-angle shots perfect for landscapes, architecture, street photography, and group portraits. Zooming in to 240mm transitions it into telephoto mode, making it ideal for sports, wildlife, or any scenario where you need to capture distant subjects.

This lens is particularly well-suited for travel, as it enables you to quickly adapt to a variety of scenes, from expansive landscapes in the morning to detailed shots of birds in trees in the afternoon. The all-in-one zoom capability ensures that you won't miss any important moments, making it a great choice for photographers who want to be ready for anything.

Image Stabilization

When using a wide lens range like the Canon RF 24-240mm, particularly at the longer telephoto end (240mm), camera shake can become more noticeable. Fortunately, this lens features built-in image stabilization (IS) of 5 stops, which helps maintain stability in your shots, even when shooting handheld. This is especially crucial in low-light situations or when zooming in on distant subjects.

The in-body image stabilization (IBIS) of the EOS R5 Mark II complements the lens's stabilization, providing even greater stability for clear images without the need for a tripod. This enhancement is also beneficial for videographers; if you're shooting video with your EOS R5 Mark II, you won't have to worry about shake compromising your footage. This capability is particularly useful for creating travel videos, covering events, or simply capturing memorable family moments.

Compact and Lightweight Design

When selecting an all-in-one lens, flexibility is key. You want something that strikes a balance between lightweight and durable. The Canon RF 24-240mm f/4-6.3 IS USM fits the bill perfectly. Weighing in at about 750g (1.65 lbs), it may not be the lightest option, but it's compact enough for travel and versatile enough for a wide range of shooting situations.

Even after a full day of photography with the Canon EOS R5 Mark II and this lens, you won't feel overwhelmed by the weight. This makes it an ideal choice for holidays, hiking, or simply exploring your surroundings. With just one lens in your bag, you can seamlessly switch between wide-angle and zoom shots without the hassle of changing lenses.

USM Autofocus System

The Canon RF 24-240mm f/4-6.3 IS USM lens features a fast and quiet Ultra-Sonic Motor (USM) autofocus system, which is essential for photographers who need quick focus—whether they're capturing moving subjects like athletes or animals, or trying to seize candid moments in bustling environments like weddings or street scenes.

This autofocus system is particularly advantageous because it operates silently, ensuring it won't interfere with video recordings. The last thing you want during an important interview or live event is the distracting buzz of a lens motor. With this lens, you can concentrate on achieving high-quality sound and video without any interruptions, making it an excellent choice for both photography and videography.

Aperture and Low Light Performance

The Canon RF 24-240mm f/4-6.3 IS USM lens features an aperture range from f/4 to f/6.3. At its widest setting of 24mm, it opens up to f/4, which is suitable for everyday shooting, especially in well-lit environments. However, when you zoom in to 240mm, the maximum aperture narrows to f/6.3, allowing less light to enter the lens.

While this aperture range is not as favorable for low-light conditions compared to lenses with a constant f/2.8 aperture, it's a trade-off for the versatility of an all-in-one lens. If you often find yourself shooting in low light, the high ISO performance of the EOS R5 Mark II and its in-body stabilization can still yield good results. You can achieve decent images by increasing the ISO or slowing down the shutter speed, but it's worth considering this limitation if low-light photography is a regular part of your work.

Build Quality

The Canon RF 24-240mm lens is built to a high standard, even though it isn't part of Canon's premium L-series. While it may not be fully weather-sealed like the more expensive options, the materials used are robust, and it can withstand certain weather conditions. This durability is important for outdoor use, where you might encounter dust or light rain.

While it's always wise to exercise caution in harsh weather, this lens is well-equipped to handle typical outdoor scenarios, making it a reliable choice for various shooting environments.

What are the Best Prime Telephoto Lenses for the Canon EOS R5 Mark II?

When selecting a telephoto prime lens for the Canon EOS R5 Mark II, your choice will largely depend on your specific photography needs, whether that's capturing wildlife, sports, birds, or distant landscapes. Canon's RF lineup includes several impressive lenses designed for mirrorless systems, offering exceptional sharpness, image stabilization, and a variety of shooting options. Here, we'll explore the Canon RF 600mm f/11 IS STM, Canon RF 800mm f/11 IS STM, Canon RF 400mm f/2.8 L IS USM, and Canon RF 600mm f/4L IS USM.

Each lens offers unique focal lengths and features, making them suited for different types of photography. This allows you to choose the one that aligns best with your style and requirements. Let's delve into each lens in more detail.

1. **Canon RF 600mm f/11 IS STM Lens**

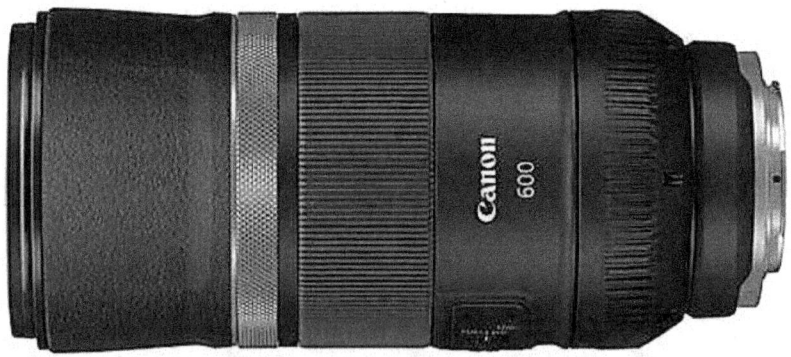

The Canon RF 600mm f/11 IS STM is a standout lens for photographers looking to explore telephoto photography without the burden of heavy equipment or a hefty price tag. Its fixed f/11 aperture and relatively lightweight design make it an excellent choice for those wanting to capture distant subjects.

Key Features:

- **Focal Length:** 600mm
- **Aperture:** Fixed f/11
- **Image Stabilization (IS):** Yes, with up to 5 stops of compensation
- **Autofocus:** STM (Stepping Motor) for smooth and quiet operation, ideal for both stills and video
- **Weight:** A manageable 930g (2.05 lbs)

What's Great About It?

- **Lightweight and Portable:** One of the major advantages of this lens is its portability. Unlike many 600mm lenses, which can be cumbersome, the RF 600mm f/11 maintains a compact size due to its fixed aperture. This makes it an excellent option for photographers who want a super-telephoto lens without the hassle of heavy gear.
- **Affordable:** The price point is another significant benefit. While many 600mm lenses can run into the thousands, the RF 600mm f/11 is much more budget-friendly, making it accessible for those new to long telephoto photography.
- **Ideal for Wildlife and Bird Photography:** This lens is particularly well-suited for wildlife and bird enthusiasts. The 600mm focal length allows you to capture subjects from a distance without disturbing them. Paired with the EOS R5 Mark II, known for its excellent image quality and fast autofocus, it enables clear shots of animals in their natural habitat.
- **Fixed Aperture Limitations:** The fixed f/11 aperture does limit light intake, making it less ideal for low-light situations. However, the EOS R5 Mark II's impressive high ISO performance helps mitigate this by allowing you to adjust the ISO in well-lit environments.

Next Up:

2. **Canon RF 800mm f/11 IS STM Lens.**

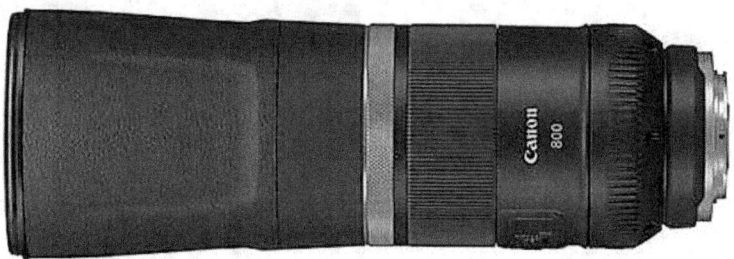

The Canon RF 800mm f/11 IS STM lens is an excellent option for those needing extreme telephoto reach, particularly for wildlife and distant subjects. Its design mirrors that of the RF 600mm but extends the focal length for even greater distance capabilities.

Key Features:

- **Focal Length:** 800mm
- **Aperture:** Fixed f/11
- **Image Stabilization (IS):** Yes, with up to 4 stops of stabilization
- **Autofocus:** STM motor for smooth and quiet focusing
- **Weight:** Lightweight for an 800mm lens at 1260g (2.78 lbs)

What's Great About It?

- **Extreme Reach:** The 800mm focal length allows you to capture details from incredible distances, making it ideal for photographing birds in flight, safari animals, or distant landscapes where you want to zoom in on specific features.
- **Compact for the Focal Length:** Despite being an 800mm lens, its fixed f/11 aperture keeps the size and weight manageable. This portability is a significant advantage over traditional 800mm lenses, which can be bulky and heavy.
- **Affordable Super-Telephoto Option:** While professional-grade 800mm lenses often come with steep price tags, this lens offers a much more budget-friendly alternative, making it accessible for photographers wanting to experiment with extreme telephoto photography without breaking the bank.
- **Fixed Aperture Limitations:** Like the 600mm variant, the fixed f/11 aperture limits low-light performance. It is best suited for well-lit environments or daytime shooting.

Next Up:

3. **Canon RF 400mm f/2.8 L IS USM Lens.**

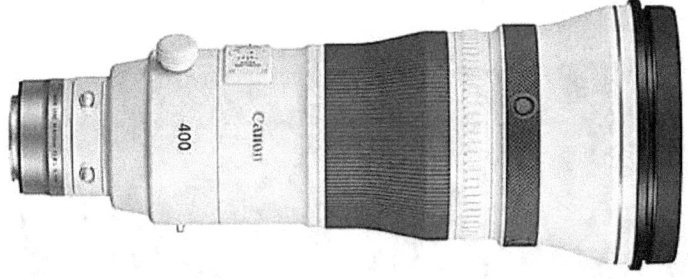

The Canon RF 600mm f/4L IS USM is another professional-grade telephoto lens that delivers exceptional performance, particularly in challenging shooting conditions. As part of Canon's esteemed L-series, this lens is engineered for serious photographers who demand quality and versatility.

Key Features:

- **Focal Length:** 600mm
- **Aperture:** f/4
- **Image Stabilization (IS):** Yes, with up to 5 stops of stabilization
- **Autofocus:** USM motor for fast and precise autofocus
- **Weight:** Heavier than the RF 400mm at 3020g (6.67 lbs)

What's Great About It?

- **Exceptional Low-Light Performance:** With a maximum aperture of f/4, this lens excels in low-light conditions, allowing you to capture clear images without needing to increase ISO excessively. This is especially beneficial for wildlife and sports photography, where light conditions can vary.
- **Stunning Background Blur:** The f/4 aperture also provides excellent control over depth of field, creating beautiful background blur (bokeh) that isolates your subject and adds a professional touch to your images.
- **Superior Image Quality:** As an L-series lens, the RF 600mm f/4 is built with high-quality optics, ensuring sharpness, contrast, and color accuracy throughout the frame. This level of quality is essential for professional work, where detail matters.
- **Rugged Build and Weather Sealing:** Designed to withstand harsh conditions, this lens features robust construction and weather sealing, making it suitable for outdoor photography, even in inclement weather.
- **Versatile Use:** The 600mm focal length is ideal for a wide range of applications, from wildlife photography to sports, providing the reach needed to capture distant subjects without compromising image quality.
- **Price Consideration:** As with the RF 400mm f/2.8, this lens is a significant investment. However, for professional photographers, the quality and performance may justify the cost.

With its combination of reach, speed, and professional quality, the Canon RF 600mm f/4L IS USM lens is an excellent choice for those serious about telephoto photography.

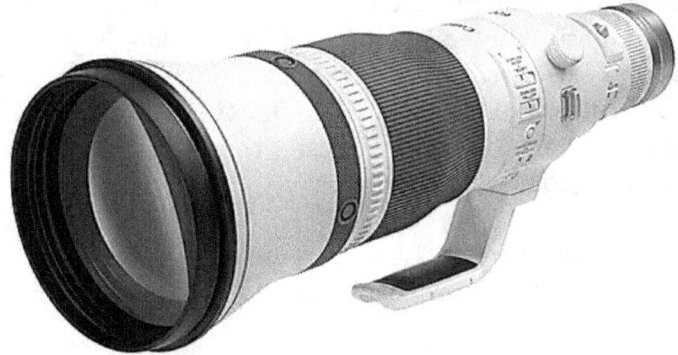

The Canon RF 600mm f/4L IS USM truly stands out as a top choice for professional telephoto photography. Here's a more detailed breakdown of its features and advantages:

Key Features:

- **Focal Length:** 600mm – Perfect for capturing distant subjects, particularly in wildlife and sports photography.
- **Aperture:** f/4 – Offers excellent light-gathering capabilities, enabling low-light shooting while maintaining sharpness.
- **Image Stabilization (IS):** Up to 5 stops – Essential for reducing camera shake at long focal lengths, allowing for clearer shots without a tripod.
- **Autofocus:** USM motor – Ensures fast and accurate focusing, critical for tracking moving subjects.
- **Weight:** 3090g (6.81 lbs) – While on the heavier side, the quality and performance justify the weight for dedicated users.

What's Great About It?

- **Incredible Reach with Fast Aperture:** The combination of a 600mm focal length and f/4 aperture is ideal for wildlife photographers who need to maintain distance from their subjects without sacrificing exposure quality. This allows for shooting in varying light conditions while ensuring sharp, well-exposed images.
- **Image Stabilization and Autofocus:** The 5-stop IS helps mitigate blurriness caused by hand movement, which is especially important when shooting at long distances. The fast and precise autofocus is crucial for capturing action shots, ensuring you won't miss fleeting moments.
- **Professional Build Quality:** As an L-series lens, it boasts a robust construction and weather sealing, making it suitable for outdoor use in diverse conditions. This durability is important for professionals who often work in challenging environments.
- **Versatile Applications:** Whether photographing wildlife, sports events, or distant landscapes, this lens excels across various scenarios, offering flexibility and reliability.
- **Investment Worth Making:** While the RF 600mm f/4L IS USM comes with a premium price tag, its performance and durability make it a valuable investment for serious photographers looking to elevate their work.

In summary, the Canon RF 600mm f/4L IS USM is an exceptional telephoto lens that combines reach, speed, and professional quality, making it a must-have for any serious photographer in the field.

Best Telephoto Zoom Lenses for Canon EOS R5 Mark II

1. Canon RF 100-500mm f/4.5-7.1 L IS USM Lens

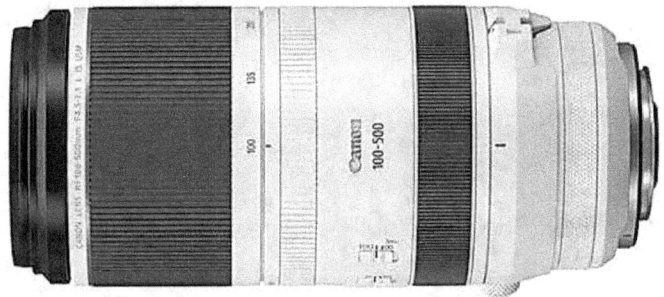

The Canon RF 70-200mm f/2.8 L IS USM lens is a premium telephoto zoom option known for its versatility and performance, making it a favorite among professionals and serious enthusiasts. Here's a closer look at its features and benefits:

Key Features:

- **Focal Length:** 70-200mm – Ideal for a variety of photography styles, from portraits to sports and wildlife.
- **Aperture:** Constant f/2.8 – Provides excellent low-light performance and allows for beautiful background blur (bokeh).
- **Image Stabilization (IS):** Yes, with up to 5 stops of compensation – Helps to minimize camera shake for clearer shots.
- **Autofocus:** Dual Nano USM motors – Ensures fast, smooth, and silent focusing, making it great for both stills and video.
- **Weight:** 1030g (2.27 lbs) – Relatively compact for a lens of this caliber, making it easier to handle for extended shoots.

What's Great About It?

- **Versatile Focal Range:** The 70-200mm range is incredibly flexible, making it suitable for various types of photography, including portraits, events, and sports. The ability to zoom in allows photographers to frame subjects tightly without needing to change lenses.
- **Exceptional Low-Light Performance:** The constant f/2.8 aperture is beneficial for shooting in dim conditions, providing greater control over exposure and depth of field. This is particularly useful for indoor events or low-light environments.
- **Superior Optical Quality:** As an L-series lens, the RF 70-200mm boasts high-quality optics that minimize distortion and ensure sharp images across the zoom range. This is crucial for maintaining detail, especially in professional work.
- **Durable Build with Weather Sealing:** Designed for rugged use, this lens is weather-sealed, which protects against dust and moisture. This makes it a reliable option for outdoor photographers who face varying conditions.

- **Efficient Image Stabilization:** The 5-stop IS works seamlessly with the in-body stabilization of the EOS R5 Mark II, enabling handheld shooting even at slower shutter speeds. This is essential for capturing sharp images at longer focal lengths.

Ideal for:

- **Portrait Photography:** The lens's ability to produce stunning background blur makes it perfect for isolating subjects in portraits.
- **Sports Photography:** Its fast autofocus and zoom range are excellent for capturing action shots, whether on the field or in the arena.
- **Event Coverage:** The flexibility of the zoom allows for quick adjustments to framing, making it ideal for weddings, concerts, and other events.
- **Wildlife and Nature Photography:** The lens can be used to capture wildlife from a distance without disturbing the subjects.

In summary, the Canon RF 70-200mm f/2.8 L IS USM is a top-tier lens that combines versatility, performance, and durability, making it a valuable tool for a wide range of photography styles.

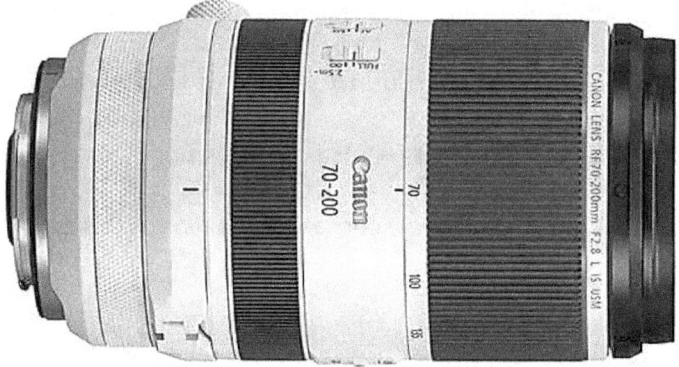

The Canon RF 70-200mm f/2.8 L IS USM lens is indeed a favorite among professional photographers for its versatility and outstanding performance. Here's a more detailed look at its features and what makes it an essential tool for various photography genres.

Key Features:

- **Focal Length:** 70-200mm – A versatile range suitable for portraits, events, and sports.
- **Aperture:** Constant f/2.8 – Maintains light-gathering ability throughout the zoom range, ideal for low-light conditions.
- **Image Stabilization (IS):** Yes, with up to 5 stops of compensation – Helps reduce camera shake for clearer images, especially at longer focal lengths.

- **Autofocus:** Dual Nano USM motors – Provides fast, accurate, and quiet autofocus performance, making it perfect for both stills and video.
- **Weight:** 1070g (2.36 lbs) – Surprisingly lightweight for a lens of this caliber, enhancing portability and ease of use.

What's Great About It?

- **Constant f/2.8 Aperture:** This feature is key for achieving shallow depth of field and excellent bokeh, making it perfect for portrait work. It allows photographers to work in varying light conditions without losing shutter speed or image quality.
- **Exceptional Image Quality:** As part of the L-series, this lens utilizes advanced optics to minimize distortion and aberration, ensuring sharp, vibrant images. This is particularly crucial for professionals who demand high standards in their work.
- **Compact and Lightweight Design:** Compared to traditional 70-200mm f/2.8 lenses, the RF version is impressively compact. This makes it easier to carry on long shoots, reducing fatigue and allowing for more spontaneous photography.
- **Fast and Accurate Autofocus:** The dual Nano USM motors provide rapid focusing, which is essential for capturing fast-moving subjects in sports or dynamic event settings. The quiet operation is a bonus for video recordings, preventing distracting noises during important moments.

Ideal For:

- **Portrait Photography:** The lens excels in creating beautiful background blur, making it perfect for isolating subjects and achieving professional-looking portraits.
- **Sports Photography:** With its fast autofocus and long reach, this lens is ideal for capturing fast action, whether on the field or in the arena.
- **Event Photography:** Its low-light capability and versatility make it a go-to choice for weddings, parties, and other events where lighting can vary.
- **General-Purpose Photography:** The RF 70-200mm f/2.8 is reliable for a wide range of scenarios, allowing photographers to adapt quickly to different situations without switching lenses.

In summary, the Canon RF 70-200mm f/2.8 L IS USM lens is a top-tier choice for any professional or serious enthusiast looking for a high-performance telephoto zoom that combines excellent optical quality with a practical design. Its versatility and exceptional features make it a valuable addition to any photographer's toolkit.

1. **Canon RF 70-200mm f/4 L IS USM Lens**

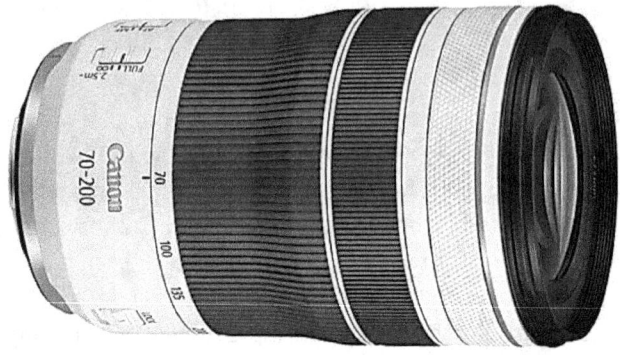

The Canon RF 70-200mm f/4 L IS USM offers a lighter and more affordable alternative to the f/2.8 version. While it shares many advantages with its counterpart, its maximum aperture is smaller. This lens is perfect for photographers who desire a high-quality, versatile telephoto zoom without needing the faster f/2.8 aperture.

Key Features:

- **Focal Length:** 70-200mm
- **Aperture:** Constant f/4
- **Image Stabilization (IS):** Yes, providing up to 5 stops of stabilization
- **Autofocus:** Nano USM motors ensure quick and smooth focusing
- **Weight:** 695g (1.53 lbs)

Highlights:

- **Lightweight and Portable:** The RF 70-200mm f/4 is significantly smaller and lighter than the f/2.8 version, making it an excellent option for photographers who need to carry their gear for extended periods or those who travel frequently. It fits easily into most bags, making it convenient for on-the-go shooting.
- **Constant f/4 Aperture:** The f/4 aperture is sufficient for most lighting conditions, though it may not create as much background blur or perform as well in low light as the f/2.8. However, for many photographers, this aperture is more than adequate.
- **Exceptional Image Quality:** Despite the smaller aperture, this lens delivers outstanding image quality, maintaining the sharpness, color accuracy, and clarity associated with Canon's L-series lenses, making it ideal for professional use.

Ideal For:

- Travel photographers seeking a lightweight lens
- Portrait photographers who don't require a fast aperture
- General photographers looking for a budget-friendly alternative to the f/2.8 version

The Canon RF 100-400mm f/5.6-8 IS USM lens is an excellent option for those wanting a long telephoto zoom without breaking the bank. With its extensive zoom range, it's ideal for wildlife, sports, or outdoor photography.

Key Features:

- **Focal Length:** 100-400mm
- **Aperture:** Variable f/5.6-8
- **Image Stabilization (IS):** Yes, offering up to 5.5 stops of stabilization
- **Autofocus:** Nano USM motor for smooth and rapid focusing
- **Weight:** 635g (1.4 lbs)

Highlights:

- **Affordable Telephoto Zoom:** This lens is one of Canon's more budget-friendly options, allowing more photographers to access quality telephoto capabilities. It delivers impressive image quality, making it suitable for beginners or those on a budget.
- **Compact and Lightweight:** Weighing just 635g, this lens is easily portable, especially considering its 400mm reach, making it perfect for photographers who want to travel light with a telephoto option.
- **Impressive Image Stabilization:** With up to 5.5 stops of image stabilization, this lens helps ensure sharp images at slower shutter speeds, particularly beneficial at 400mm. It works well with the in-body stabilization of the EOS R5 Mark II for enhanced steadiness.

Ideal For:

- Beginners and hobbyists seeking an affordable telephoto zoom lens
- Travel photographers needing a lightweight long-reach option
- Wildlife photographers who don't require premium aperture speeds

The Best Standard Prime Lenses for the Canon EOS R5 Mark II

1. **Canon RF 50mm f/1.2 L USM Lens**

One of the standout lenses in Canon's RF lineup is the RF 50mm f/1.2 L USM, designed for professionals and serious photographers who demand top-notch image quality, performance, and durability. As part of Canon's L-series, this high-end, fast prime lens excels in sharpness, offers smooth bokeh, and performs exceptionally well in low-light conditions.

Key Features:

- **Focal Length:** 50mm
- **Maximum Aperture:** f/1.2
- **Autofocus Motor:** USM (Ultrasonic Motor) for rapid and quiet focusing
- **Lens Elements:** Advanced optics with aspherical and UD elements
- **Weather Sealing:** Yes
- **Weight:** 950g (2.1 lbs)

What Sets It Apart?

- **Outstanding Sharpness:** The RF 50mm f/1.2 delivers incredible sharpness even when shot wide open at f/1.2, capturing detailed images ideal for fine art and professional photography.
- **Ultra-Wide Aperture:** The fast f/1.2 aperture allows for low-light shooting without increasing ISO, producing a shallow depth of field that beautifully blurs backgrounds, making it perfect for portrait photography.
- **Professional Build Quality:** Being part of the L-series, this lens is built to withstand challenging conditions, with weather sealing that protects against rain and dust, making it suitable for outdoor shoots.
- **Fast and Quiet Autofocus:** The USM autofocus system ensures quick and quiet focusing, ideal for both still photography and videography, even in low-light situations, making it great for dynamic environments like events and street photography.
- **Size and Weight:** Its primary downside is its bulk and weight—at 950g, it may not be the best choice for photographers who prioritize portability. However, for those focused on image quality, the trade-off is worthwhile.

Ideal For:

- Portrait photographers who seek beautiful subject separation and bokeh.
- Wedding photographers needing low-light performance.

- Professionals who prioritize top-quality images and can manage the lens's weight and cost.

The Canon RF 50mm f/1.8 STM, often referred to as the "nifty fifty," offers excellent image quality at an affordable price. This lens is perfect for beginners or those seeking a compact, lightweight prime lens that still delivers great results.

Key Features:

- **Focal Length:** 50mm
- **Maximum Aperture:** f/1.8
- **Autofocus Motor:** STM (Stepping Motor) for smooth and silent autofocus
- **Lens Elements:** Aspherical element to minimize aberrations
- **Weight:** 160g (0.35 lbs)

What Makes It Unique?

- **Compact and Lightweight:** Weighing just 160g, this lens is highly portable, making it an excellent choice for photographers who prefer not to carry heavy gear during outings or travels.
- **Affordable Price:** The RF 50mm f/1.8 is one of the most budget-friendly options in the RF lineup, making it ideal for beginners or photographers on a budget, yet it delivers impressive image quality.
- **Sharpness:** While it may not be as sharp as the f/1.2 version, the f/1.8 lens still offers excellent clarity, especially when stopped down to f/2.8 or f/4, making it suitable for everyday and semi-professional use.
- **f/1.8 Aperture:** This aperture allows for good low-light performance and a decent depth of field, providing enough background blur for effective subject separation, though with less bokeh than the f/1.2 version.
- **STM Autofocus:** The STM autofocus system provides quiet and smooth focusing, making it suitable for both stills and video. While not as fast as the USM system, it performs well for general photography needs.

Ideal For:

- Beginners and hobbyists looking for an affordable, versatile prime lens.
- Budget-conscious photographers seeking good value for their investment.
- Travel and street photographers needing a lightweight and compact lens for casual shooting.

Best For:

- Everyday photography
- Budget-friendly portraits
- Travel and street photography
- Video projects

Comparison: Canon RF 50mm f/1.2 L USM vs Canon RF 50mm f/1.8 STM

Both the RF 50mm f/1.2 L and the RF 50mm f/1.8 STM serve as standard prime lenses with a 50mm focal length, closely matching the human eye's natural perspective. However, they target different audiences and have distinct characteristics:

- **Image Quality:** The RF 50mm f/1.2 L stands out in image quality, offering sharper images, superior bokeh, and better low-light performance due to its wider f/1.2 aperture. While the RF 50mm f/1.8 also produces good images, especially for its price, it doesn't quite reach the same level of clarity and detail.
- **Aperture:** The f/1.2 aperture of the L-series lens excels in low-light situations and provides more pronounced subject separation. It's ideal for photographers who frequently work in dim environments or desire beautiful background blur. Conversely, the f/1.8 aperture remains sufficiently fast for most scenarios, delivering pleasing background blur as well.
- **Build and Durability:** The RF 50mm f/1.2 is constructed for professional use, featuring robust weather sealing that protects against harsh conditions. In contrast, the RF 50mm f/1.8 has a plastic build and lacks weather resistance, making it less suitable for challenging environments.
- **Size and Weight:** The RF 50mm f/1.8 is significantly lighter and more compact, making it an excellent choice for photographers who prioritize portability or are traveling. The f/1.2 version is bulkier and heavier, reflecting its professional-grade construction and larger aperture.
- **Price:** There's a substantial price difference between the two. The RF 50mm f/1.2 is a premium lens with a higher cost, while the RF 50mm f/1.8 is much more budget-friendly, making it accessible to a wider range of photographers.

Best Standard Zoom Lenses for Canon EOS R5 Mark II

1. **Canon RF 24-70mm f/2.8 L IS USM Lens**

Canon RF 24-70mm f/2.8 L IS USM Lens

The Canon RF 24-70mm f/2.8 L IS USM is a go-to zoom lens for professional photographers, offering versatility and exceptional image quality across a wide range of focal lengths. As part of Canon's L-series, it's built to perform in challenging conditions, making it ideal for various photography styles, from portraits to events.

Key Features:

- **Focal Length:** 24-70mm
- **Maximum Aperture:** Constant f/2.8 throughout the zoom range
- **Autofocus Motor:** USM (Ultrasonic Motor) for fast and accurate focusing
- **Image Stabilization:** Yes, up to 5 stops
- **Weather Sealing:** Fully weather-sealed for dust and moisture resistance
- **Weight:** 900g (2 lbs)

Why It Stands Out:

- **Versatile Focal Range:** The 24-70mm range allows for both wide-angle and short-telephoto shots, making it perfect for diverse shooting scenarios, from landscapes to close-up portraits.
- **Constant f/2.8 Aperture:** The f/2.8 aperture provides consistent exposure and depth of field control across the zoom range, enhancing performance in low-light situations.
- **Advanced Image Stabilization:** With up to 5 stops of stabilization, this lens is great for handheld shooting in low light, especially when paired with in-body stabilization systems like those in the EOS R5 Mark II.
- **Superb Optical Performance:** Designed for outstanding sharpness, contrast, and color accuracy, it minimizes chromatic aberrations and distortion, ensuring high-quality images even at f/2.8.
- **Durability:** The lens is fully weather-sealed, making it reliable for outdoor photography in various conditions without worrying about dust or moisture.
- **Fast, Quiet Autofocus:** The USM motor ensures quick and silent focusing, making it suitable for both photography and video work.

Ideal For:

- Event photographers capturing weddings and concerts

- Travel photographers needing a versatile, all-in-one lens
- Portrait photographers seeking beautiful background blur
- Professional photographers who require reliability and high-quality performance

Canon RF 28-70mm f/2 L USM Lens

The Canon RF 28-70mm f/2 L USM lens offers a unique approach to zoom photography with its constant f/2 aperture, making it one of the fastest standard zooms available. This lens is designed for photographers who prioritize low-light performance and image quality, and while it's bulkier, many find the trade-off worthwhile.

Key Features:

- **Focal Length:** 28-70mm
- **Maximum Aperture:** Constant f/2 throughout the zoom range
- **Autofocus Motor:** USM (Ultrasonic Motor) for quick and accurate focusing
- **Weather Sealing:** Fully weather-sealed
- **Weight:** 1430g (3.15 lbs)

Why It Stands Out:

- **Ultra-Wide f/2 Aperture:** The f/2 aperture excels in low-light conditions, allowing for faster shutter speeds and beautiful subject separation, similar to that of prime lenses.
- **Exceptional Image Quality:** Known for its sharpness and detail even at f/2, this lens features advanced optical elements to minimize distortion and chromatic aberration.
- **Unique Focal Range:** While not as wide as the 24-70mm, the 28-70mm range is still versatile enough for most everyday shooting scenarios, from landscapes to portraits.
- **Solid Build Quality:** This lens is robust and weather-sealed, designed to withstand the rigors of professional use in various environments.
- **Fast, Silent Autofocus:** The USM autofocus system is quick and discreet, making it suitable for both photography and videography.

Ideal For:

- Portrait photographers looking for beautiful bokeh
- Low-light photographers needing superior performance
- Professional photographers who require top image quality and don't mind the heft of the lens

Both lenses cater to different needs, with the RF 24-70mm f/2.8 offering a versatile all-rounder option, while the RF 28-70mm f/2 focuses on exceptional low-light capabilities and depth of field control.

Comparison: Canon RF 24-70mm f/2.8 L IS USM vs Canon RF 28-70mm f/2 L USM

Both of these lenses appeal to different types of photographers, each with its strengths:

Aperture:

- **RF 28-70mm f/2**: With its wide f/2 aperture, this lens excels in low-light situations and offers greater control over depth of field. It's ideal for those who frequently shoot in dim conditions or want stunning subject isolation.
- **RF 24-70mm f/2.8**: While the f/2.8 aperture is still fast and performs well in low light, this lens is lighter and more versatile for various shooting scenarios.

Focal Range:

- **RF 24-70mm f/2.8**: Starting at 24mm, this lens provides a wider angle, making it more suitable for landscapes and architecture. If you need that extra width, this is the better option.
- **RF 28-70mm f/2**: Although it begins at 28mm, this lens delivers exceptional image quality, perfect for those who don't require ultra-wide angles.

Portability:

- **RF 24-70mm f/2.8**: Lighter and easier to carry, this lens is ideal for extended shoots or travel.
- **RF 28-70mm f/2**: While it's heavier, many photographers find the added weight worthwhile for the f/2 benefits it offers.

Final Thoughts:

- **Canon RF 24-70mm f/2.8 L IS USM**: A fantastic choice for those seeking a lightweight, versatile lens suitable for various tasks, including events and travel, enhanced by its image stabilization.
- **Canon RF 28-70mm f/2 L USM**: Perfect for photographers who prioritize image quality and performance in low light, this lens combines the quality of a prime lens with the flexibility of a zoom, making it ideal for portraits, weddings, and fine art.

Best Wide-Angle Zoom Lenses for Canon EOS R5 Mark II

1. **Canon RF 15-35mm f/2.8 L IS USM Lens**

Here's a breakdown of the three Canon wide-angle zoom lenses, each catering to different needs and preferences:

1. Canon RF 15-35mm f/2.8 L IS USM

Key Features:

- **Focal Length:** 15-35mm
- **Maximum Aperture:** f/2.8 constant
- **Autofocus Motor:** USM (Ultrasonic Motor)
- **Image Stabilization:** Up to 5 stops
- **Weather Sealing:** Fully weather-sealed
- **Weight:** 840g (1.85 lbs)

Why It Stands Out:

- **Fast f/2.8 Aperture:** Excellent for low-light situations and allows for a shallow depth of field, which is rare for wide-angle lenses.
- **Exceptional Image Quality:** Sharp across the frame with advanced optical elements to minimize chromatic errors and flare.
- **Versatile Focal Range:** Great for landscapes, architecture, and event photography, providing a mix of wide and closer shots.
- **Durable Construction:** Fully weather-sealed for outdoor shooting in various conditions.

Ideal For:

- Landscape and nature photography
- Real estate and architecture
- Wedding and event photography
- Street photography

2. Canon RF 14-35mm f/4 L IS USM

Key Features:

- **Focal Length:** 14-35mm

- **Maximum Aperture:** f/4 constant
- **Autofocus Motor:** USM (Ultrasonic Motor)
- **Image Stabilization:** Up to 5.5 stops
- **Weather Sealing:** Fully weather-sealed
- **Weight:** 540g (1.19 lbs)

Why It Stands Out:

- **Ultra-Wide 14mm Focal Length:** Perfect for capturing expansive scenes and tight indoor spaces.
- **Lightweight and Compact:** Easier to carry for long shoots or travel.
- **Constant f/4 Aperture:** Adequate for most lighting conditions, with consistent exposure across the zoom range.
- **Excellent Sharpness:** High-quality optics provide great performance with minimal distortion and flare.

Ideal For:

- Travel and street photography
- Real estate and architecture
- Landscape photography
- General wide-angle shooting

3. Canon RF 10-20mm f/4 L IS STM (Hypothetical)

Key Features:

- **Focal Length:** 10-20mm
- **Maximum Aperture:** f/4
- **Autofocus Motor:** STM (Stepping Motor)
- **Image Stabilization:** Expected up to 5 stops
- **Weather Sealing:** Likely weather-sealed
- **Weight:** Estimated around 500g

Why It Would Stand Out:

- **Ultra-Wide Field of View:** Excellent for architectural and creative wide-angle compositions, perfect for capturing vast landscapes.
- **STM Autofocus for Video:** Ideal for videographers needing quiet and smooth focus transitions.
- **Lightweight and Versatile:** A compact option for photographers seeking portability without sacrificing performance.

Ideal For:

- Architecture and interior photography
- Real estate photography
- Creative landscape photography
- Vlogging and video work

Conclusion

- **Choose the RF 15-35mm f/2.8** if you need versatility and performance in low light, making it suitable for a wide range of applications.
- **Opt for the RF 14-35mm f/4** if you prioritize portability and are working in good lighting, making it perfect for travel and everyday use.
- **The hypothetical RF 10-20mm f/4** would cater to those needing an ultra-wide option, especially for architectural photography and vlogging.

Each lens offers unique advantages, so your choice should reflect your specific photography needs and style!

Best Wide-Angle Prime Lenses for Canon EOS R5 Mark II

1. **Canon RF 16mm f/2.8 STM Lens**

Canon RF 16mm f/2.8 STM Lens

The Canon RF 16mm f/2.8 STM is an ultra-wide-angle prime lens designed for the Canon RF mount. It provides photographers with a compact and lightweight option for capturing expansive scenes, making it ideal for landscape, architecture, and astrophotography. Its fast f/2.8 maximum aperture and wide focal length enhance its versatility.

Key Features:

- **Focal Length:** 16mm
- **Maximum Aperture:** f/2.8
- **Autofocus Motor:** STM (Stepping Motor) for quiet and smooth focusing
- **Weight:** Approximately 165g (0.36 lbs)
- **Close Focusing Distance:** 0.13m (5.1 inches)

Why the Canon RF 16mm f/2.8 STM Stands Out:

- **Ultra-Wide Perspective:** With a wide field of view at 16mm, it excels in capturing expansive landscapes, tall buildings, and starry skies, allowing for rich detail and dramatic compositions.
- **Compact and Lightweight:** At just 165g, it's one of the lightest lenses in the RF series, making it perfect for travel photographers who prefer minimal gear without sacrificing quality.
- **Fast f/2.8 Aperture:** The f/2.8 aperture is beneficial in low-light conditions, providing sharp images and creative depth-of-field options.
- **Macro Capability:** With a close focusing distance of 0.13m, it allows for detailed shots of small subjects, ideal for capturing textures and nature's intricacies.
- **Affordable:** A great option for those looking to expand their wide-angle lens collection without a hefty price tag.

Who Should Buy It:

- **Landscape Photographers:** Perfect for capturing vast scenes and dramatic skies.
- **Travel Photographers:** Ideal for those who want a quality wide-angle lens without added weight.
- **Astrophotographers:** Its low-light performance is excellent for night sky photography.

Best For:

- Landscapes
- Travel photography
- Night sky and astrophotography

Canon RF 35mm f/1.8 Macro IS STM Lens

The Canon RF 35mm f/1.8 Macro IS STM Lens is user-friendly and versatile, offering a standard focal length with macro capabilities. It's perfect for photographers who wish to explore both wide-angle and close-up photography.

Key Features:

- **Focal Length:** 35mm
- **Maximum Aperture:** f/1.8
- **Autofocus Motor:** STM (Stepping Motor) for smooth and silent focusing
- **Image Stabilization:** Yes, up to 5 stops
- **Weight:** Approximately 405g (0.89 lbs)
- **Close Focusing Distance:** 0.17m (6.7 inches)

Why the Canon RF 35mm f/1.8 Macro IS STM Stands Out:

- **Versatile Focal Length:** The 35mm focal length is ideal for street photography, portraits, and nature shots, offering a good balance between wide-angle and normal perspectives.
- **Fast f/1.8 Aperture:** This allows for great performance in low-light situations and creates beautiful background blur (bokeh), enhancing portrait and artistic photography.
- **Macro Capability:** The ability to focus as close as 0.17m lets you capture intricate details of small subjects like flowers and insects.
- **Image Stabilization:** The built-in stabilization reduces camera shake, improving handheld shooting, especially in low-light and macro settings.
- **Compact Design:** Weighing around 405g, it's portable and easy to carry for extended shoots.

Who Should Buy It:

- **Street Photographers:** Its focal length and aperture make it suitable for spontaneous and natural captures.
- **Macro Enthusiasts:** The close-focusing feature is perfect for detailed close-ups.
- **Portrait Photographers:** The f/1.8 aperture is excellent for low-light conditions and beautiful background separation.

Best For:

- Street and environmental photography
- Macro and close-up photography
- Portraits

Canon RF 24mm f/1.8 Macro IS STM Lens

The Canon RF 24mm f/1.8 Macro IS STM Lens combines wide-angle capabilities with macro features, making it a flexible choice for various photographic situations.

Key Features:

- **Focal Length:** 24mm
- **Maximum Aperture:** f/1.8
- **Autofocus Motor:** STM (Stepping Motor) for smooth and silent focusing
- **Image Stabilization:** Yes, up to 5 stops
- **Weight:** Approximately 325g (0.72 lbs)
- **Close Focusing Distance:** 0.14m (5.5 inches)

Why the Canon RF 24mm f/1.8 Macro IS STM Stands Out:

- **Wide-Angle Flexibility:** The 24mm focal length is excellent for capturing landscapes, architecture, and urban scenes, providing a broad view without excessive distortion.
- **Fast f/1.8 Aperture:** Ideal for low-light conditions and creating depth-of-field effects, it allows for focused subjects against blurred backgrounds.
- **Macro Capability:** With a close focusing distance of 0.14m, it excels at capturing fine details in small subjects, enhancing its utility as a prime lens.
- **Compact and Lightweight:** Weighing only 325g, it's easy to carry for daily use and travel.
- **Image Stabilization:** Helps ensure clear images, especially in low light, providing confidence for handheld shooting.

Who Should Buy It:

- **Landscape and Nature Photographers:** The 24mm length is perfect for expansive views.
- **Street Photographers:** Versatile for both wide-angle and close-up shots.
- **Macro Enthusiasts:** Its macro features allow for detailed close-up photography.

Best For:

- Landscapes and architecture
- Street photography
- Macro photography

Best Portrait Lenses for Canon EOS R5 Mark II

Canon RF 85mm f/1.2 L USM Lens

The Canon RF 85mm f/1.2 L USM Lens is a premier portrait lens specifically designed for the Canon RF mount. Highly regarded among portrait photographers, it excels at creating stunning images with beautifully soft backgrounds.

Key Features:

- **Focal Length:** 85mm
- **Maximum Aperture:** f/1.2
- **Autofocus Motor:** Ring USM (Ultrasonic Motor) for rapid and quiet focusing
- **Weight:** Approximately 1,195g (2.63 lbs)
- **Close Focusing Distance:** 0.85m (2.79 feet)

Why the Canon RF 85mm f/1.2 L USM Stands Out:

- **Exceptional Image Quality:** Even at wide apertures, this lens delivers sharp, clear images, capturing fine details and vibrant colors in subjects' faces.
- **Stunning Bokeh:** The f/1.2 aperture creates a smooth, creamy background blur, enhancing depth and ensuring the subject stands out beautifully.
- **Fast Autofocus:** The Ring USM system provides quick and accurate focusing, making it easy to capture fleeting moments in both posed and candid shots.
- **Versatile Applications:** While primarily a portrait lens, it is also suitable for fashion, events, and product photography, offering flattering perspectives for both portraits and full-body shots.
- **Weather-Sealed Design:** Built to withstand challenging conditions, this lens is ideal for outdoor portraits.

Who Should Buy It:

- **Professional Portrait Photographers:** Its outstanding image quality and beautiful bokeh make it an excellent choice for creating striking portraits.
- **Wedding Photographers:** Ideal for capturing both spontaneous moments and formal portraits during weddings.
- **Fashion Photographers:** The lens enhances clothing and accessories, making them stand out with its beautiful background blur.

Best For:

- Portraits
- Weddings and events
- Fashion and editorial photography

Canon RF 135mm f/1.8 L IS USM Lens

The Canon RF 135mm f/1.8 L IS USM Lens is another exceptional portrait lens, offering a longer focal length that makes it perfect for capturing stunning close-up images. With impressive sharpness and image stabilization, it's a valuable tool for any portrait photographer.

Key Features:

- **Focal Length:** 135mm
- **Maximum Aperture:** f/1.8
- **Autofocus Motor:** Ring USM for fast and quiet focusing
- **Image Stabilization:** Yes, up to 5 stops
- **Weight:** Approximately 1,020g (2.25 lbs)

- **Close Focusing Distance:** 0.8m (2.62 feet)

Why the Canon RF 135mm f/1.8 L IS USM Stands Out:

- **Longer Focal Length:** The 135mm focal length allows you to get close to your subject without distortion, making it ideal for flattering portraits and full-body shots.
- **Fast f/1.8 Aperture:** While not as wide as f/1.2, the f/1.8 aperture still performs well in low light and produces lovely background bokeh.
- **Image Stabilization:** The built-in stabilization minimizes camera shake, resulting in sharper images, especially useful in low light or handheld shooting.
- **High Image Quality:** The lens delivers exceptional sharpness and clarity, reducing chromatic aberration and distortion for crystal-clear images.
- **Versatile Applications:** Beyond portraits, this lens is great for sports, wildlife, and event photography due to its longer reach.

Who Should Buy It:

- **Professional Portrait Photographers:** A favorite among pros for its ability to produce outstanding portrait images.
- **Event Photographers:** The longer focal length allows for capturing candid moments from a distance.
- **Wildlife Photographers:** Its versatility and reach make it suitable for wildlife photography as well.

Best For:

- Portraits
- Events and candid shots
- Wildlife photography

Best Macro Lenses for Canon EOS R5 Mark II

Canon RF 100mm f/2.8 L Macro IS USM Lens

The Canon RF 100mm f/2.8 L Macro IS USM Lens is a premier choice for serious macro photographers. It boasts excellent image quality and a range of useful features, making it ideal for capturing intricate details, from insects to product photography.

Key Features:

- **Focal Length:** 100mm
- **Maximum Aperture:** f/2.8

- **Autofocus Motor:** Ring USM (Ultrasonic Motor) for quick and quiet focusing
- **Image Stabilization:** Yes, up to 5 stops
- **Weight:** Approximately 505g (1.11 lbs)
- **Close Focusing Distance:** 0.26m (10.2 inches)
- **Maximum Magnification:** 1.0x (life-size)

Why the Canon RF 100mm f/2.8 L Macro IS USM Stands Out:

- **Impressive Magnification:** With a maximum magnification of 1.0x, this lens allows for life-size captures of small subjects, revealing details not visible to the naked eye.
- **Outstanding Image Quality:** Known for its exceptional optical performance, the lens produces sharp, vibrant images with minimal artifacts, meeting Canon's high L-series standards for durability and reliability.
- **Effective Image Stabilization:** The built-in stabilization enhances macro photography by enabling slower shutter speeds without camera shake, particularly useful in natural light or when photographing delicate subjects.
- **Versatile Applications:** While primarily a macro lens, its focal length is also suitable for portraits, providing a good working distance for capturing moving subjects like insects or animals.
- **Weather-Sealed Design:** As part of Canon's L series, this lens is weather-sealed, making it a robust choice for outdoor photography in various conditions.

Who Should Buy It:

- **Professional Macro Photographers:** Ideal for those seeking high-resolution images with versatility.
- **Nature and Wildlife Photographers:** The close-focusing capabilities and longer focal length allow for capturing subjects without disturbance.
- **Product Photographers:** Excellent for highlighting textures and intricate details in commercial photography.

Best For:

- Macro photography
- Nature and wildlife photography
- Product and commercial photography

Canon RF 85mm f/2 Macro IS STM Lens

The Canon RF 85mm f/2 Macro IS STM Lens is a more compact option that still delivers impressive macro capabilities. It's designed for photographers seeking a lightweight solution for capturing details in various environments.

Key Features:

- **Focal Length:** 85mm
- **Maximum Aperture:** f/2
- **Autofocus Motor:** STM (Stepping Motor) for smooth and quiet focusing
- **Image Stabilization:** Yes, up to 5 stops
- **Weight:** Approximately 500g (1.1 lbs)
- **Close Focusing Distance:** 0.35m (1.15 feet)
- **Maximum Magnification:** 0.5x

Why the Canon RF 85mm f/2 Macro IS STM Stands Out:

- **Compact and Lightweight:** At just 500g, this lens is easier to carry than longer macro options, making it ideal for fieldwork or travel.
- **Decent Magnification:** Although it offers 0.5x magnification, it excels at capturing detailed close-ups of flowers and small objects, emphasizing texture and intricacies.
- **Good Low-Light Performance:** The f/2 aperture allows for effective shooting in dim conditions without excessive ISO increases, making it perfect for indoor or shaded environments.
- **Smooth Autofocus:** The STM motor ensures quiet and fluid focusing, beneficial for both macro and video work. It also allows for easy switching between autofocus and manual focus for more control.
- **Versatile for Different Photography Styles:** The 85mm focal length makes it suitable for portrait photography, providing flattering compression for facial features, making it a great dual-purpose lens.

Who Should Buy It:

- **Photographers Seeking Portability:** Ideal for those who want a lightweight lens for macro photography without sacrificing performance.
- **Portrait Photographers:** The lens also excels in portraiture, offering a versatile option for different shooting styles.
- **Nature Enthusiasts:** Great for capturing details in nature, whether in the field or at home.

Best For:

- Macro photography
- Portrait photography
- General detail-oriented photography

Chapter 2

Initial Setup: Charging the Battery and Attaching the Lens

Charging the Battery

- Take off the protective cover of the battery.

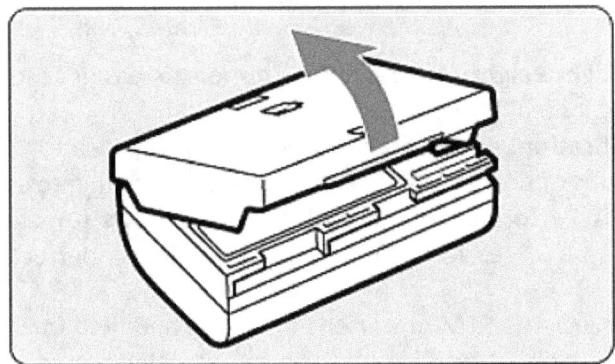

- Fully place the battery into the charger.

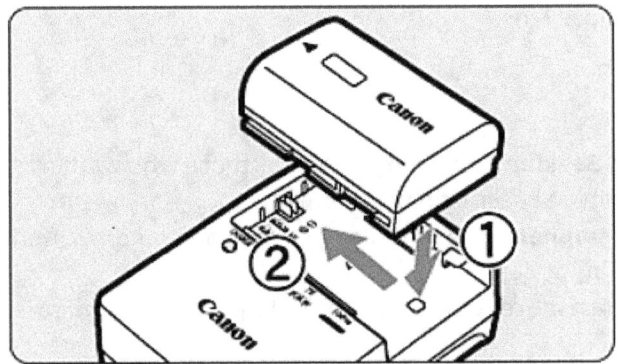

To put the battery back in, follow these steps in reverse:

1. **Align the battery:** Position the battery so that the connectors match up with the contacts in the device.
2. **Insert the battery:** Gently push the battery into place until it clicks securely.
3. **Close any covers:** If there's a battery cover or compartment door, make sure to close it properly.

This will complete the reinstallation of the battery.

1. Get the battery charged.

LC-E6

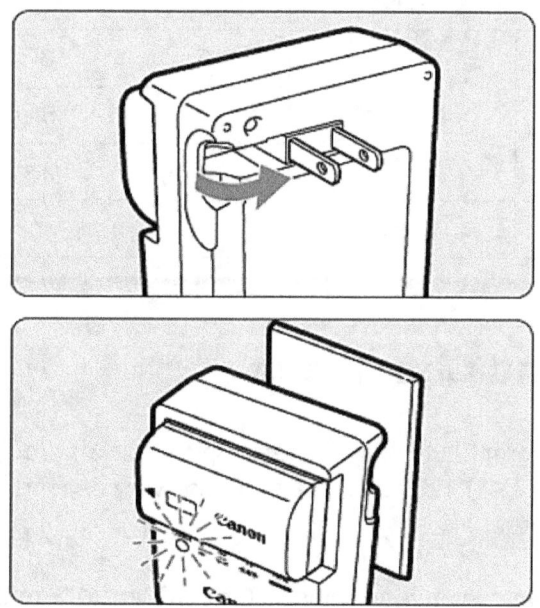

- **Extend the prongs:** Flip out the prongs as demonstrated.

- **Plug in the charger:** Insert the charger into a wall outlet.

LC-E6E

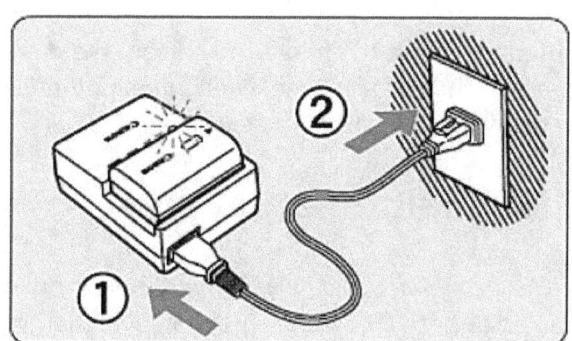

- **Plug in the charger:** Connect the charger's power cord to a power source.

- **Charging indicator:** The charging process will begin automatically, and the charge lamp will blink orange.

Charge Level	Charge Lamp	
	Color	Display
0–49%	Orange	Blinks once per second
50–74%	Orange	Blinks twice per second
75% or higher	Orange	Blinks three times per second
Fully charged	Green	Turned on

Charge Time and Conditions

- **Charging duration:** A completely dead battery typically takes around three hours to charge at room temperature (23°C/73°F). However, the time may vary depending on the remaining battery power and external temperature.

- **Cold weather effects:** In cooler conditions (5°C to 10°C or 41°F to 50°F), charging may take up to four hours. The charging speed may slow down in cold temperatures to protect the battery.

Pre-charging requirements

- **Battery condition upon purchase:** The battery is not fully charged when you first buy it. For optimal performance, always charge it before use.

- **Charging recommendations:** It's best to charge the battery the day before or the day of your intended use. Batteries can lose charge over time, even when not in use. By charging just before use, you'll ensure it's fully ready for your shoot or session.

Safety and Battery Maintenance Tips

- **Removing the battery:** Once the battery is fully charged, take it out of the charger and unplug the charger from the power outlet. This helps prevent overcharging and conserves power, extending the lifespan of both the charger and the battery.

⬛ **Battery charge indicator:** Using the protective cover helps keep your batteries organized. You can attach the cover in various ways to indicate whether a battery is charged or not, making it easy to check while in the studio or out in the field.

Putting in the Battery.

1. **Unlock the cover:** Slide the Battery Compartment Cover Lock to release it.
2. **Open the cover:** Once unlocked, lift the cover to access the battery compartment.

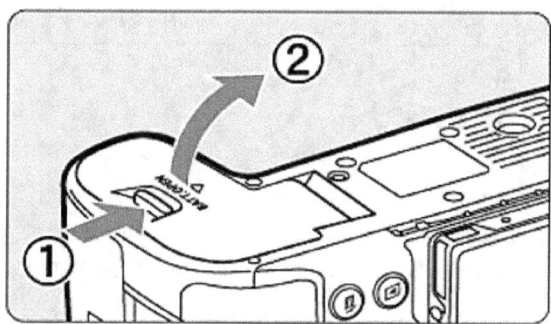

Insert the battery: Take your fully charged LP-E6P Battery Pack and carefully place it into the slot.

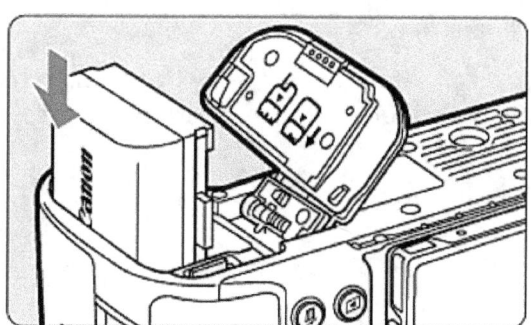

- **Orientation:** Insert the battery with the electrical connections facing in first.
- **Secure the battery:** Gently push the battery until it clicks, indicating that the lock is secure.

3. **Close the lid:** After inserting the battery, press down on the compartment lid until it snaps shut. This ensures the cover is securely closed, protecting the battery from exposure to air and accidental removal.

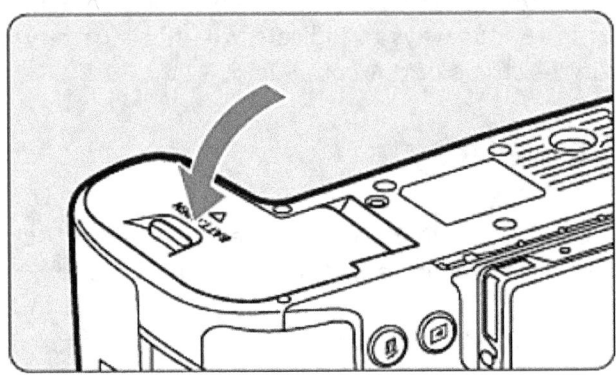

4.

Removing the Battery.

5. **Access the battery:** Slide the compartment lock to unlock it, then open the cover.
6. **Release the battery:** Locate the battery lock lever inside the compartment and press it. Push the lever in the direction indicated by the arrow (usually outward) to release the battery.
7. **Remove the battery:** Once the lock lever is pressed, gently pull the battery out. Handle it carefully, especially around the electrical contacts.
8. **Attach the protective cover:** After removing the battery, promptly replace the cover to prevent damage and avoid short circuits.

By following these steps, you can safely and correctly insert and remove your camera's battery, ensuring the performance of both your camera and battery are preserved.

Chapter 3
Camera Setup

Step 1: Inserting the Battery and Memory Card

To set up your Canon EOS R5 Mark II camera, start by inserting the battery and memory card. The memory card slot is located on the side, while the battery compartment is at the bottom.

- Open the battery compartment and insert the LP-E6P battery with the connections facing the camera. Ensure it clicks into place before closing the compartment.
- For the memory card, open the memory card slot cover, making sure the label faces the camera. Push the card in firmly until it is secure before closing the lid.

Step 2: Charging the Battery

Before first use, ensure the battery is fully charged. Connect the battery to the charger and plug it into a power source. The charger will indicate when the battery is fully charged.

Step 3: Attaching the Lens

The Canon EOS R5 Mark II features interchangeable lenses. Align the lens mount with the camera mount, then turn the lens clockwise until it clicks into place. Ensure the lens is securely attached before use.

Step 4: Turning on the Camera

To power on the camera, press the power button located on top. It may take a moment for the camera to fully turn on.

Step 5: Choosing Language and Time Zone

Upon turning on, you'll be prompted to select your preferred language and time zone. Use the touch screen to make your selections.

Step 6: Setting the Time and Date

Next, set the time and date on your Canon EOS R5 Mark II. Make sure the time zone is correct as you enter the information via the touch screen.

Step 7: Configuring the Camera's Settings

After setting the time and date, adjust the camera settings to fit your preferences. Access the settings menu by pressing the menu button on the back of the camera. You can navigate using the touch screen or control knobs. Consider these key settings:

- **Shooting Mode:** Choose from program, manual, aperture priority, or shutter priority modes.
- **Autofocus Options:** Select how the camera focuses on subjects, with options like single-point AF, zone AF, and face recognition AF.
- **Image Quality Settings:** Adjust the resolution and compression options, including RAW, JPEG, and HEIF formats.
- **Custom Functions:** Personalize settings like buttons, shooting modes, and white balance to suit your style.

Step 8: Customizing the Quick Control Screen

The Quick Control Screen enhances usability by allowing quick adjustments to key settings like ISO, shutter speed, and aperture. To customize it:

1. Press the **Q** button on the back of the camera to access the Quick Control Screen.
2. Tap the "Customize" icon in the top right corner.
3. Use the joystick or touch screen to add settings to the Quick Control Screen.
4. Click the **Set** button to save your changes.
5. Rearrange the order of settings as desired.
6. Press the **Menu** button to exit customization.

Customizing the Quick Control Screen helps streamline your workflow, enabling faster and more accurate shooting. You can also save and switch between up to three different Quick Control Screen setups based on your shooting needs. Just select "Save/Load Settings" from the customization menu to store your preferred setup.

The Set-up Menu

Set-up Menu Overview for the Canon EOS R5 II

The Set-up Menu on your Canon EOS R5 II is essential for customizing how your camera operates and ensuring it meets your needs. Here's a breakdown of its key features:

1. **Basic Settings:**
    - **Formatting the Memory Card:** Prepare your card for use by erasing existing data and ensuring optimal performance.

- o **Date and Time Adjustment:** Set the correct date and time to keep your images accurately timestamped.
2. **Power-Saving Features:**
   - o Control how the camera conserves battery life, including settings for auto shut-off and display timing.
3. **Information Display:**
   - o Customize how information is shown on the screen, such as grid lines, shooting data, and levels.
4. **Screen Brightness:**
   - o Adjust the brightness of the LCD screen for optimal visibility in different lighting conditions.
5. **Connectivity Options:**
   - o Manage Bluetooth and Wi-Fi settings to connect your camera to smartphones, tablets, or other devices for easy sharing and remote control.
6. **Software Updates:**
   - o Keep your camera's firmware up to date to benefit from the latest features and improvements.

Goals of the Set-up Menu

- **Personalization:** Tailor the camera settings to fit your shooting style and preferences.
- **Performance Optimization:** Ensure your camera operates smoothly and efficiently, prolonging its lifespan.
- **User Convenience:** Streamline access to important settings, making it easier to adjust configurations on the fly.

By utilizing the Set-up Menu effectively, you can enhance your photography experience with the Canon EOS R5 II, making it a truly personalized tool for capturing stunning images.

Set-up Menu Options

Amber-Coded Set-up Menu Options for Canon EOS R5 II

The amber-coded Set-up menu screens on the Canon EOS R5 II allow you to customize various operational aspects of your camera while shooting. Here are some of the key options available:

1. **Custom Functions:**
   - o Adjust specific camera settings to suit your shooting style, such as button assignments and control settings.
2. **Display Options:**
   - o Change the way information is displayed on the screen, including grids, histogram views, and shooting data overlays.

3. **Power Settings:**
    - Control the camera's power-saving features, including sleep timers and auto shut-off intervals.
4. **Connectivity Settings:**
    - Manage Wi-Fi and Bluetooth connections, enabling easy sharing and remote control capabilities.
5. **Firmware Update:**
    - Access options for updating the camera's firmware to ensure you have the latest features and fixes.

Important Note

Remember, these Set-up menu options differ from the Shooting menu, which directly affects how photos and videos are captured. The Set-up menu focuses on the camera's functionality and user interface, enhancing your overall shooting experience.

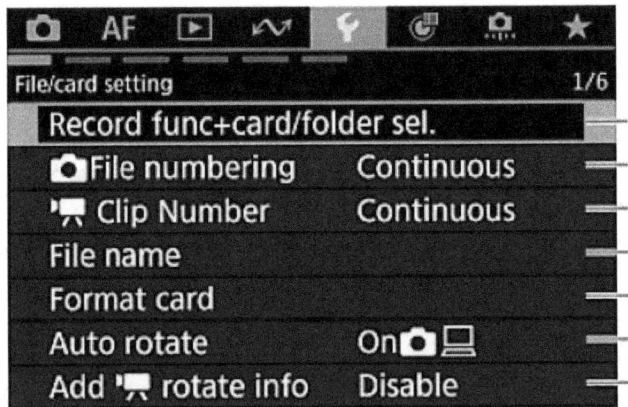

Record Functions+Card/Folder Sel.

Set-up 1 Menu: Card and Folder Management for Canon EOS R5 II

The Set-up 1 menu on the Canon EOS R5 II provides extensive options for managing how your photos and videos are stored on the memory cards. Here are the key features:

1. **Card Selection:**
    - Choose which card (Card 1 or Card 2) will be the primary storage for images and videos. This allows you to prioritize one card over the other based on your needs.
2. **Separate Storage:**
    - You can configure the camera to store photos on one card and videos on another, enabling better organization and management of your files.

3. **Folder Naming:**
   - Customize how folders are named by default. This helps in organizing your images and videos systematically, making it easier to find specific files later.
4. **Automatic Switching:**
   - Set the camera to automatically switch between cards when one fills up. This ensures that you don't run out of storage space during a shoot.

These options give you greater flexibility in managing your storage, helping you to streamline your workflow and keep your media organized.

Record Stills/Movies Separately

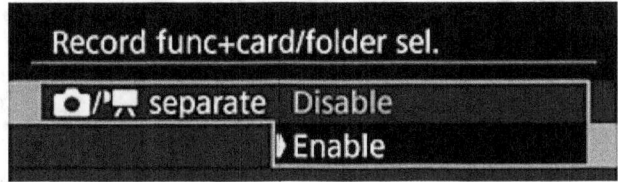

Storage and Playback Separation

When you enable the strict storage and playback separation on the Canon EOS R5 II, it effectively manages how your photos and videos are stored and accessed. Here's a breakdown of how this feature works:

1. **Storage Allocation:**
   - **Photos on Card 1:** All still images will be saved to Card 1.
   - **Videos on Card 2:** All video files will be stored on Card 2.
   - This ensures that there is a clear division between your photo and video files.
2. **Playback Limitations:**
   - When in **Movie Mode**, playback will only show video files from Card 2.
   - When in **Still Photo Mode**, playback will only show images from Card 1, with no access to video files.
3. **Card Capacity Management:**
   - If either card becomes full, the camera will not automatically switch to the other card for recording. This means you need to monitor your storage to avoid missing shots.
   - There are no backup options available; the camera won't copy files from one card to the other.
4. **Speed Considerations:**
   - It's recommended to use a fast memory card in Slot 1, especially for recording high-resolution 4K or 8K video.

- o A fast card in Slot 2 is also important to maintain high-speed shooting capabilities.
5. **Feature Restrictions:**
   - o When this separation is enabled, the Recording options and Record/Play options will be disabled. This means you won't have the flexibility to switch recording modes or create backups between the cards.

This setup is beneficial for those who want clear organization between different types of media, but it does require careful management of card space and speed.

Recording Options

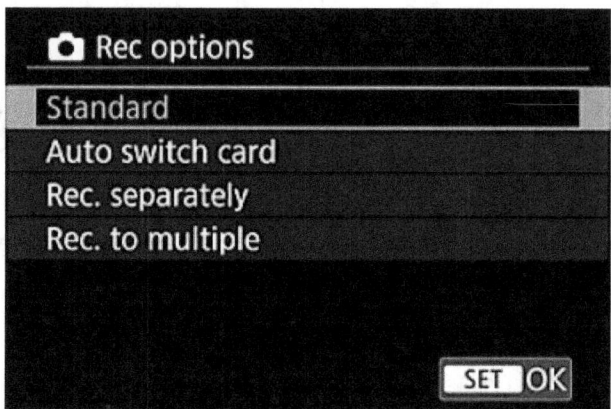

Handling Still Photos on the Canon EOS R5 II

The EOS R5 II provides four options for managing how still photos are saved, allowing photographers to choose the setup that best fits their workflow:

1. **Standard:**
   - o **Storage Location:** Photos are saved to the card designated in the Stills Record/Play setting.
   - o **Limitations:** If the selected card becomes full, you cannot take any more still photos until a new card is inserted.
2. **Auto Switch Card (Overflow):**
   - o **Functionality:** This option allows the camera to automatically switch to the other card once the designated card fills up. It enables continuous shooting without the need to change cards manually.
   - o **Caveat:** While convenient, this setting means that photos and videos will not be kept separate, as both types of files may end up on either card.
3. **Record Separately (Backup):**

- **Backup Feature:** Each photo is saved on both cards, allowing for an identical backup. You can also set different qualities for each file, such as saving a RAW file on one card and a JPEG on the other.
- **File Numbering:** The images will share the same file number, making it easy to identify which pairs belong together.
- **Flexible Quality Options:** You can choose different formats for each card, such as RAW on Card 1 and JPEG on Card 2, or create smaller versions (S1/S2) for easy sharing.

4. **Record to Multiple (Backup):**
    - **Exact Copies:** This option creates identical copies of photos on both cards, maintaining the same quality level for both.
    - **Space Considerations:** The number of photos you can take will depend on the available space on the cards. If one card becomes full, you'll need to replace it to continue recording.
    - **Redundancy:** This setting offers a straightforward backup solution, ensuring you have duplicate files.

Conclusion

These settings give you flexibility and control over your photography workflow, allowing you to choose between ease of use and backup security based on your shooting needs. Whether you prefer to keep files separate or want redundancy in your captures, the EOS R5 II offers a configuration that can fit various styles of photography.

Movie Recording Options

Managing Movie Clips on the Canon EOS R5 II

The Canon EOS R5 II provides several options for handling movie clips, enhancing flexibility for video recording. Here's a breakdown of the available settings:

1. **Standard:**
    - **Storage Location:** Movies are saved to the card designated in the Movies Record/Play setting.
    - **Limitations:** If the selected card becomes full, you will be unable to record any additional video clips until a new card is inserted.
2. **Auto Switch Card (Overflow):**
    - **Functionality:** This setting allows movies to be recorded on the primary card. Once that card is full, the camera automatically switches to the second card, saving clips in a new folder.
    - **Convenience:** This feature enables continuous recording without interruptions, making it useful for longer shoots.
    -

3. **Main Proxy:**
    - **Dual Recording:** In this mode, both main and proxy video files are saved simultaneously. The main video is saved under the standard file name, while proxy files are marked with "_Proxy."
    - **File Naming:** You can customize the file name for the recordings in the [Movies] setting under [File name], helping you to manage and organize your clips effectively.
4. **Rec. to Multiple:**
    - **Identical Copies:** Both cards will record the same movie file, creating a backup in real-time.
    - **Recording Restrictions:** Note that video cannot be recorded on SD or SDHC cards when using this option, so ensure you're using compatible media.

Conclusion

These settings provide a comprehensive approach to managing video recordings on the EOS R5 II, catering to different shooting scenarios. Whether you prefer straightforward recording, dual backups, or overflow capabilities, you can customize your setup to fit your video production needs.

Recording/Playback Selection with Two Cards Inserted

You can customize the recording settings for your Canon EOS R5 II to prioritize which card is used for stills and movies. Here's how to manage these settings using the INFO button:

Default Settings

- **Movies:** Saved to Card 2 by default.
- **Stills:** Recorded on Card 1 by default.

Customization Options

You can rearrange the labels and choose which card to prioritize for still image capture. Here are the options you can select:

1. **Card Priority Settings:**
    - **Select Card for Stills:** Use the INFO button to access the settings and choose which card will be used for still photo storage.
    - **Select Card for Movies:** You can similarly designate which card will be the default for video recordings.
2. **Options for Card Settings:**
    - **Stills Record/Play:** Choose either Card 1 or Card 2 for capturing still images.

- **Movies Record/Play:** Set your preferred card for recording video clips.

Customization Tips

- **Visual Indicators:** Highlight your preferred card choice to make it easily identifiable during shooting.
- **Consider Speed:** Ensure you use fast memory cards, especially in Card 1, if you plan to shoot high-resolution images or 4K/8K video.

By adjusting these settings, you can tailor your camera's performance to suit your shooting style and workflow.

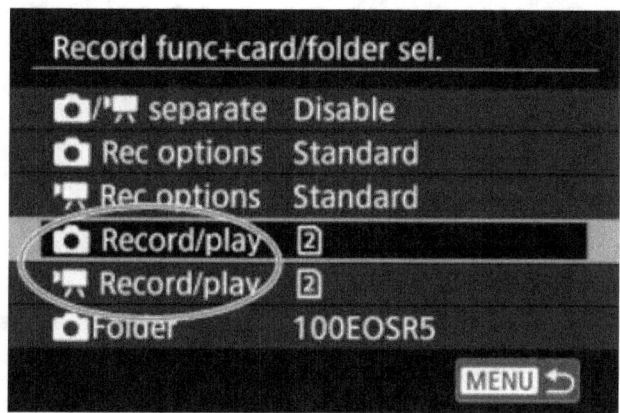

Card Priority Settings for Video Recording

When using the Canon EOS R5 II, you can customize how your camera handles video recording and playback through various settings. Here's a breakdown of your options:

Standard/Auto Switch Card Modes

- **Standard Mode:** Choose which card will record and play back video files. The selected card remains the default until changed.
- **Auto Switch Card Mode:** If the primary card becomes full, the camera automatically switches to the secondary card for continued recording.
- **Setting Card Priority:**
  - Press the **INFO** button to set a card as a priority. This feature ensures that whenever a card is added or removed, the camera will automatically switch to the designated priority card for recording.

Record Separately/Record to Multiple/1 Main 2 Proxy

- **Record Separately:** This setting allows you to save two versions of each video (one on each card).
- **Record to Multiple:** Both cards will create exact copies of the video, ensuring redundancy.
- **1 Main 2 Proxy:** The main video is recorded on one card, while a lower-resolution proxy file is saved on the other (useful for editing).
- **Playback Options:** When using these settings, only playback options will be visible. You can select either Card 1 or Card 2 as the primary for playback by pressing the **INFO** button.

Tips for Effective Use

- **Priority Settings:** Enabling card priority ensures seamless operation, particularly useful during long recording sessions where card changes may occur.
- **Check Card Status:** Regularly verify the available space on your cards to prevent interruptions during shooting.

Folder Settings

Creating and Managing Folders on Your Canon EOS R5 II

This menu option allows you to organize where your photos and videos are saved on your memory card. Here's how to create a new folder or navigate existing ones:

Default Folder Structure

- Each folder is automatically assigned a three-digit number followed by five letters (e.g., CANON).
- Each folder can hold up to **9999 photos**.
- When a folder reaches capacity, a new folder is created automatically.
- You can create folders numbered from **100 to 999**.

Steps to Create and Navigate Folders

1. **Pick Folder:**
   - Access the folder option by selecting **Record Function + Card/Folder Sel**.
2. **Navigate Folders:**
   - Use the camera's menu to scroll through existing folders.
   - Select a folder to view its contents or set it as the destination for new files.
3. **Create a New Folder:**
   - If you wish to create a new folder, ensure your memory card is formatted correctly and located within the main **DCIM** folder.

- Follow the on-screen prompts to designate a folder number (between 100 and 999) and confirm.
4. **Finalize:**
    - Once you have selected or created a folder, you can exit the menu. The camera will now save new photos and videos in the designated folder.

Tips for Folder Management

- **Regularly Check Space:** Monitor the contents of your folders to avoid hitting capacity unexpectedly.
- **Organize by Date/Event:** Consider creating folders based on dates or specific events for easier retrieval later.
- **Backup Your Data:** Regularly transfer files from your memory card to a computer or external storage to free up space and ensure your photos and videos are safely stored.

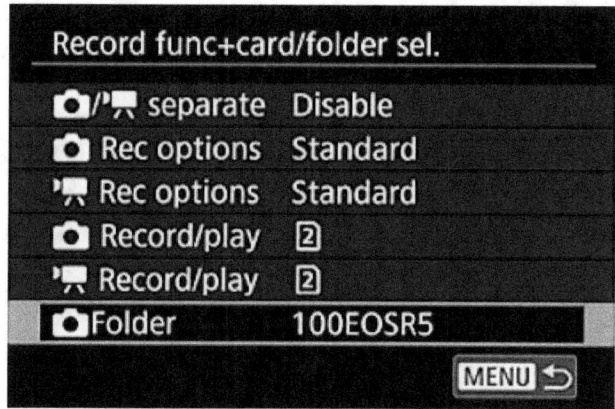

Viewing Available Folders on Your Canon EOS R5 II

To manage your files effectively, you can easily view the list of available folders on your memory card. Here's how to do it:

Steps to View Available Folders

1. **Access the Select Folder Screen:**
    - Navigate to the **Record Function + Card/Folder Sel** option in the menu.
2. **View Folder List:**
    - Once in the Select Folder screen, you will see a list of all folders available on your memory card.
    - Folder names typically appear in a format like **100EOSR5**, **101CANON**, etc.

Select a Folder:

- Use the camera's navigation controls (joystick or touch screen) to scroll through the list of folders.
- Highlight the desired folder you wish to access or set for saving new files.

3. **Confirm Your Selection:**
   - Press the **Set** button to confirm your selection. The camera will now use the chosen folder for saving new images and videos.

Tips for Folder Management

- **Naming Convention:** Familiarize yourself with the folder naming convention to easily identify the right folder.
- **Regular Checks:** Periodically check the folder contents to manage your space effectively and prevent overflow.
- **Delete Unused Folders:** If there are folders you no longer need, consider deleting them (ensure the files are backed up first).

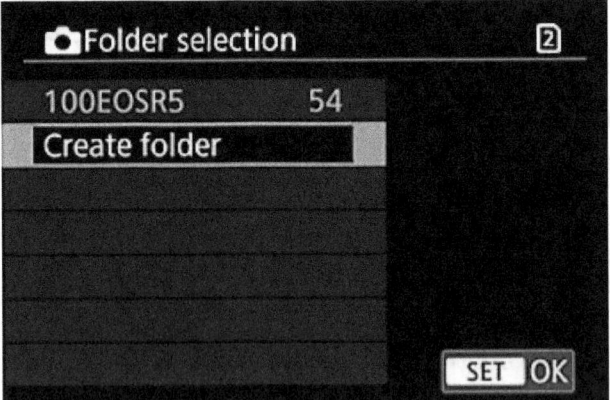

Selecting or Creating a Folder on Your Canon EOS R5 II

To manage where your images and videos are saved, you can select an existing folder or create a new one. Here's how to do it:

Steps to Select or Create a Folder

1. **Select a Different Folder:**
   - Use the **directional keys** or the **touch screen** to scroll through the folder options.
   - As you highlight each folder, you'll see two thumbnails of the images stored in that folder on the right side of the screen.

2. **Confirm the Folder:**
   - Once you've chosen the desired folder, press the **SET** button to confirm your selection. The camera will now save new photos to this folder.
3. **Create a New Folder:**
   - If you wish to create a new folder, highlight **Create Folder** in the Select Folder box and press **SET**.
   - You will be prompted to enter a **Folder Name**. Here, you can:
     - Change the default name if desired.
     - Select **Cancel** to abort the creation process.
     - Choose **OK** to create the folder with the specified name.
4. **Confirm Folder Creation:**
   - After entering the desired folder name, press **SET** to confirm your choice and create the folder.

Tips for Effective Folder Management

- **Organize by Event or Date:** Consider naming folders based on events, dates, or subjects for easier retrieval later.
- **Regular Maintenance:** Periodically review and clean up your folders to keep your memory card organized.
- **Backup Important Files:** Always back up important photos and videos before deleting folders to avoid losing valuable content.

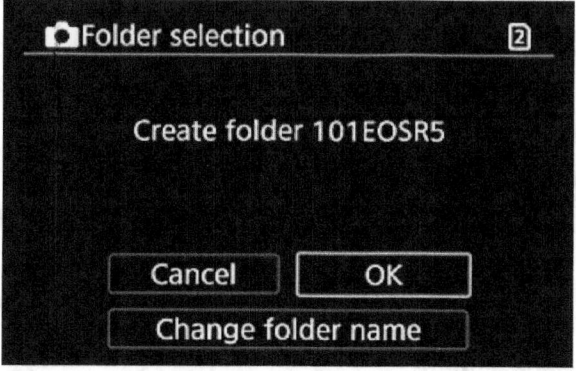

Changing a Folder Name on Your Canon EOS R5 II

If you want to give your folder a new name, follow these steps:

1. **Select "Change Folder Name":**
   - After choosing the option to create a new folder, select **Change Folder Name**.
2. **Enter a New Name:**

- You'll see a keyboard interface on the screen.
- Use the **directional keys** or **touch screen** to navigate through the available characters, which include uppercase and lowercase letters, numbers, and the underscore character (_).

3. **Confirm Your Selection:**
   - Once you've entered your desired name (e.g., **101EOSR5**), navigate to the **OK** option and press **SET** to confirm the new name.
4. **Complete the Process:**
   - The folder will now be created with your specified name. You can continue to use this folder for organizing your photos and videos.

Tips for Naming Folders

- **Be Descriptive:** Use names that reflect the content or event to make it easier to locate files later.
- **Keep It Simple:** Shorter names are often easier to manage and remember.
- **Avoid Special Characters:** Stick to letters, numbers, and underscores to ensure compatibility across devices.

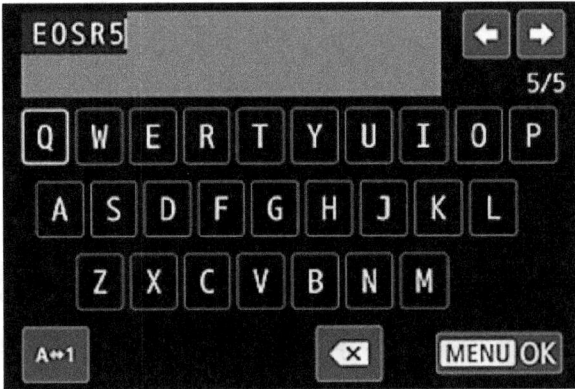

Exiting the Folder Management

1. **Exit the Folder Management:**
   - After you've created or selected your folder, press the **MENU** button to return to the Set-up 1 menu.

Tips for Creative Folder Naming

- **Use Themes:** Consider naming folders based on themes like events (e.g., **Wedding2024**, **VacationParis**) or subjects (e.g., **Wildlife, Landscapes**).
- **Incorporate Dates:** Including the date can help with organization (e.g., **2024-10-28_Trip**).

- **Location-Based Names:** Use location names to easily identify where the photos were taken (e.g., **BeachDay**, **MountainHike**).

Benefits of Organizing Folders

- **Easier Navigation:** With well-organized folders, you can quickly find specific images, especially on larger memory cards.
- **Slideshow Creation:** You can easily create slideshows from selected folders, allowing for quick reviews of specific events or themes.
- **Efficient Management:** Organizing by date or location helps in maintaining a clear record of your photography journey.

By following these steps and tips, you can make the most of your Canon EOS R5 II's folder management system!

File Numbering

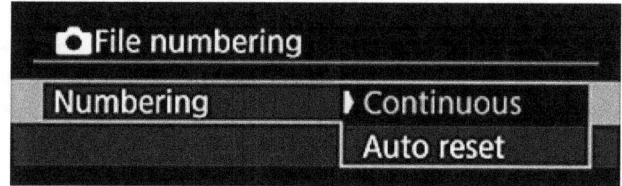

File Numbering System on the Canon EOS R5 II

Every photo you take with the Canon EOS R5 II is assigned a unique file number. This system allows for consistent organization across multiple memory cards. Here's how it works:

File Numbering Basics

- **Number Range:** Each folder can contain images numbered from **0001 to 9999**. After reaching 9999, the camera creates a new folder (e.g., **100, 101, 102**).
- **Resetting Numbers:** The numbering resets when:
    - You insert a new memory card.
    - You manually change the numbering settings.

Internal Memory

The camera retains the last used number in its internal memory. If you use a memory card previously utilized in another camera, the numbering may start from the last used number on that card, which can lead to unexpected file numbers.

Numbering Modes

You have three options for how the camera handles file numbering:

1. **Continuous**
   - **Functionality:** The camera uses the next available number based on the internal memory or the highest number on the current card.
   - **Examples:**
     - New blank card: Next number is one higher than the last used number.
     - Card with images: Next number is one more than the highest existing number on that card.
   - **Tip:** To maintain continuity, use a blank or formatted card regularly.
2. **Automatic Reset**
   - **Functionality:**
     - On a blank or formatted card, the next photo is numbered **0001**.
     - If the card has images, numbering starts at one more than the highest number on that card.
   - **Limitations:** Once the folder reaches 999 (which allows for 9999 images each), you won't be able to take more photos unless you switch to a new card.
3. **Manual Reset**
   - **Functionality:** Resets numbering to **0001** and creates a new folder with a higher number.
   - **Effect on New Cards:** When inserting a different memory card, it will follow the previously set mode (either Continuous or Automatic Reset).
   - **Custom Folder Names:** You can rename the default CANON folder to anything you prefer when performing a manual reset.

Conclusion

Understanding the file numbering system helps keep your photography organized. Choose the mode that best suits your workflow, especially if you frequently switch memory cards or shoot in varying environments. By staying aware of these settings, you can ensure a smooth shooting experience with your Canon EOS R5 II!

Movie Clip Numbering

Movies stored in a folder are assigned clip numbers ranging from 001 to 999. You have the option to modify the numbering of the clips.

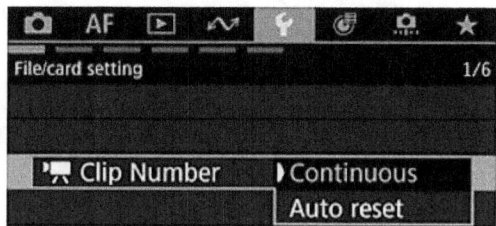

Continuous

For continuous file numbering regardless of switching cards

The clip numbering continues sequentially up to 999, regardless of whether you switch target cards (like from card 1 to card 2) or replace a card. This feature is useful when saving movies numbered 001 to 999 from various cards into a single folder on a computer.

It's important to note that the numbering can extend beyond the numbers of any previously recorded movies on the cards you intend to use. For uninterrupted movie numbering, consider using a card that has been freshly formatted each time.

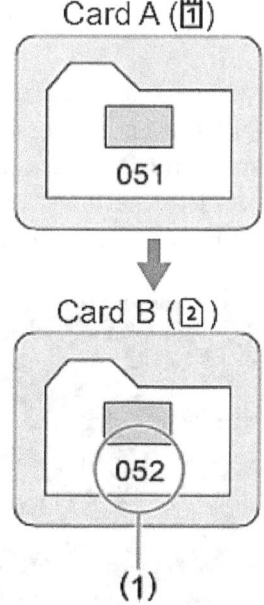

Auto Reset

To restart clip numbering from 001 after switching cards

The clip numbering resets to 001 whenever you switch target cards (like from card 1 to card 2) or insert a new card. This can be useful for organizing movies based on the cards.

Keep in mind that the numbering can continue beyond the numbers of any previously recorded movies on the cards you wish to use. If you prefer the file numbering to start at 001, use a new card each time you save a movie.

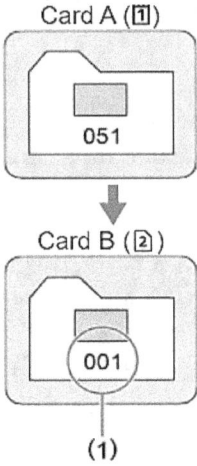

File Name

Similar to other Canon cameras, the R5 II assigns a four-digit alphanumeric string to your picture files upon creation. For instance, you might see file names like BE3B0001.jpg, BE3B001.hif, or BE3B0001.cr3. The initial four characters are unique to your camera and are preset at the factory. Alternatively, you can configure two custom User Settings: User Setting 1 allows you to choose four characters, while User Setting 2 lets you select three characters.

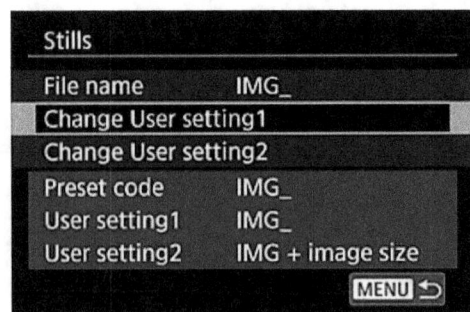

You can modify the names associated with your pictures through this menu option, but there are specific limitations to keep in mind.

DCF restricts file names created by compliant digital cameras to a maximum of eight characters, followed by a three-character extension (like .jpg, .hif, or .cr3) to indicate the file type. This eight-plus-three (or 8.3) limitation originates from the outdated D.O.S. operating system, which many seasoned photographers would prefer to forget, yet it remains a standard for file naming.

Four of the eight characters are designated to identify the camera used for the shot, with Canon using a unique four-character code set by the manufacturer. When the numbering reaches 9999, it resets to aaaa4000, as the last four digits accommodate numbers from 0000 to 9999.

Upon leaving the factory, the camera is configured to offer three different file naming options:

1. **Factory Preset Code**: Each camera has its unique preset code. For example, files may be named aaaa0001.jpg when using the sRGB color space. If you switch to Adobe RGB, the first character changes to an underscore, resulting in names like _EOS0001.jpg or _EOS001.cr3. Although you cannot alter the factory preset code, you can select one of the alternative naming systems.
2. **User Setting 1**: Users can define two naming schemes. By default, the camera is set to IMG_0001.jpg for JPEGs or _IMG0001.jpg for Adobe RGB. If you use sRGB, you can customize the initial four characters to get something like EOSR0001.jpg. The underscore will replace the initial characters when using Adobe RGB. For example, if you choose "OHIO," the file names will be _HIO0001.jpg for Adobe RGB and OHIO0001.jpg for sRGB.
3. **User Setting 2**: In this setting, you can customize only the first three of the four initial characters, with IMG as the default. The fourth character indicates the image quality. For example, if you set the first three characters to ABC, your file names might look like _BCL0001.jpg or ABCL001.jpg. Here are the codes as they appear:
   - **L**: RAW, Large Fine JPEG, or Large Standard JPEG.
   - **M**: M RAW, Medium Fine JPEG, or Medium Standard JPEG.
   - **S**: Small 1 Fine JPEG, Small 1 Standard JPEG, or S RAW.
   - **T**: Small 2 JPEG.
   - **_ (underscore)**: Indicates a movie file, with no quality setting specified.

Redefining User Settings 1 and 2

You can modify the two User Settings from their default values by navigating to the File Name menu. Follow these steps:

1. **Access Menu Entry**: Select the setting you wish to change and press the SET button.
2. **Delete Old Entry**: To remove the previous entry, press the Trash button located in the bottom right corner of the camera's back panel, or tap the <x (backspace icon) at the

bottom right of the screen multiple times. A vertical line will appear where the cursor is positioned.

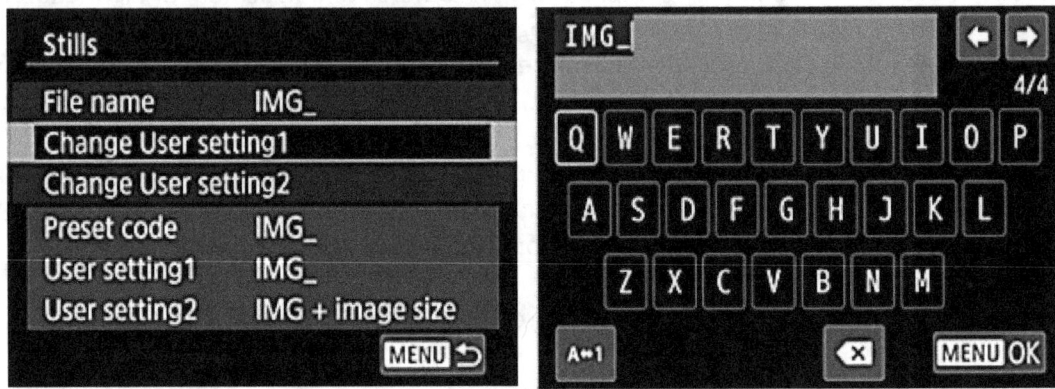

⬚ **Choose Characters**: Use the Multi-controller joystick or the touchscreen to select the first character. You can only input numbers, capital letters, and an underscore. You can also navigate using the Main Dial and select characters with the QCD-2 or QCD-1. Press the character or the SET button to enter the highlighted character.

⬚ **Choose Remaining Characters**: Repeat Step 3 to enter the remaining characters (four for Setting 1 and three for Setting 2). The pointer will then move to the next position. If you make an error, you can use the Trash button to delete any incorrect characters. Note that only the camera can use an underscore; no other characters can include it.

⬚ **Finish**: Press the MENU button to confirm your entries, or press INFO to cancel.

⬚ **Review**: The latest definitions will be displayed at the bottom of the screen.

Movie File Name Settings

You can customize the names of your movie files (clips).

Movie file name structure

	Item	Description
(1)	Camera index	Two letters in the range A–Z. An underscore (_) can also be used as the second character. Identifies the camera used.
(2)	Reel number	A 4-digit number from 0001 to 9999. A different number is automatically assigned to identify the card used. You can set the default value. Advances by one when the first recording on a new card* is made. * Newly purchased or formatted card
(3)	Clip number	A 3-digit number from 001 to 999 preceded by C, as in C001–C999. After C999, D is used at the beginning. Automatically assigned to each clip (movie file). You can set the default value.
(4)	Codec identifier	"A" (as in AVC) is automatically set for H.264 main movies, "H" for HEVC, and "X" for RAW.
(5)	Recording date	Year, month, and day, set automatically based on when recording began.
(6)	Recording time	Hour, minute, and second, set automatically based on when recording began.
(7)	Random component	Two characters, from A to Z and 0 to 9, randomly set for each clip (movie file).
(8)	User-defined field	Five characters, from A to Z and 0 to 9. Default: CANON.
(9)	Proxy identifier	_Proxy is automatically appended to proxy movie files.

Format Card

You can completely erase everything on your memory card and create a new, efficient file system using this option. When you select "Format Card," a screen will appear where you can choose between Card 1 and Card 2. After selecting your card, the screen will display the current storage usage and present two options at the bottom: Cancel or OK (to proceed with the format). Press the Trash button for a low-level format. If a card is running slowly, this type of format can improve its performance by erasing all sectors and creating new ones, helping the camera avoid bad sectors from previous use. An orange progress bar will appear on the screen to indicate the formatting progress.

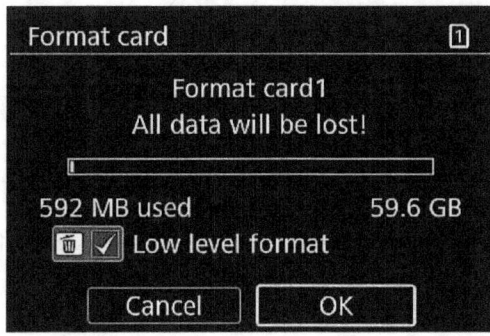

Auto Rotate

You have the option to enable or disable this feature. When turned on, it allows you to view vertically oriented pictures without needing to rotate the camera; the images will automatically rotate on the screen. However, this setup displays the picture with the smallest dimension, resulting in a smaller view. You can do three things with this feature: set your photo-editing or viewing program to automatically rotate the image for display in the camera and on your computer screen. This capability is indicated by two icons: one for the camera and one for the computer screen.

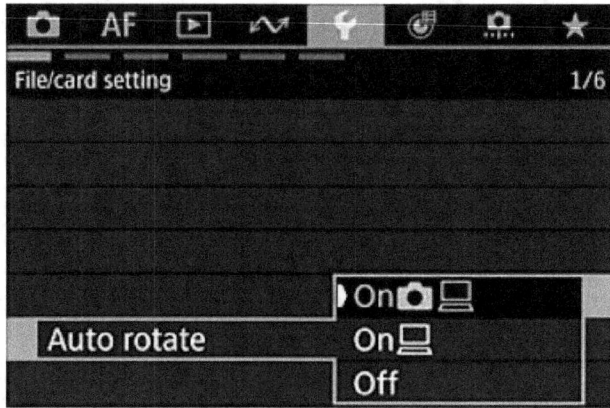

You can't mark an image for auto-rotation until you've viewed it in an image editor or viewing program (indicated by a computer screen icon). This feature allows your camera images to look their best on your screen while still rotating when viewed on your computer.

The third option is to disable auto-rotation, meaning the picture won't rotate whether you're viewing it on your computer or the camera. It's important to note that if you turn off Auto Rotate, any pictures taken during that period won't be automatically rotated once you turn it back on. Auto-rotation is determined by the data stored in the image file at the time of capture.

Add Movie Rotate Information

Cell phones have transformed how movies are displayed, allowing for both horizontal and vertical orientations. Users of smartphones and tablets often rotate their devices to record videos in either mode, even though videos have traditionally been shot in landscape. You can configure your video clips to automatically include information about their orientation, ensuring that when played back on devices, they appear correctly. This setting does not alter how the video is viewed on the camera or on an external screen connected via HDMI.

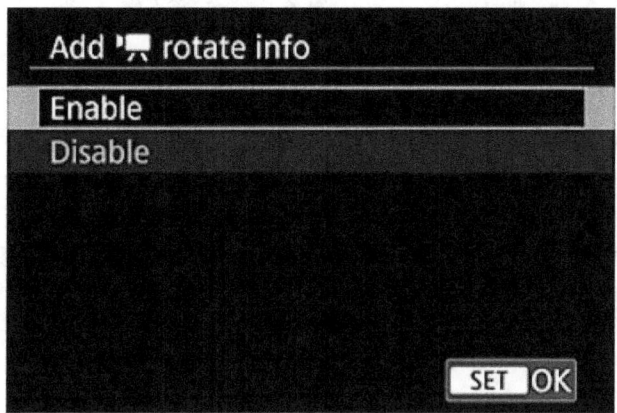

Date/Time/Zone

This option allows you to set the time and date, which will be saved in the image file along with exposure and other details. Here's how to access it:

1. Navigate to the Set-up 2 menu.
2. Use the QCD-1 to highlight the Date/Time field.
3. Press the SET button, located in the center of the QCD-1, to open the Date/Time setting screen.
4. Rotate the QCD-1 to select the number you want to adjust. When the gold box highlights the month, day, year, hour, minute, or second you wish to change, press the SET button to confirm your selection. Two triangles pointing up and down will appear above the value you're adjusting.

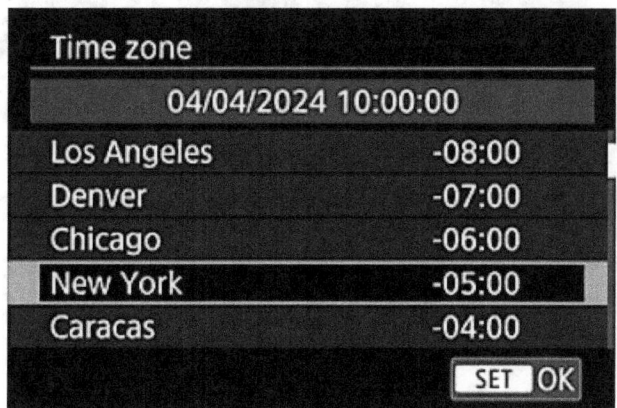

⬚ Use the QCD-1 to adjust the number. Once you've entered the correct value, press the SET button to confirm.

⬚ Repeat steps 4 and 5 for any other numbers you want to change. You can also switch the date format between mm/dd/yy, yy/mm/dd, or dd/mm/yy. Additionally, you can select the appropriate time zone and toggle Daylight Saving Time on or off.

⬚ Rotate the QCD-1 to choose OK (if you're satisfied with the changes) or Cancel (if you want to return to the Set-up 2 screen without making changes). Press SET to confirm your selection.

⬚ After setting the date and time, you can exit by pressing the shutter release or the MENU button.

Language

To change the menu display language among 29 options, rotate the Quick Control Dial 1 or use the Multi-controller joystick to highlight your desired language. Once selected, press the SET button to confirm and activate it.

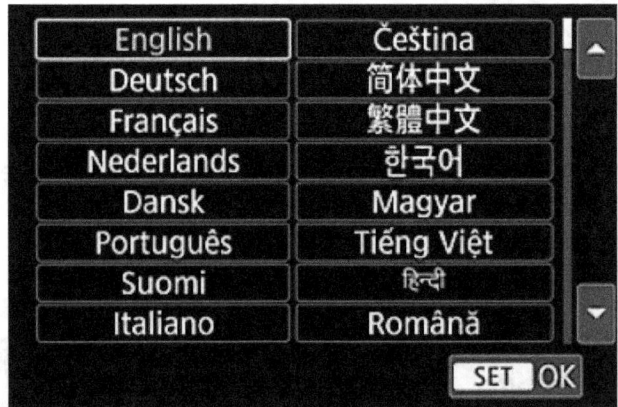

System Frequency

Any television intended for display must have its video system configured properly. This setting determines the frame rates available for recording movies.

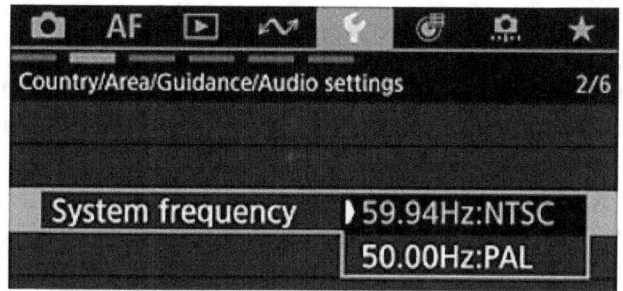

- **59.94Hz: NTSC**

Used in regions with the NTSC television system, including North America, Japan, South Korea, and Mexico.

- **50.00Hz: PAL**

Applicable in areas where the PAL television system is standard, such as Europe, Russia, China, and Australia.

Help Text Size

When you power on your camera for the first time, you may see the INFO Help message displayed behind a menu. To view it, simply press the INFO button. This will bring up a screen with instructions on how to select options for that menu item. While you may not need this assistance after some time, it can be helpful to have it displayed in a large, easy-to-read format initially. You can navigate the help text window using the up and down arrow keys.

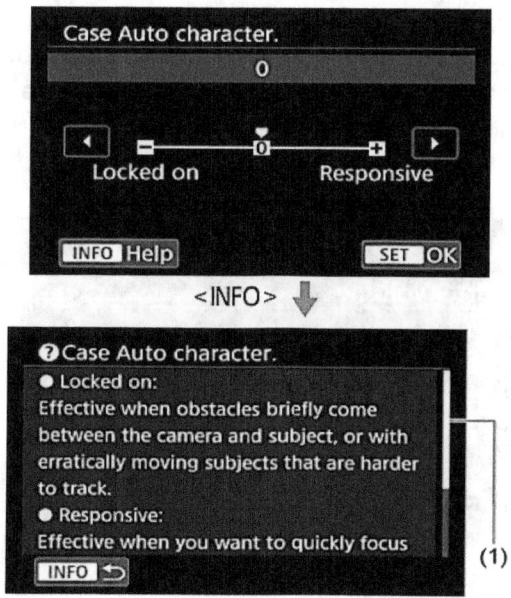

Beep

The internal beeper provides helpful notifications, such as when the self-timer is counting down, when a picture is in focus, and when you interact with the screen. If the beeping is bothersome, inappropriate, or distracting (like in a concert or museum), you can turn it off completely. On the Beep screen, you can select from the following options: Enable to turn the sound on, Disable to mute all beeps, or Touch To Silence to silence the sound only when using the touch screen. Press SET to apply your choice and exit the menu.

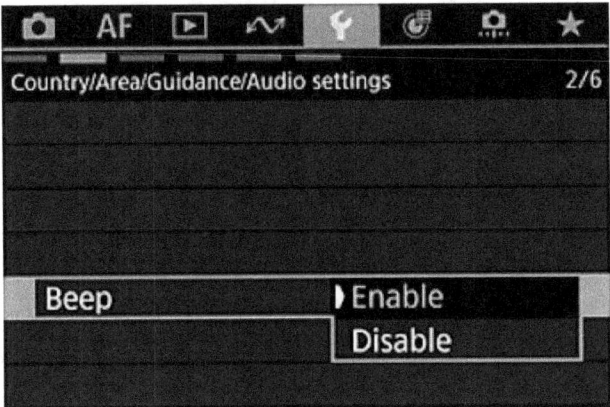

Volume

You can adjust the headphone volume through the camera's headphone port by using the QCD-2 or QCD-1 dials, or by navigating with the Multi-controller joystick. The volume levels range from 0 to 15, giving you a total of 16 options. Headphones are ideal for monitoring the sound quality of recordings made with either an external microphone or the camera's built-in mic when Sound Recording is enabled and High Frame Rate is turned off. You can find these settings in the Movie Shooting 1 menu.

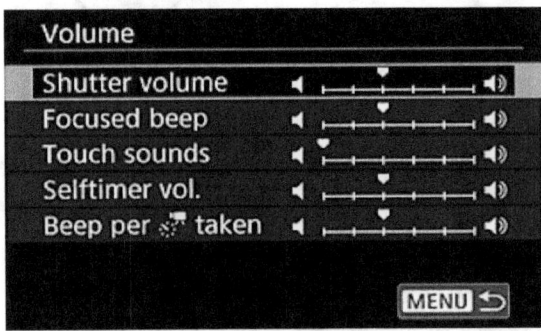

Screen Brightness/Viewfinder Brightness

The next two options allow you to adjust the brightness of the LCD screen and the viewfinder. Typically, you'll need to modify the LCD screen more frequently to improve visibility outdoors or reduce glare indoors. At concerts, I often prefer using the electronic viewfinder to review my shots. If I want to share a picture with a friend, I dim the LCD screen to its lowest setting to avoid disturbing others who may not be as interested.

To ensure the brightness is correct, use the example picture and the highlighted gray areas as a reference. You can calibrate your screen based on your shooting conditions by viewing the thumbnail of the most recent picture while the video is playing back. It's crucial to maintain visibility of all steps in the grayscale, particularly the lightest and darkest areas at the top and bottom. Increasing the brightness helps you see the LCD screen clearly in bright sunlight, but it will also drain the battery more quickly. To confirm your chosen brightness setting, press the SET button, then return to the menu.

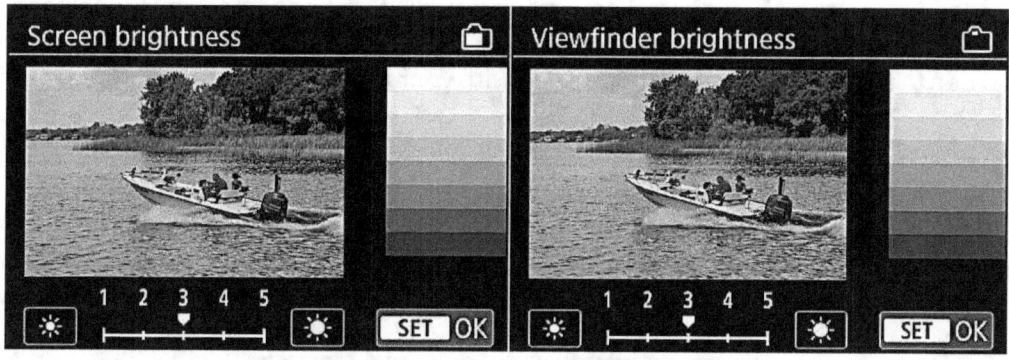

Screen/Viewfinder Color Tone

This setting allows you to fine-tune the color balance of the LCD screen and camera to suit your preferences. It functions similarly to the Display Brightness option: hold the camera up to your eye to adjust the viewfinder and check the LCD screen for color tone changes. Opt for this setting if you want a preview image that more closely resembles reality, especially if your photos tend to appear warmer or cooler than what you see. Keep in mind that neither display will perfectly match the final image, particularly when shooting in RAW, as the screen will always show a JPEG version, regardless of your chosen format.

To adjust the color balance, enable this option, which will display the most recent picture you played back. Make sure to consider the room's lighting conditions for consistency. You can select from the following options: 1 for warm tone, 2 for standard, 3 for cool tone 1, or 4 for cool tone 2. Finally, press SET to save your choice.

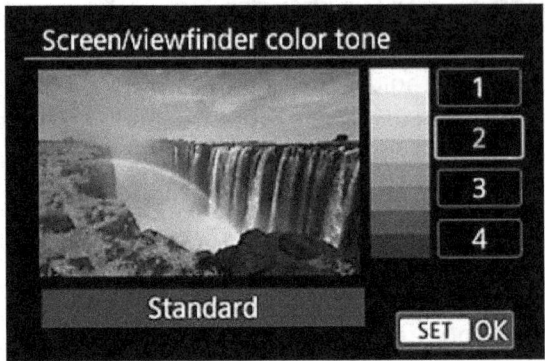

Fine-Tune Viewfinder Color Tone

This option allows you to adjust the color tone of the viewfinder similarly to how you would with color balance settings. It works by adjusting the bias along the blue/amber and green/magenta axes. You can move the Multi-controller joystick in four directions to achieve a balanced color while viewing the video image in the viewfinder. A grayscale reference is displayed at the bottom of the screen to assist you. Once you're satisfied with your adjustments, press SET to confirm your settings.

Screen and Viewfinder Display

You can select whether to use the screen or the viewfinder for viewing, preventing the viewfinder sensor from activating accidentally when the screen is open.

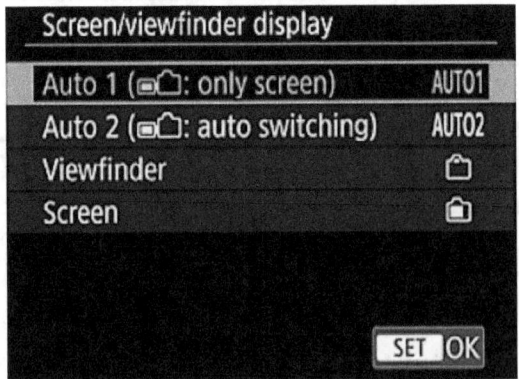

This option is the first item in the Set-up 3 menu. Many mirrorless camera users experienced issues with the display unexpectedly switching between the LCD screen and the viewfinder. Canon has addressed this problem. The eye sensor beneath the viewfinder window activates the lens when your face (or anything else) gets close. If your camera is on a stand, you can easily activate the switch by pressing the MENU button.

This setting offers four useful modes:

- **Auto1:** When the LCD screen is extended from the camera body, Auto1 mode remains active, even if something is near the eye sensor. The viewfinder will activate only when the screen is returned to its normal position and your eye approaches the sensor. Essentially, the EVF can only be engaged when the screen is swiveled out.
- **Auto2:** This mode uses the LCD to indicate whether the screen is swiveled out or back in. If your eye or an object touches the camera/eye sensor, it will switch to the viewfinder, meaning the image will change regardless of the display's position.
- **Viewfinder:** This option always displays information through the viewfinder.
- **Screen:** This option ensures that the LCD screen is always used for displaying information.

Additionally, the Customize Button option in the Custom Functions 3 menu allows you to assign a button to toggle between this setup and the previous one.

UI Magnification

If you find that the regular user interface (UI) makes it difficult to view menus in challenging conditions, you can enable this option to make the menu screens twice as large. To further enlarge the LCD screen, simply double-tap it. Tapping it again will return it to normal size. Keep in mind that when the UI is expanded, other touchscreen features become unavailable, so you'll need to use the camera controls to adjust settings.

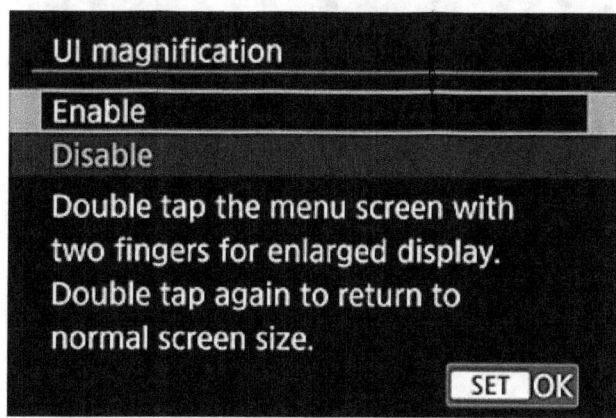

HDMI Resolution

An HDMI Mini-C connector on one end of the cable connects to the camera, while a standard HDMI connector on the other end connects to your device. This setup allows you to send video to an external monitor or recorder. When set to Auto, the camera attempts to detect the connected device's size and output the appropriate format. If you're confident your device can handle it, you can bypass the delay by selecting 1080p video. However, this may involve a brief wait as it adjusts to the correct resolution.

One of the main issues with this approach is that you can't manually select the resolution, which complicates matters for devices that require different settings. For instance, my BlackMagic Intensity Shuttle capture device needs a specific configuration that Canon doesn't allow you to change manually, and the camera can't automatically detect those settings either. I reached out to Canon for assistance, but they couldn't provide a solution since there's no option to choose a format other than 1080p. Ultimately, I opted for the $20 MavisLink USB-to-HDMI video capture device along with the free OBS Studio app to record the displays.

Cooling Fan Settings

- **Fan**

- **Fan Rotation Speed**

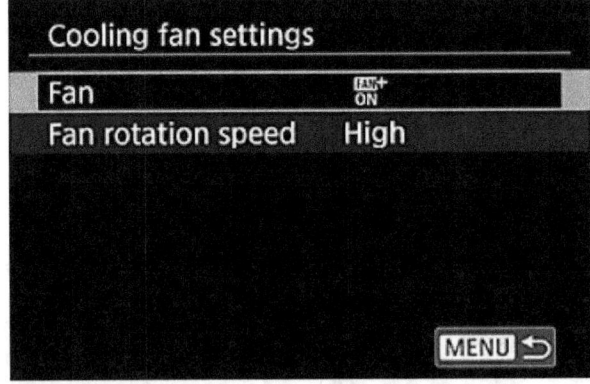

When using an optional cooling fan, you can adjust its operation through the camera settings. Make sure to connect the cooling fan before modifying any settings.

Shutter at Shutdown

Some users feel uneasy when they remove the lens from their first compact camera and see the exposed image sensor. However, those with an EOS R5 II don't have to worry, as Canon has designed it to close the shutter when the camera is off, preventing dust or debris from settling on the sensor. I typically disable this feature only when shooting acoustic shows or in quiet environments where the camera may turn off to conserve battery. When using the electronic shutter with the camera open, the only sound you'll hear is a faint whirring from the autofocus motor.

Sensor Cleaning

The automatic sensor cleaning feature is very useful, as it minimizes or even eliminates the need for manual cleaning with brushes, swabs, or blowers. Canon has applied an anti-static coating to the sensor and other internal components to prevent dust accumulation from static charges. Each time the camera is turned on or off, ultrasound waves move a separate filter above the sensor, dislodging any dust stuck to a sticky strip below it.

In this menu, you can choose to have the sensor cleaned automatically when the camera is turned on (Auto Cleaning) or during a shooting session (Clean Now).

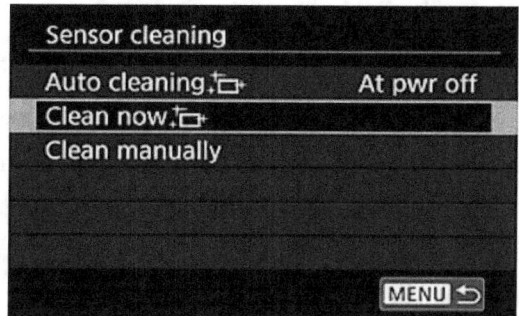

You can also select the **Clean Manually** option, which opens the shutter, allowing you to use a cleaner, brush, or swab. The camera will alert you if the battery level is too low to complete the cleaning safely and will not proceed further unless you connect the optional AC Adapter Kit ACK-E6N with the DC Coupler DR-E6.

Power Saving

When the camera is not in use, you can adjust the timing for when the screen dims and turns off, as well as when the camera itself powers down and when the viewfinder turns off. These settings include Screen Dimming, Screen Off, Auto Power Off, and Lens Off.

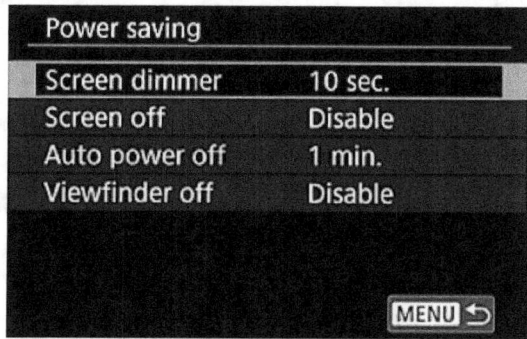

- **Auto Power Off:** This setting determines how long the camera waits before automatically turning off. When you press the shutter button, the system will reactivate. I typically keep this setting at five minutes, but for sports or street photography, where I need quick access, I set it for a longer duration.
- **Viewfinder Off:** Turning off the electronic viewfinder doesn't save much battery, which is why there are only three options: 1 minute, 3 minutes, or Disable. Regardless of the setting, the viewfinder will turn back on when you bring the camera up to your eye, so I find it reasonable to choose a three-minute timeout.

Reset Camera

This option allows you to reset most settings to their original defaults. If you want to revert the camera and menus to their default configuration, you can select **Basic Settings**. If no changes have been made, the camera will automatically switch to One-Shot AF mode, Evaluative metering, Single Shot drive mode, JPEG Fine Large image quality, Automatic ISO, sRGB color mode, Automatic White Balance, Auto Lighting Optimizer Off, and Standard Picture Style.

You can also undo any adjustments made to white balance, exposure compensation, or flash exposure compensation, which will reset any bracketing used for exposure or white balance. Custom white balances and Dust Delete Data will also be erased.

Other settings that can be reset include Root Certificate, Communications Settings, Shooting Information Display, Custom Shooting Modes, and Copyright Information. Note that while Custom Functions (Customize Buttons and Customize Dials) will be retained, the Custom Controls setting will clear any changes made to Customize Buttons and Customize Dials, as well as My Menu.

Custom Shooting Mode (C1–C3)

Custom shooting modes cannot be reset using the camera's general reset commands. Instead, you can save your current settings to C1, C2, or C3 using this option, which allows quick access by pressing the MODE button. This will overwrite any previously saved settings in those slots. Additionally, you can clear the settings for all three positions, returning them to their original factory defaults.

It's useful to save your preferred settings for specific situations, such as sports, portraits, or landscapes. If you forget the settings for a particular mode, you can press the INFO button while in C1, C2, or C3 to view them. Keep in mind that the settings for My Menu are not saved separately; each Mode Dial position can only have one list of My Menu items.

In this menu, you'll find three options: **Clear Settings**, **Register Settings**, and **Auto Update Settings**. **Register Settings** saves your current configurations to C1, C2, or C3. **Clear Settings** deletes the settings from those positions. If **Auto Update Settings** is set to "Enable," any changes made in C1, C2, or C3 will automatically save to that memory slot. If set to "Disable," your registered settings will remain unchanged, regardless of any adjustments made while in those modes. You must use this menu item to clear your choices.

To complete these tasks, follow these steps:

1. Adjust your settings and set the camera to a different exposure mode than Scene Intelligent Auto.
2. Access the camera user settings by going to the Set-up 5 menu and selecting **Custom Shooting Mode**, then press SET.
3. Choose the desired function: select **Register Settings** to save your current settings to C1, C2, or C3, or select **Clear Settings** to delete settings from those locations. Press SET to access the settings screen you need.

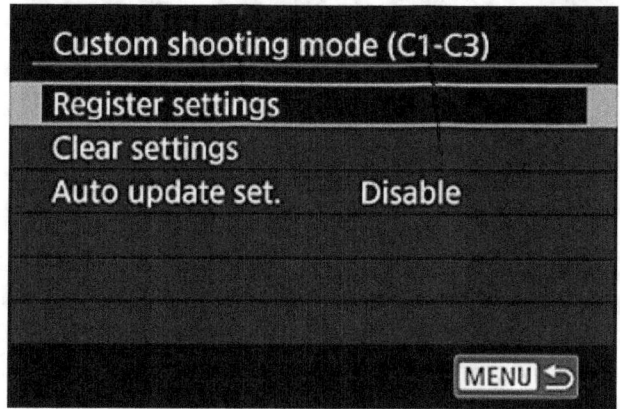

⬚ **Store/Clear Settings:** The screens for saving and clearing settings are quite similar. Select either Custom Shooting Mode: C1, Custom Shooting Mode: C2, or Custom Shooting Mode: C3 using the QCD-1, then press SET to save or clear the settings for that mode. You'll first be prompted to confirm your choice to proceed or cancel.

⬚ **Auto Update:** If you modify a setting in one of the custom shooting modes and want to retain that change, you can easily update your saved settings. Select **Auto Update Set** and choose **Enable** to turn this option on. If you prefer to keep your current custom settings until you decide to update them, select **Disable** instead of Update.

⬚ **Exit:** After confirming your changes, you will return to the Set-up 5 menu. To exit the menu system completely, press the MENU button or the camera release button.

Save/Load Camera Settings On Card (R5 II only)

With this feature, you can save your current settings—such as shooting modes, menu configurations, and Custom Function settings—onto a memory card as a specific file. This file can then be restored to your R5 II or transferred to another R5 II. There are two options available: **Save to Card** and **Load from Card**. While saving, you can use the standard text-entry screen and the INFO button to assign a unique 8-character name to your settings.

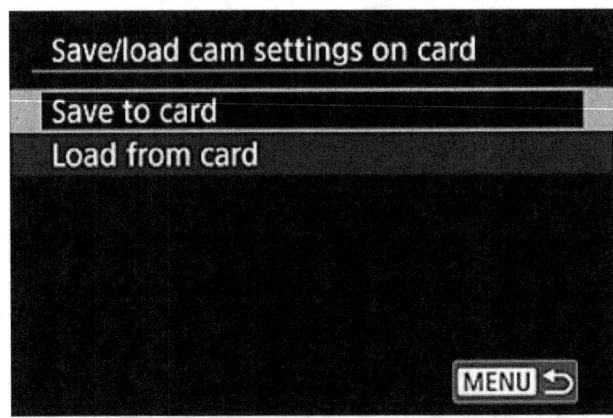

Please note that you can only load settings onto an R5 II or another R5 II; settings from other Canon cameras that support saving won't be compatible. Additionally, if you update the software on this or any other camera, you won't be able to restore the previous settings. The camera must have the same firmware as it did when the settings were saved for them to be loaded successfully. You can store up to ten sets of settings on a single memory card.

Battery Information

This tool is essential for monitoring the state and performance of your batteries, allowing you to track data from multiple units. Each LP-E6, LP-E6N, or LP-E6NH battery has a unique serial number, enabling your camera to manage several batteries simultaneously. When you use a battery, it becomes "registered" with the camera, which records its serial number and relevant information.

I recommend having at least two batteries, with three or more being even better, especially when using a power grip. Since I have other Canon cameras that utilize the same battery, I find it beneficial to keep four batteries on hand to power multiple devices.

This tool provides insights into the condition of each battery, allows you to rotate them to ensure balanced usage, and helps determine when a battery needs replacing. When you select this menu item, you'll see details for both LP-E6/E6N batteries if you're using two in a grip, such as the BG-R10:

- **Battery Position:** An icon indicates which battery slot is currently being monitored.
- **Power Type:** Next to the position icon, a symbol displays the model number of the inserted battery or indicates a connected DC power adapter.
- **Remaining Capacity:** The battery check icon shows the remaining power along with a percentage displayed in 1-percent increments. This helps you gauge how much power is left. If you're in a shooting session, consider switching to a fully charged battery when your current one drops between 25% and 33% to avoid interruptions.
- **Shutter Count:** This indicates how many times the shutter has been activated with the fully charged battery. This information helps you understand power consumption; for example, if your battery is half full but you've taken only a few shots, it suggests that power is being drained by functions like reviewing images, frequent autofocus use, image stabilization, or using the flip-up flash. Being aware of this can help you conserve battery life by minimizing power-hungry features.
- **Recharge Performance:** This indicator shows how effectively your battery can be charged and how well it holds that charge. Three green bars indicate optimal performance, while two bars suggest reduced efficiency. A red light means the battery is nearly dead and needs replacing. To prolong battery life, consider rotating different packs to ensure they age at a similar rate.

Registering Your Battery Packs

The camera can store information for up to six LP-E6 battery packs and provide updates on their status. To register your camera's current battery level, follow these steps:

1. Access the **Battery Information Screen**.
2. Press the **INFO** button on the left side of the LCD panel.
3. A new screen will appear, displaying details about the current battery, including its date and serial number.

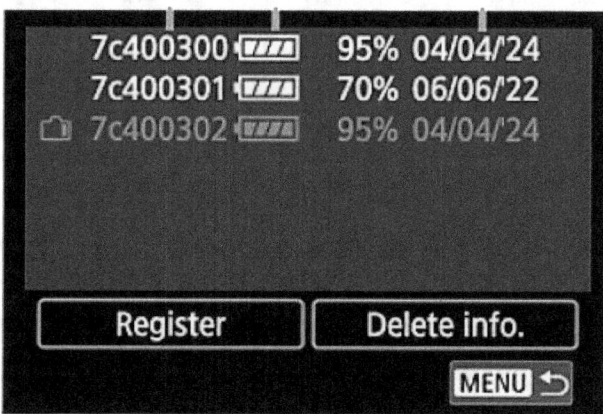

4. To log a battery that has already been registered, select **Delete Info** instead of **Register**. This option allows you to remove a battery from the list, which is useful if you've already registered six batteries and want to add a new one.
5. Press **SET** to add the battery to the register.
6. When you delete a battery, the camera will show the **Battery Info** screen. You can delete a battery pack even if it's not currently in the camera, which is helpful if you've lost one. Simply select the battery by its serial number and click **Delete**.
7. To exit any of the Battery Info screens, press **MENU**.
8. You can check the Battery Info page at any time, even if the battery isn't in the camera, to see how much power is left after registering it. The camera updates the status of registered batteries every time one is added and displays the date of the last use.

TIP: Keep in mind that this information may not always be accurate, as a battery might have fully charged since its last use or could have self-discharged while in storage. However, this data can help you track the remaining power in multiple battery packs during a shooting session or over a few days if they haven't been charged between uses.

Copyright Information

This section allows you to take pride in your photography by managing copyright information for your images:

- **Display Copyright Info:** Enable or disable the option to include copyright information in your image files. If you're a covert agent sharing sensitive photos, you might want to turn this feature off.
- **Enter the Author's Name:** You can add your name (up to 63 characters) to each image file.
- **Enter Copyright Details:** Provide additional information using an extended character set, also limited to 63 characters. Note that there's no copyright symbol; while some use a lowercase "c" in brackets, the proper formats are (Copyright) or (Copr.).
- **Delete Copyright Information:** This option removes all previously entered copyright details, giving you a clean slate to start fresh.

Manual/Software URL

In this section, you can enter the URL to access the page containing your camera's instructions and software. Additionally, there's a QR code available that you can scan with your phone to reach the same page.

Certification Logo Display

With a software update, Canon can incorporate certification data (similar to what is displayed on the bottom panel of the camera) into this information screen. This allows them to avoid creating new stickers for the camera's base.

Firmware

In the menu, you can check for the latest firmware releases for compatible accessories. To update the software, insert a memory card containing the binary file and press the **SET** button to begin the update process.

Chapter 4
Working with the AF System

Now that you have a foundational understanding of the autofocus system, you can explore the various settings and options available. To achieve consistently sharp focus, it's important to understand how to utilize different focus modes and select the desired focus area effectively.

AF Operation

The AF Operation focus modes dictate when the camera focuses, but not where. Other features manage the focus area. These modes allow you to choose whether the camera locks focus with a half-press of the shutter button or continuously tracks moving subjects. The two main AF modes are One-Shot AF (single autofocus) and Servo AF (continuous autofocus). You can also manually focus with up to 10X zoom. Selecting the appropriate autofocus setting and focus point is crucial for capturing clear images of your intended subject. I learned this the hard way while photographing sports: using the wrong setting can result in sharp images of the wrong subject.

If you don't select Continuous AF in the AF 1 menu, the camera will only focus when you partially depress the shutter button. Autofocus isn't automatic; you can adjust the settings for greater control. Press the **Q** button to access the Quick Control menu, then navigate to **AF Operation** and use the dial to select your desired mode. Also, ensure the AF/M switch on the lens is set to AF to toggle between focusing modes.

One-Shot AF.

In single autofocus mode, focus locks in once and remains until the shutter button is fully pressed to take a picture or released without capturing an image. This mode is ideal for stationary subjects, making it great for non-action photography, as it reduces the chances of blurry shots. However, you must first lock the focus before taking a photo, which is why it's often referred to as focus priority. While it conserves battery life compared to other autofocus settings, this brief delay can lead to shutter lag.

If the beep feature is enabled, the camera will beep and the focus point will light up green on the screen upon achieving focus. When using Evaluative metering, the exposure locks simultaneously. You can half-press the shutter button to reframe the shot while maintaining the same focus and exposure. Additionally, the AE/FE Lock buttons can lock in brightness as you adjust your composition. If the camera fails to find focus, the focus point will turn orange, and you won't be able to take a picture even if the shutter button is pressed.

To switch to release priority, simply press the shutter button more quickly. This is helpful for capturing quick moments, prioritizing the shot over perfect focus. You can find this setting in the AF 4 menu under One-Shot AF Release Priority, allowing the camera to take a picture even if it hasn't confirmed crisp focus.

Servo AF.

Continuous autofocus, or Servo AF, is ideal for fast-moving subjects like in sports or continuous video modes. When you press the shutter button halfway, the camera locks onto your chosen focus point and continuously adjusts as either you or the subject moves. The focus point glows blue to indicate it's in focus, but there are no beep sounds to avoid distractions during constant refocusing.

Unlike single autofocus, focus and exposure aren't locked until you fully press the shutter button. With Servo AF, there's virtually no shutter lag; the camera starts capturing images immediately when you press the button. However, this mode consumes more battery power since the autofocus system remains active even with a half-press.

In Scene Intelligent Auto mode, the camera automatically switches to Servo AF when it detects motion. Additionally, the camera can capture images even if the focus isn't perfect, known as Release Priority. This utilizes predictive autofocus to adjust focus as the subject moves closer or farther away.

Setting the release priority allows the camera to take a picture even if it's not perfectly focused, but this doesn't lead to many out-of-focus shots. Generally, images remain sharp or very close to sharp throughout the exposure time.

Manual Focus.

To switch to manual focus, slide the AF/MF switch on your lens to the MF position. This allows you to adjust the focus manually. While manual focus can extend battery life, it may slow down your shooting process since you need to adjust the focus yourself.

Canon provides helpful features for manual focusing:

- **Focus Peaking**: In the AF 2 menu, you can enable MF Peaking, which highlights the edges of your subject with a distinct color, making it easier to see what's in focus. You can also adjust the intensity of the peaking effect to High, Medium, or Low. Note that peaking is not visible when the image is magnified.

- **Magnified View**: Using the magnified view (also accessible in autofocus modes) simplifies manual focusing. This feature allows you to zoom in on your subject, providing a clearer view for precise adjustments.

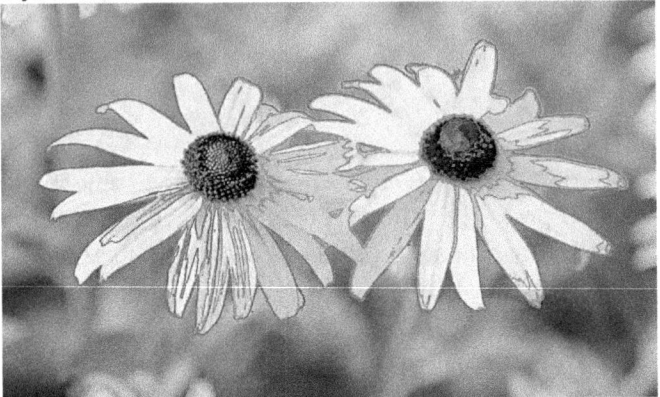

AF Method

- Canon's AF Method tool allows you to select how autofocus information is gathered by choosing from seven AF area options. You can set a specific starting point or zone, and you can adjust which other points are activated as needed. The eighth mode, **Face+Tracking**, enables the camera to automatically select and track the focus point, prioritizing faces and eyes of people or animals.
- Switching between AF modes is straightforward: just press the AF selection button on the upper-right corner of the back panel, right next to the * button. Then, keep pressing the M-Fn button to cycle through the available modes.
- In the AF 4 menu, you can find the **AF Method Selection Control** option, which allows you to change AF methods using the Main Dial instead of the M-Fn button. If you only use a few modes frequently, you can simplify your workflow by hiding the others. Just go to the AF 4 menu and select **Limit AF Methods** to customize your options.

Face+Tracking AF

In **Face+Tracking** mode, the camera actively searches for faces to focus on. If it detects a face, it will lock onto it and track its movement, displaying a box around the face on the screen. If no faces are found, the camera will utilize the entire autofocus area.

You can specify where the Servo AF starts by selecting the initial AF point. The camera will prioritize that point for face detection, and if no face is found there, it will scan the rest of the frame. This feature is particularly useful for scenarios where your main subject might move around, allowing the camera to quickly adjust focus while minimizing interference from other moving objects in the frame. This setup helps maintain sharp focus on your subject, even in dynamic environments.

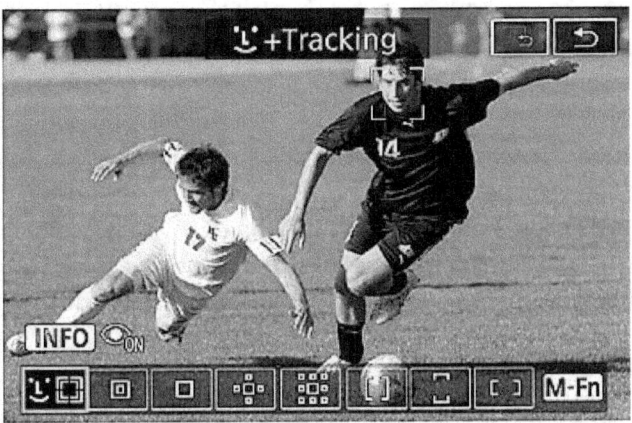

Here are some practical tips for using **Face + Tracking AF** effectively:

1. Pick a Subject to Detect

- **Subject Type**: Use the AF 1 menu to specify whether the camera should focus on faces, heads of people, or animals. The system excels at distinguishing between different subjects like dogs, cats, and birds.
- **Mode Compatibility**: This feature works well in **Zone AF** or **Large Zone AF** (horizontal/vertical) modes, allowing flexibility depending on your shooting situation.

2. Enable/Disable Eye Detection

- **Eye Detection AF**: When activated, the camera will highlight an eye with a small box in One-Shot mode. You can also select which eye to focus on by tapping the LCD screen.
- **Quick Toggle**: Press the **INFO** button to turn eye recognition on or off while using Face + Tracking. You can also manage this feature using the AF Point Selection button, the M-Fn button, and the INFO button.

3. Faces Detected

- **Face Tracking**: Detected faces will be highlighted with a box. You can switch between recognized faces by pressing the AF Selection button again and using the Multi-controller key.
- **Manual Selection**: Touching the screen allows you to select a specific face for tracking. To stop tracking, simply press the Off icon in the bottom left corner of the screen.

4. Set Initial Focus Point

- **Initial Focus Setup**: In the AF 5 menu, choose where you want the face tracking to start in Servo AF mode. Ensure Face + Tracking and Servo AF are enabled.
- **Selection Process**: Press the AF Point Selection button and either tap the screen or use the Multi-controller joystick to set your desired starting point, then confirm with SET.
- **Focus Point Options**:
    - **Specified Point**: Choose a specific location in the frame that the camera will prioritize for tracking.
    - **Retain Manual Point**: If you were using 1-Point AF, Expand AF Area, or Expand AF Area: Around, the camera will keep that point for Servo AF.
    - **Auto Selection**: If you want simplicity, let the camera automatically choose the first AF point when Face + Tracking is activated.

These tips should help you utilize Face + Tracking AF to its fullest potential, ensuring that your subjects are consistently in sharp focus, especially in dynamic shooting environments.

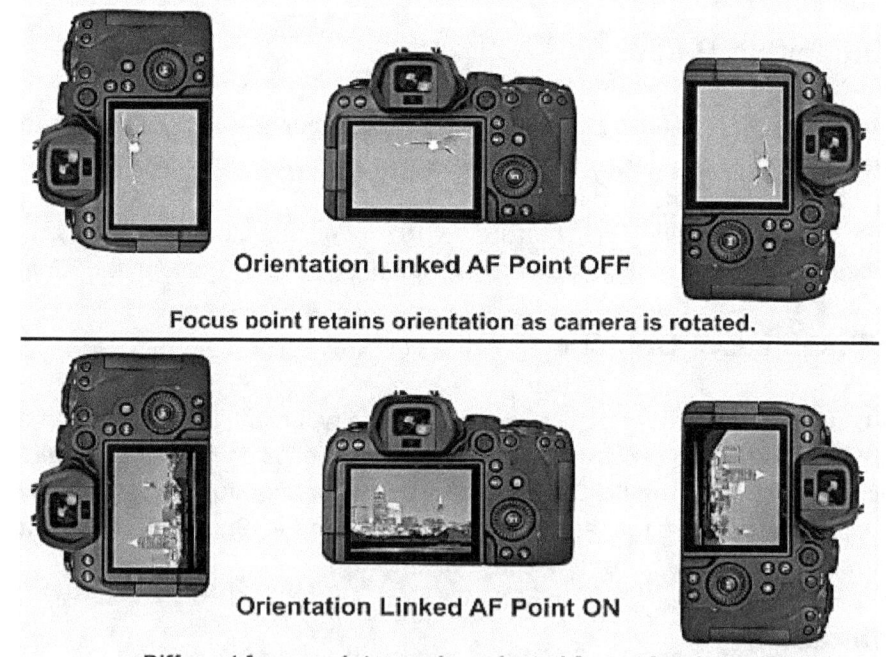

Orientation Linked AF Point OFF
Focus point retains orientation as camera is rotated.

Orientation Linked AF Point ON
Different focus points can be selected for each orientation.

Spot AF

In this mode, you can easily focus on and zoom in on a specific area using the following controls:

Moving the Focus Point

1. **Activate Focus Point Selection**: Press the **AF Point Selection** button to enter focus point adjustment mode.
2. **Adjust Focus Area**:
   - Use the **Multi-controller joystick** to move the focus box to your desired location on the screen with precision.
   - Alternatively, use the **Main Dial** for horizontal movements and **QCD-1/QCD-2** for vertical adjustments.

Resetting the Focus Point

- To quickly return the focus point to the center of the frame, press the **Multi-controller button** or tap the **Return to Center** icon located in the top right corner of the LCD screen.

This functionality allows for precise control over your focus point, ensuring you can easily target specific areas of interest in your composition.

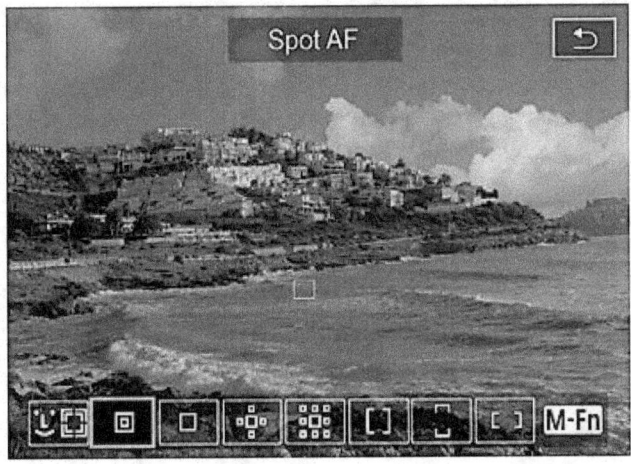

Using Spot AF can indeed provide the precision you need for focusing on a specific area, especially in detailed scenes. However, as you mentioned, if the camera or subject moves, this precision can lead to missed focus on your main subject. Here are some alternative modes to consider for better adaptability:

Alternative AF Modes

1. **1-Point AF**:
   - This mode allows you to select a specific focus point while still enabling the camera to utilize adjacent points if the chosen area isn't solid. It provides a

balance between precision and flexibility, ensuring that even if the subject moves slightly, the camera can still maintain focus.
2. **Zone AF**:
    - With Zone AF, you can select a larger area of focus around your main subject. This is particularly useful when you're shooting moving subjects or in situations where quick adjustments are necessary. The camera will prioritize focus within the selected zone while allowing for some leeway.
3. **Large Zone AF**:
    - Similar to Zone AF but with an even broader area, this mode is ideal for fast-moving subjects or when you want to ensure that focus is maintained despite minor movements. It can capture a subject effectively within a larger frame.

Recommendations

- **Choose the Right Mode**: For static subjects or when precision is critical, Spot AF is excellent. However, for moving subjects or dynamic environments, consider switching to 1-Point AF or Zone AF for more adaptability.
- **Practice with Modes**: Experiment with different AF modes in various shooting conditions to understand their strengths and find the best fit for your style.

Using the right AF mode will help you achieve sharper images while maintaining the flexibility needed for dynamic shooting situations.

1-Point AF

Using the **Expanded AF Area** is indeed a great choice for scenarios where you need both speed and precision, especially in sports or other dynamic settings. Here's how to effectively utilize this mode:

Expanded AF Area Benefits

- **Larger Focus Area**: This mode allows you to focus on a wider area while still keeping precision, which is useful for subjects that might not be moving quickly or are partially obstructed.
- **Faster Acquisition**: The expanded area makes it easier to lock onto moving subjects quickly, reducing the chances of losing focus during fast-paced action.

Tips for Using Expanded AF Area

1. **Track Moving Subjects**: Ideal for sports where you need to keep an eye on a player, like an infielder, as they shift positions but remain relatively stationary.

2. **Easily Move Focus Point**: Use the Multi-controller joystick or touch screen to quickly reposition the focus area as your subject moves, allowing for swift adjustments.
3. **Combine with Servo AF**: Pairing this mode with Continuous AF (Servo AF) allows the camera to maintain focus on moving subjects, ensuring you capture sharp images even as they shift around the frame.

By leveraging the Expanded AF Area, you can enhance your shooting efficiency, especially in fast-moving environments, while still achieving the accuracy needed for great shots.

Expand AF Area

Using the **Expanded AF Area** effectively can make a significant difference in tracking moving subjects. Here are some key points to keep in mind:

Expanded AF Area Details

- **Focus Point Array**: This mode activates the main focus point you select, along with the adjacent points above, below, and on either side. This creates a larger effective area for focus, which is particularly useful for moving subjects.
- **Tracking Movement**: The additional focus points help maintain tracking if the subject shifts outside the primary focus point. This is particularly valuable in dynamic scenarios like sports or wildlife photography.
- **Visual Feedback**: In One-Shot AF mode, you'll see the selected focus point highlighted alongside the expanded points that were engaged during the focus acquisition.

Tips for Using Expanded AF Area

1. **Ideal for Moving Subjects**: Use this mode when photographing athletes, wildlife, or any subject that may move unpredictably within the frame.
2. **Quick Adjustments**: If the subject moves quickly, having additional focus points means you're less likely to lose track of them, as the camera can continue to adjust focus automatically.
3. **Practice with Different Scenarios**: Experiment with this mode in various shooting conditions to understand how the camera responds and refine your technique for better results.

Incorporating the Expanded AF Area into your shooting strategy can greatly enhance your ability to capture sharp images of moving subjects.

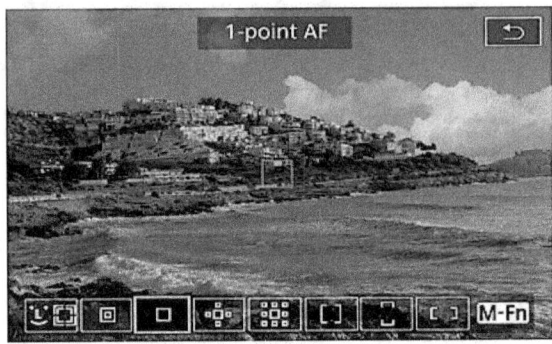

Using a focus area that covers a somewhat larger portion of the frame is beneficial for several reasons:

Benefits of a Larger Focus Area

- **Increased Flexibility**: A larger focus area allows you to maintain focus on subjects that might move around within the frame, making it easier to capture sharp images of dynamic scenes.
- **Better for Group Shots**: When photographing multiple subjects, such as in group portraits or crowded events, a wider focus area ensures that more faces are likely to be in focus.
- **Less Sensitivity to Camera Movement**: A larger focus area can compensate for slight camera movements, making it easier to maintain focus, especially when shooting handheld.

How to Use a Larger Focus Area

1. **Select the Mode**: Choose a focus mode that allows for a broader area, like **Zone AF** or **Large Zone AF**.
2. **Position the Focus Area**: Move the focus area to the desired part of the frame using the Multi-controller or touch screen.
3. **Monitor Your Subject**: Keep an eye on your subject's movements, and be ready to adjust the focus area as needed.

Tips for Success

- **Experiment with Different Subjects**: Test the larger focus area with various types of subjects to see how it performs in different scenarios.
- **Use for Action Shots**: This setting works well for sports and fast-paced events, where subjects may not stay still.
- **Combine with Continuous Shooting**: Pair a larger focus area with continuous shooting to increase your chances of capturing the perfect moment.

By effectively using a larger focus area, you can enhance your photography, especially in situations where subjects are moving or when you need to capture multiple elements in the frame.

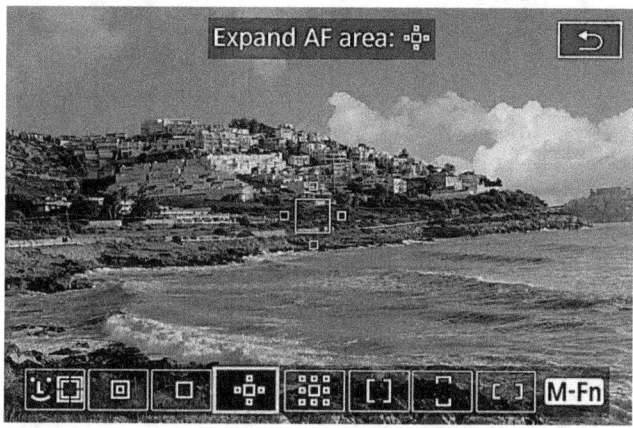

When using the **Expand AF Area**, the camera's autofocus system utilizes a larger focus zone that includes the selected point and surrounding points. This is particularly useful for tracking moving subjects, as it provides more flexibility in maintaining focus when the subject shifts slightly or moves quickly across the frame.

Key Features of Expand AF Area

- **Increased Coverage**: The expanded area allows for more points to engage, making it easier to lock focus on a moving subject.
- **Better Tracking**: If your main focus point loses the subject, the additional points can help keep track of it, ensuring it remains in focus even if it drifts from the center.
- **Versatility**: This mode is excellent for various scenarios, including sports, wildlife photography, or any situation where subjects may not stay perfectly still.

How to Use Expand AF Area Effectively

1. **Select the Mode**: Choose the Expand AF Area option in the camera's AF settings.
2. **Position the Focus Point**: Start by positioning your primary focus point on the subject you want to track.
3. **Track Movement**: As the subject moves, the camera will use the surrounding points to adjust focus dynamically, increasing your chances of capturing sharp images.

Tips for Optimal Performance

- **Practice Panning**: If you're photographing fast-moving subjects, practice panning with your camera to maintain focus.

- **Stay Alert**: Keep an eye on the subject's movements to anticipate changes, allowing for smoother tracking.
- **Use in Appropriate Lighting**: This mode can be more effective in good lighting conditions, where the autofocus system can operate optimally.

Using the Expand AF Area enhances your ability to capture sharp images of moving subjects, making it a valuable tool in your photography toolkit.

Expand AF Area: Around

The **Expand AF Area: Around** mode enhances your autofocus capabilities by incorporating not just your selected focus point but also eight additional points surrounding it. This setting is particularly useful for subjects that may lack distinct detail at the chosen focus point, as the extra points provide better overall accuracy and tracking.

Key Features of Expand AF Area: Around

- **Enhanced Tracking**: The surrounding points help maintain focus on larger, less detailed subjects, making it easier to track movement.
- **Greater Flexibility**: This mode allows for more dynamic shooting, as it can adjust focus if the subject shifts slightly.
- **Visual Feedback**: The active focus points are displayed in the center of the frame, making it easy to see what the camera is using to achieve focus.

When to Use This Mode

- **Larger Subjects**: Ideal for tracking larger subjects, such as animals or vehicles, where precision isn't as critical, but the ability to maintain focus is.
- **Dynamic Scenes**: Perfect for situations where subjects may move erratically or unpredictably, such as in sports or wildlife photography.

Tips for Using Expand AF Area: Around

1. **Adjust Focus Point**: Position your primary focus point on your main subject.
2. **Monitor Movement**: Keep an eye on the subject's motion, allowing the camera to adjust focus using the additional points.
3. **Use in Varying Conditions**: This mode can be beneficial in both good and challenging lighting, but be aware that its effectiveness may vary depending on the complexity of the scene.

By using the Expand AF Area: Around mode, you can effectively capture sharp images of larger, moving subjects while maintaining a balance between precision and flexibility.

Zone AF

The **Zone AF** mode offers a practical solution for focusing on subjects within a defined area of the frame. By spreading the AF points across about one-sixth of the viewfinder, this mode allows for quicker adjustments and is particularly useful when you anticipate your subject's location.

Key Features of Zone AF

- **Coverage Area**: The focus zone encompasses a significant portion of the frame, making it easier to track subjects within that area.
- **Ease of Use**: You can easily reposition the focus zone as needed, which is beneficial for scenes with predictable subject movement.
- **Subject Detection**: The camera prioritizes focusing on the closest subject within the zone, including any people detected.

When to Use Zone AF

- **Predictable Subjects**: Ideal for situations where you have a good sense of where your subject will be, such as in sports or event photography.
- **Moderate Movement**: Suitable for tracking subjects that may move within a certain area but aren't darting around erratically.

Tips for Using Zone AF

1. **Position the Zone**: Before taking your shot, move the focus zone to cover the area where you expect your subject to be.
2. **Monitor Focus**: Keep an eye on the subject's position, as the camera will focus on the closest object within the zone.
3. **Combine with Other Modes**: If you find that Zone AF isn't providing the accuracy you need, consider switching to a more precise mode like Spot AF or Expand AF Area.

By utilizing Zone AF, you can streamline your shooting process while still maintaining reasonable focus accuracy, especially in dynamic environments.

Large Zone AF (Vertical)/(Horizontal)

The **Large Zone AF** modes—Horizontal and Vertical—are excellent for capturing larger subjects or scenes, making them particularly effective for events like basketball games or motorsports.

Key Features of Large Zone AF

- **Rectangular Zones**: Each mode uses a large rectangular area, which can be oriented either horizontally or vertically, allowing for flexible composition based on your subject's orientation.
- **Automatic Point Selection**: The camera automatically selects the necessary AF points within the defined zone, usually focusing on the closest subject detected.
- **Face Detection**: Both modes actively scan for faces, prioritizing them for focus when detected, which is beneficial for capturing action in crowded settings.

When to Use Large Zone AF

- **Sports Photography**: Ideal for fast-paced sports where subjects can move quickly within a larger area.
- **Dynamic Environments**: Great for scenes with multiple subjects, ensuring that the camera can adjust focus as needed.

Tips for Using Large Zone AF

1. **Choose the Right Orientation**: Select between Horizontal and Vertical mode depending on your subject's orientation—whether you're capturing tall players or wide action scenes.
2. **Focus on Movement**: Since the camera automatically selects the focus points, you can concentrate on composing your shot and tracking action.
3. **Be Aware of Depth**: In scenes with multiple subjects at different distances, ensure that the camera's automatic selection aligns with your intended focus.

Using Large Zone AF effectively can enhance your ability to capture sharp images of larger subjects in fast-paced environments, allowing for more creativity and spontaneity in your shooting.

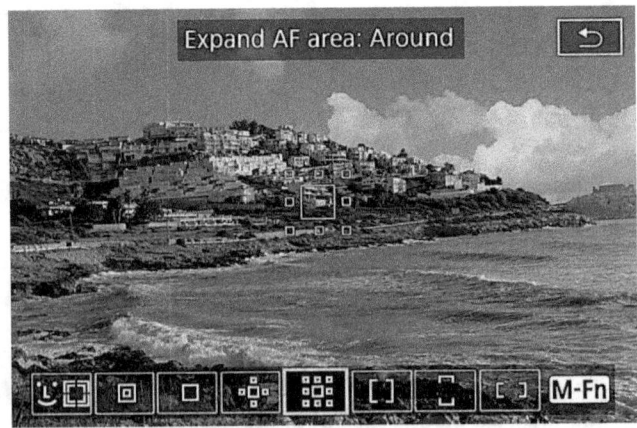

In the **Expand AF Area** mode, the camera activates four additional focus points around your selected point. This broader coverage helps improve autofocus accuracy, especially for moving subjects.

Key Features of Expand AF Area

- **Additional Points**: Alongside your manually selected focus point, the surrounding four points assist in tracking movement, making it easier to maintain focus on a subject that's shifting within the frame.
- **Improved Tracking**: This mode is beneficial for subjects that may not have a lot of detail at the focus point, allowing the camera to grab focus from nearby points.
- **Versatility**: It works well for various subjects, especially in dynamic situations like sports or wildlife photography, where movement is unpredictable.

When to Use Expand AF Area

- **Moving Subjects**: Ideal for tracking athletes or animals that may dart in and out of the selected focus area.
- **Complex Backgrounds**: Helps when your subject is surrounded by intricate details, ensuring that focus remains locked on the intended subject.

Tips for Using Expand AF Area

1. **Monitor Movement**: Stay aware of your subject's motion, as the extra points will help maintain focus if the subject moves away from the central point.
2. **Combine with Servo AF**: Pair this mode with Continuous AF (Servo) for even better tracking of fast-moving subjects.
3. **Adjust as Needed**: If you find the camera occasionally focusing on nearby distractions, consider refining your focus area or switching modes based on your shooting conditions.

This mode strikes a balance between precision and flexibility, making it a powerful option for capturing sharp images of dynamic subjects.

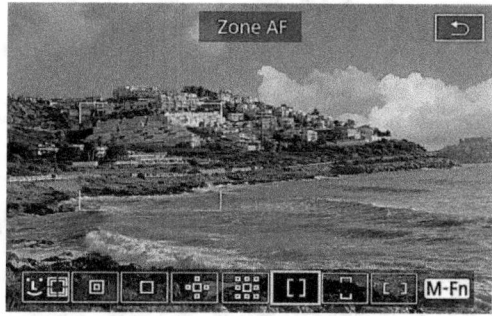

In **Zone AF** mode, a larger focus area is utilized, covering about a sixth of the frame. This method is particularly useful for situations where you have a good idea of where your subject will be but need more flexibility in tracking it.

Key Features of Zone AF

- **Larger Coverage**: The AF points are arranged in a rectangular zone, allowing for broader focus capabilities.
- **Automatic Selection**: The camera automatically chooses which AF points within the zone to use, typically prioritizing the closest subject.
- **Face Detection**: Zone AF can recognize and focus on faces, enhancing accuracy when photographing people.

When to Use Zone AF

- **Predictable Subjects**: Great for events like sports or gatherings where subjects are likely to remain within a certain area.
- **Quick Adjustments**: Useful when you need to adjust focus quickly without the precision of a single point.

Tips for Using Zone AF

1. **Anticipate Movement**: Position the zone where you expect your subject to move, which helps the camera lock onto the subject as it enters the area.
2. **Combine with Continuous AF**: Using Zone AF with Continuous (Servo) mode allows the camera to track moving subjects effectively.
3. **Monitor Background Distractions**: While this mode provides a larger area, ensure there are no distracting elements that might confuse the autofocus system.

Zone AF is a versatile option that balances focus coverage and tracking capability, making it suitable for a variety of shooting scenarios.

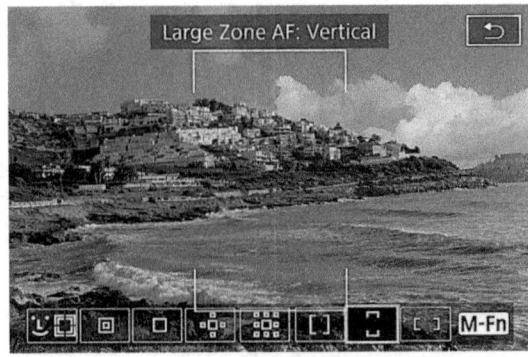

Extensive vertical area.

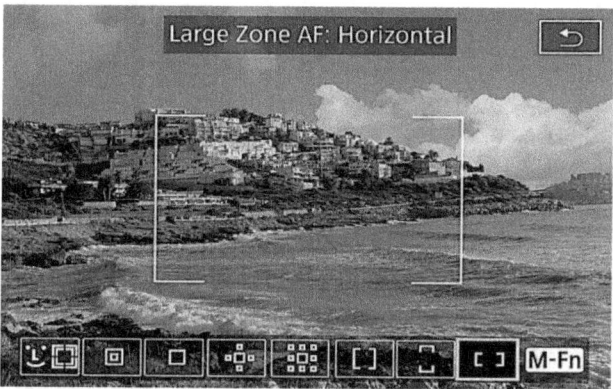

Wide horizontal area.

Magnified View

By pressing the Magnify/Reduce button, you can enlarge images to 6X or 15X (R5) or 5X or 10X (R5) in all modes except Face+ Tracking, ensuring focus accuracy. To zoom in, simply tap the button once or twice. To return to the normal view, tap it again. The zoom is centered on the AF point when using Spot AF, 1-point AF, Expand AF Area, Expand AF Area: Around, or Zone AF. In Spot AF and 1-point AF, pressing the camera button halfway allows AF to be displayed on a larger screen.

In other modes, AF occurs only after returning to the normal view. In Servo mode, the camera resets to a standard view for focusing. Note that Continuous AF and Movie Servo AF are unavailable in magnified mode, and excessive shaking can make focusing more challenging. While zoomed in, use the Multi-controller to navigate the area. To lock the enlarged area in the frame, press the Multi-controller button.

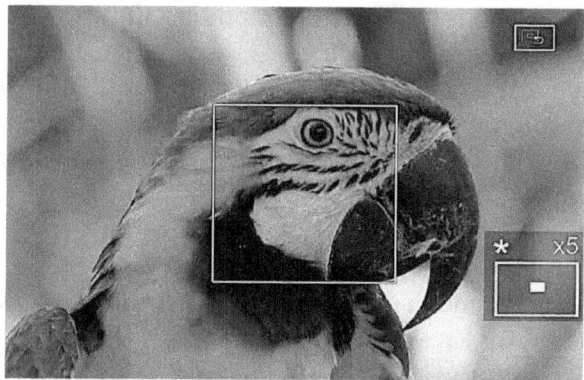

You can utilize magnified views in all AF modes except Face+ Tracking or when focusing manually.

Managing the various autofocus options can be overwhelming. Here's a concise list of your choices to help simplify things:

- **Continuous AF**: The camera continuously refocuses until you press the shutter release halfway, even in One-Shot mode. It remains in Servo AF until you fully press the shutter. Focus is locked in One-Shot mode, and while this speeds up autofocus, it can drain the battery faster. You can find this option in the AF 1 menu.
- **Touch & Drag**: Adjust the focus point on the touchscreen while composing your shot in the viewfinder. This option is also located in the AF 1 menu.
- **AF-assist Beam Firing**: This setting determines whether to use an external flash or the camera's built-in LED to illuminate a subject for easier focusing. Find it in the AF 2 menu.
- **Servo AF Characteristics**: Modify how tracking operates in Servo AF mode through the AF 3 settings, which include four preset Cases suitable for different shooting conditions. You can select Case A (Auto) for automatic adjustments to moving subjects.

    Two aspects of the preset cases can be customized:

    - **Tracking Sensitivity**: Adjust how quickly the AF system shifts focus to a new subject, with options ranging from -2 (Locked On) to +2 (Responsive). Negative values keep focus on the original subject longer, while positive values allow for quicker responses but may result in focusing on the wrong subject.
    - **Acceleration/Deceleration Tracking**: This controls the AF response to speed changes. Options range from 0 (steady pace) to 2 (quick responses to variable speeds). Lower values might misfocus if a moving subject suddenly stops.
- **Focusing Challenges**: When there's insufficient contrast or light, focusing can become difficult, particularly with long telephoto lenses or those with small apertures. Use the Lens Drive When AF Impossible (AF 4) setting to decide if the camera should keep attempting to focus or stop altogether.
- **Limit AF Methods**: You can streamline the autofocus options displayed on the selection screen, making it easier to switch between methods. However, you cannot disable 1-point AF mode. These settings are part of the AF 4 menu.
- **Orientation Linked AF Point**: Set a specific AF point for vertical or horizontal orientations in the AF 4 menu. You can either use the same AF mode or point for both orientations or differentiate them. The option "Separate AF Points: Point Only" allows you to choose distinct points for three orientations:
    - Horizontal (viewfinder and shutter button on top)
    - Vertical with the shutter release above the mode dial
    - Vertical with the mode dial above the grip/shutter release
- **Initial Servo AF Point for Face+Tracking**: Options can be found in the AF 5 menu.

Chapter 5
Autofocus Menu

AF Menu Options

The autofocus menus vary in options based on the selected shooting mode.

AF Operation

This is the first option in the AF 1 menu, allowing you to set autofocus without needing the QCD-1 or M-Fn buttons. If the lens's AF/MF switch is set to MF, only the MF option will be displayed. The focus point indicator changes color: green or blue (in Servo mode) when in focus, and orange when out of focus. Here's a summary:

- **One-Shot AF**: This mode locks onto a focus point when the shutter button is half-pressed. Green boxes indicate sharp focus at the selected points, while orange boxes indicate out-of-focus areas. If focus is achieved, you'll hear a beep (if enabled in the Set-up 2 menu). The focus remains locked until you release the button or take a shot. If the camera can't achieve proper focus, it won't take a picture, even with the shutter button pressed.
- **Servo AF**: In this continuous focusing mode, the camera maintains focus on a moving subject. There is no sound when focused, and the focus area turns blue; it changes to orange if focus is lost. You can take a picture by pressing the shutter button even if the focus isn't perfect.
- **AI Focus AF**: This mode automatically transitions between One-Shot AF and Servo AF depending on the subject's conditions, allowing for flexibility during shooting.

Subject to Detect

This option defines how the Face+Tracking, Zone AF, and Large Zone AF (Vertical or Horizontal) autofocus algorithms prioritize object tracking. Here's a breakdown of each setting:

- **Auto**: Automatically selects the main subject to track from people, animals, or vehicles in the scene.
- **People**: Focuses on detecting and tracking people as the primary subjects. The camera identifies faces, heads, or bodies, displaying tracking frames around detected faces. If it struggles to recognize a face or body, it may focus on other body parts.
- **Animals**: Detects both people and animals (like dogs, cats, birds, and horses), using this information to prioritize tracking. The camera looks for faces or bodies of animals and displays tracking frames over any faces it detects. If it can't identify the animal by its face or body, it may track other body parts.

- **Vehicles**: Identifies both people and vehicles (including cars, motorcycles, planes, and trains), using vehicle detection to determine the main subjects to track. The camera focuses on key features of the vehicle (or the front half of a train) and shows tracking frames over those details. If it can't find significant features or the entire vehicle, it may focus on other parts. Press the INFO button to enable or disable spot detection for key vehicle details.
- **None**: In this mode, the camera does not specifically search for subjects but instead determines the main focus based on your composition. Tracking frames are not displayed.

Eye Detection

You can enable or disable Eye Detection AF using this setting. When activated, an AF point appears around the identified eye of a person or animal. Only One-Shot AF and Face+Tracking AF can utilize this feature. To temporarily disable Eye Detection AF, press the AF Point Selection button followed by the INFO button. To reactivate it, simply press INFO again.

Action Priority

Soccer, volleyball, and basketball players can be grouped together as priority subjects for recognition and autofocus tracking, as their movements are similar across these sports.

MF Peaking Settings

The MF Peaking Settings can only be used in Manual focus mode. Focus peaking highlights the edges of areas in sharp focus using color (red, white, or yellow), allowing you to quickly identify what will be sharp in your shot.

If you're not satisfied with the focus, you can manually adjust the focus distance. The color outline indicates which edges are sharp, helping you get closer to the ideal focus. You can adjust the intensity of the peaking (High or Low), choose a color (Red, Yellow, or White), or disable the feature altogether.

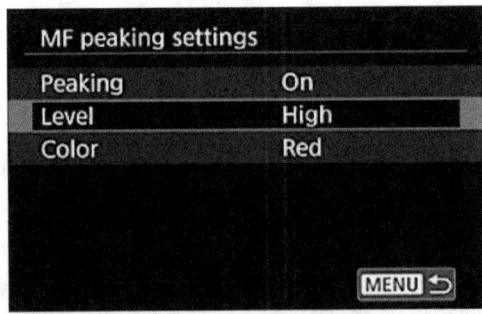

Peaking Color allows you to select the color used to indicate focus when using manual mode. While white is the default color, you can switch to a more visible option like red or yellow if it doesn't stand out against similarly colored subjects. Keep in mind that peaking is not visible when the view is expanded or when connected to an external display or recorder via HDMI. Additionally, if you're using high ISO settings or Canon Log, the peaking lines may be less discernible.

Focus Guide

This feature is an excellent aid for manual focus only. It displays a guide over the image frame, indicating how to adjust the focus ring and in which direction to move it. By pressing the AF Point button and using the directional keys or tapping the screen, you can reposition the focus guide to a specific area of the frame. The guide will return to the center when you press the SET button or the Return icon in the top right corner of the touchscreen.

AF-Assisted Beam Firing

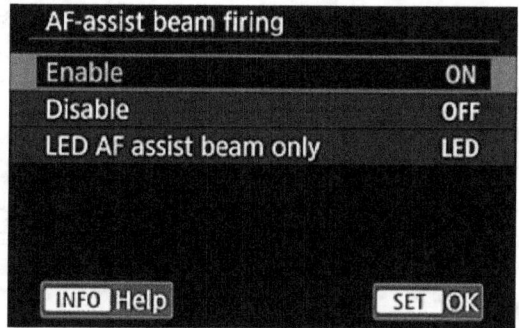

This setting determines whether to use an external electronic flash or the camera's built-in LED to emit a pulse of light, providing the necessary contrast for focusing on a subject. When enabled, you can utilize either the camera's LED or a connected Canon Speedlite to generate a focus assist beam. If this feature becomes bothersome, you can turn it off. Note that if you select "Enable" while the Speedlite's AF-Assist Beam Firing is set to "Disable," the AF-assist beam will not activate; instead, the flash option will be used.

- **Enable**: When ambient light is insufficient for proper focusing, the AF-assist light activates from either the camera's LED or a powered external flash.
- **Disable**: Turns off AF-assist lighting. This option is useful for situations like concerts or weddings, where additional light may be intrusive or distracting.
- **LED AF-Assist Beam Only**: Some Canon flash units have a built-in LED AF-assist lamp. Selecting this option activates only the Speedlite's beam. If your flash lacks this feature, the camera's LED will be used instead. This function is also turned off if you disable the external flash's AF-assist beam through its controls.

Lens Electronic MF

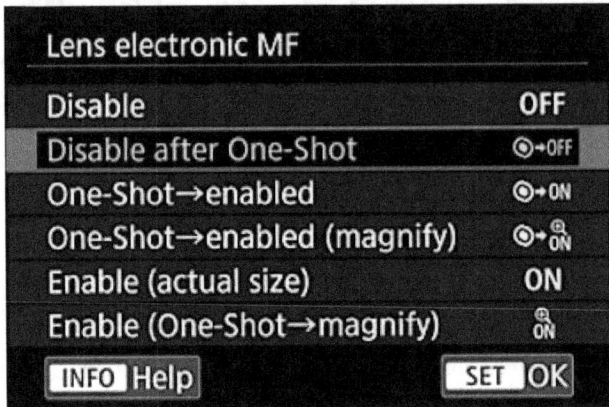

This setting is useful if you frequently use EF or EF-S mount lenses with an adapter. You may want to disable the highly sensitive manual focus rings on compatible lenses, as even slight touches can significantly alter the focus. Only certain fast Canon prime lenses and one zoom lens feature these sensitive rings, all equipped with USM or STM motors.

- **Disable after One-Shot AF**: This option disables manual focus. Use this setting if you're satisfied with the camera's autofocus and prefer not to adjust it manually. Remember, you can completely turn off the autofocus system by switching the lens's AF/MF toggle to MF.
- **One-Shot AF: Enabled**: When this feature is active, you can hold the shutter button halfway while manually adjusting the focus. This is particularly helpful for achieving precise focus on a subject positioned diagonally, such as when shooting with the EF 85mm f/1.2 lens at a wide aperture.
- **One-Shot AF: Enabled (Magnify)**: When activated, you can hold the shutter button halfway while adjusting the focus manually. This option allows you to enlarge the focused area as you make adjustments.
- **ON: Enable (Actual Size)**: When the camera is on and certain compatible lenses are attached, you can always adjust the focus manually. With other lenses, it functions similarly to the One-Shot AF setting.

Chapter 6
Exploring Canon EOS R5 Mark II's Video Capabilities

Introduction to the R5 Mark II's 8K Video Recording

The Canon EOS R5 Mark II offers a variety of movie shooting options, allowing users to customize video settings to their preferences. Here's an overview of the different features for shooting movies:

1. **Movie Recording Quality**: This option allows users to select the video recording quality and frame rate. You can record Full HD video at 120 fps and 4K video at 60 fps. Users can also choose between Canon Log mode or HDR PQ mode, both of which provide greater flexibility in post-production and a wider dynamic range.
2. **Movie Servo AF**: This setting enables you to determine how the camera focuses during video recording. Options include face recognition and tracking, subject tracking, or manual focus. In face recognition mode, the camera focuses on the subject's face regardless of its position in the frame. Subject tracking lets you select a specific subject to maintain focus on, while manual focus gives you complete control over the focus distance.
3. **AF Method**: This setting dictates how the camera focuses when shooting video. Users can choose from single-point AF, zone AF, or tracking AF. Zone AF focuses on a larger area of the frame compared to single-point AF, which focuses on a smaller area. Tracking AF allows the camera to follow a moving subject, making real-time adjustments to the focus.
4. **Movie Digital IS**: This feature controls image stabilization during video recording. You can select from normal, enhanced, or off modes. Normal mode stabilizes the entire frame, while enhanced mode provides stronger stabilization, particularly around the edges to minimize camera shake.
5. **Movie Crop**: This setting determines whether the camera crops the image during video recording. Users can choose between Super 35mm, APS-C, or full-frame modes. Full-frame captures the entire sensor area, while APS-C and Super 35mm modes crop the image, reducing the field of view.
6. **Movie Sound Recording**: This setting governs how sound is recorded during video capture. You can use the built-in stereo microphone, an external microphone, or both. The camera features a 3.5mm microphone jack for connecting additional microphones.
7. **Movie Time Code**: This feature allows you to assign a time code to your video recordings, which is useful for syncing footage from multiple cameras and organizing clips during post-production. The camera supports both free run and rec run time code modes.
8. **Movie Recommendation Size**: This option sets the maximum file size for video recordings. Users can choose standard settings, which limit each file to 4 GB, or automatic settings that allow the camera to split recordings into multiple files as needed.

9. **Movie Recording Control**: In this section, you can specify when the camera starts and stops recording. Users can initiate recording using the snap or record buttons on the camera, or via external devices like a smartphone app or remote control.
10. **Movie Playback**: This setting determines how recorded videos are displayed during playback. You can select from normal, full-screen, or auto modes for viewing your footage.

The Movie Shooting Menu

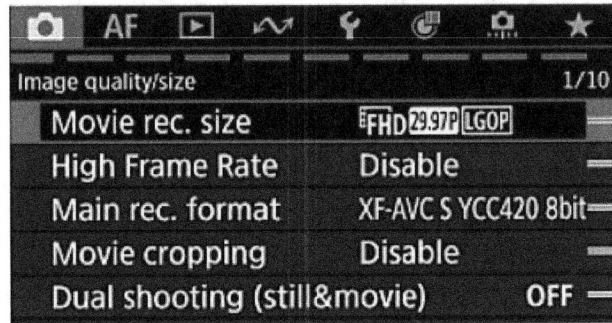

Movie Recording Size

This option is the first setting in the Movie Shooting 1 menu, allowing you to adjust various video clarity settings. The camera supports high-resolution 4K recording. Here are some key choices available:

- **Image Size**: You can choose between 4K and HD movie formats. The resolution and aspect ratio may vary based on how the video is recorded and cropped.
- **Frame Rate**: This setting indicates how many frames or fields are recorded per second. In NTSC mode (used in North America, Japan, and some other regions), you can select from 120 fps, 60 fps, 30 fps, or 24 fps. In PAL regions, the options are 100 fps, 50 fps, and 25 fps. Note that the actual fps may be slightly lower than specified.
- **Compression Method**: Each frame is compressed using either the ALL-I or IPB format before being saved to your storage device. This helps conserve space and improve transmission speeds. An icon with a downward arrow indicates IPB Lite versions that record at a lower bitrate. All video files are stored in the MP4 container format, with MPEG4 AVC/H.264 codec used for encoding and decoding. The MP4 format is widely recognized as a global standard and uses progressive scan.

Movie File Size Limitations:

- You cannot record single movie files larger than 4 GB on SD cards.

- When video files on an SDHC card exceed 4 GB, the camera automatically creates new files. During playback, these files are played in sequence.
- CFexpress or SDXC cards can record movies as a single file, even if the file size exceeds 4 GB.

High frame rate.

When set to Enable, the camera can record video at 29.97 or 25.00 fps. It also supports higher frame rates of 239.76 or 200.00 fps, as well as 119.88 or 100.00 fps.

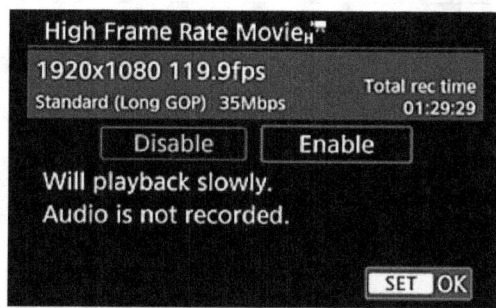

Main Recording Format:

- **Supports XF-HEVC S and XF-AVC S movie formats**: The camera is compatible with these advanced video formats for high-quality recordings.
- **Raw Movies**: It allows for recording in raw format, providing maximum flexibility in post-production.
- **Recording Proxy Movies**: The camera can create lower-resolution proxy files during recording, making editing and sharing more efficient.

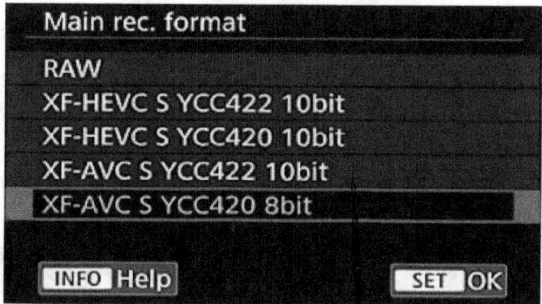

XF-HEVC S and XF-AVC S Movies: These are Canon video codecs based on H.265/HEVC and MPEG-4 AVC/H.264 standards. They maintain high image quality while significantly reducing the amount of data required for storage and transmission.

RAW Movies

The picture sensor transmits raw data in digital form to create RAW movies. You can view and edit these RAW movies using EOS Digital Photo Professional. For more information, consult the Digital Photo Professional instruction manual.

Recording Proxy Movies

Main Movie Settings		Proxy Movie Settings (Set Automatically)	
Recording Format	Image Size	Recording Format	Image Size
XF-HEVC S YCC422 10bit XF-HEVC S YCC420 10bit	4096×2160 2048×1080	XF-HEVC S YCC420 10bit	2048×1080
	3840×2160 1920×1080		1920×1080
XF-AVC S YCC420 8bit XF-AVC S YCC422 10bit	4096×2160 2048×1080	XF-AVC S YCC420 8bit	2048×1080
	3840×2160 1920×1080		1920×1080
RAW	8192×4320 4096×2160	XF-AVC S YCC420 8bit	2048×1080

Movie Cropping

When recording a movie, cropping typically reduces the overall area of the sensor used for capturing the image. Since FHD and 4K video formats use a 16:9 aspect ratio, unlike the 3:2 ratio used for still photos, some of the top and bottom of the image will be trimmed. Additionally, when using certain lenses in movie mode, the cropped area may be further minimized. This setting allows you to adjust how the image is cropped.

Here are your options:

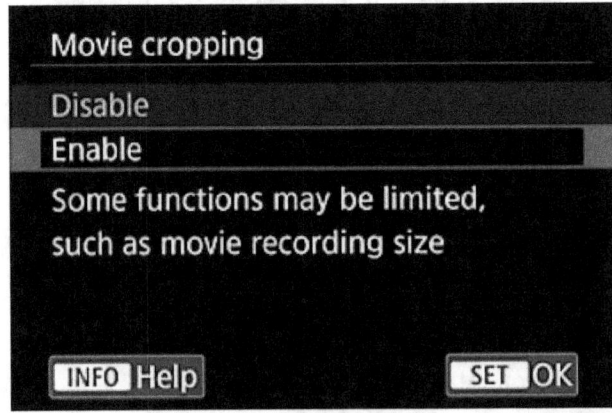

- **Disable**: In this mode, you can use RF or EF mount lenses with an adapter, typically full-frame lenses. The picture area captured by the R5 Mark II remains unaffected when Movie Cropping is not applied.
- **Enable**: Choosing this option will always crop your video, adjusting the image area to match that of Canon APS-C lenses (RF-S or EF-S). When Movie Cropping is enabled, a green box will indicate the areas of the image that have been cropped out by the camera.

Keep in mind that when using RF-S or EF-S lenses or with Movie Cropping enabled, you cannot record movies at high frame rates with the R5 Mark II. Additionally, using Movie Digital IS will introduce an extra small crop to the image.

Dual Shooting (Still Photos and Movies)

By pressing the shutter button, you can capture still images (either single or continuous shots) while the movie recording is ongoing. This allows for higher-quality still photos compared to using frames extracted from the video.

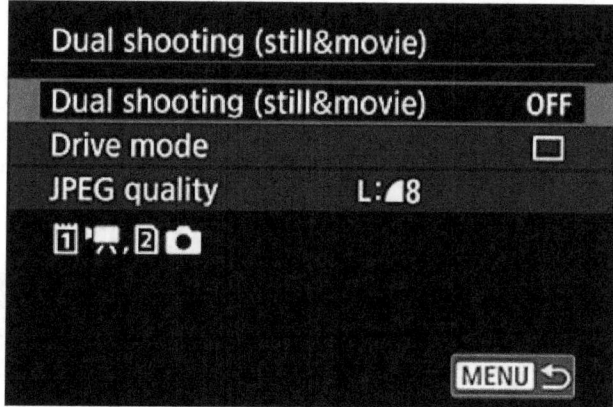

Sound Recording

While recording a movie, press [On] to start recording audio. If you do not connect an external microphone, the camera will use its built-in microphone.

Four-Channel Recording

The camera supports four audio channels for recording. You can use the following combinations for four-channel recordings:

- **Two Microphones**: One connected to the multi-function shoe and one external microphone.
- **Multi-Function Shoe Microphone** (2 channels) and **Built-In Microphone** (2 channels).
- **External Microphone** (2 channels) and **Built-In Microphone** (2 channels).
- **Two Built-In Microphones** (2 channels each).

When multiple microphones are connected, channels 1 and 2 are assigned to the highest priority microphone, while channels 3 and 4 go to the lower priority microphone. The priority ranking is as follows:

1. Microphones designed for multi-function shoes
2. External microphones
3. Built-in microphone

Audio Format:

When recording a movie, you have the option to select the audio file format.

Audio Settings:

In specific situations, set up microphones to capture sound effectively. When using external microphones or those designed for multi-function shoes, refer to the microphone's instruction manual for guidance.

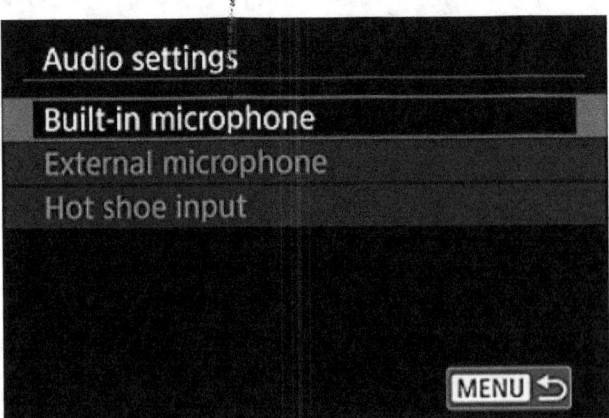

- **Built-In Microphone**: Adjust the settings for the built-in microphone.

- **External Microphone**: Use the external microphone IN terminal to set up configurations for external mics.

▣ **Hot Shoe Input**: Configure settings for microphones designed for the multi-purpose shoe.

Recording Level

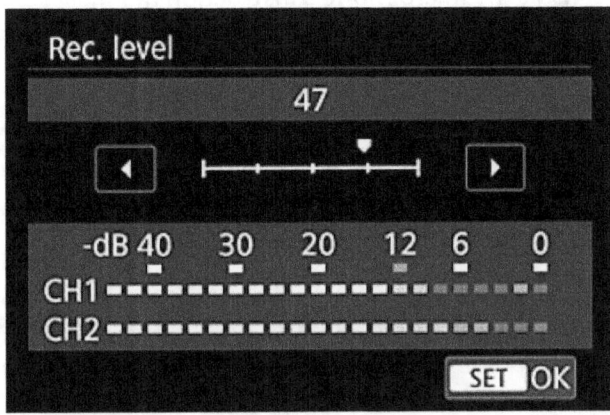

This feature is available when the recording mode is set to Manual. As you adjust the recording level using the dial, monitor the level meter. Ensure that the peak hold indicator shows levels occasionally reaching just above the -12 dB mark for the loudest sounds. Any value exceeding "0" will impact the audio quality.

Wind Filter

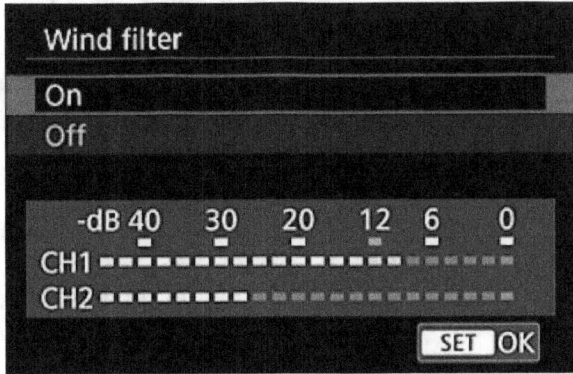

This feature can be used with the built-in microphone or multi-function shoe microphones that are compatible with windshields. If you're recording outdoors in windy conditions, set it to [Enable] to reduce wind noise. Keep in mind that using the wind filter may also attenuate some lower bass sounds.

Attenuator

When using microphones designed for multi-function shoes, you can enable or disable the attenuator. This feature helps eliminate sound distortion caused by loud noises during recording. For more information, consult the microphone's instruction manual.

Microphone Directionality

This option is available when using multi-function shoe microphones that have directional controls. For further details, please refer to the microphone's instruction manual.

Audio Status

This setting allows you to configure audio parameters, including the status of the active microphone and the volume level for headphones.

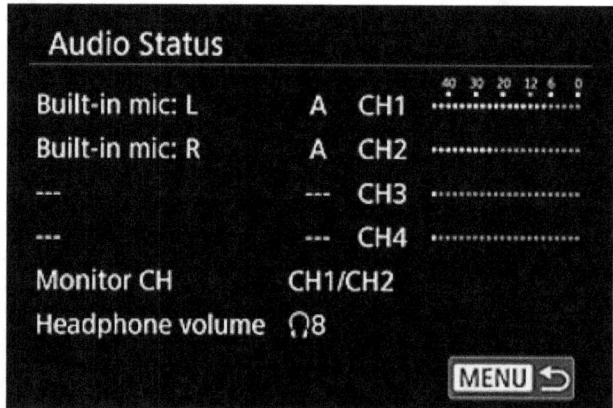

HDR Movie Mode

You can record high-dynamic-range (HDR) movies that retain details in scenes with high contrast.

Shadow Compensation

With Shadow Comp., you can enhance the brightness of shadows and other dark areas in an image.

- On the next screen, select an option to preview the results.

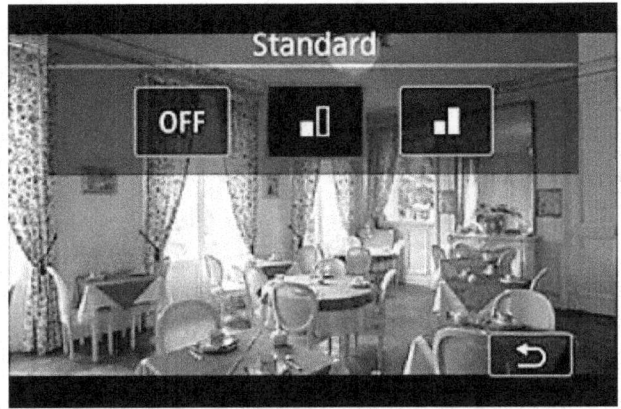

Saturation

You can adjust the overall intensity of a color by modifying the saturation levels.

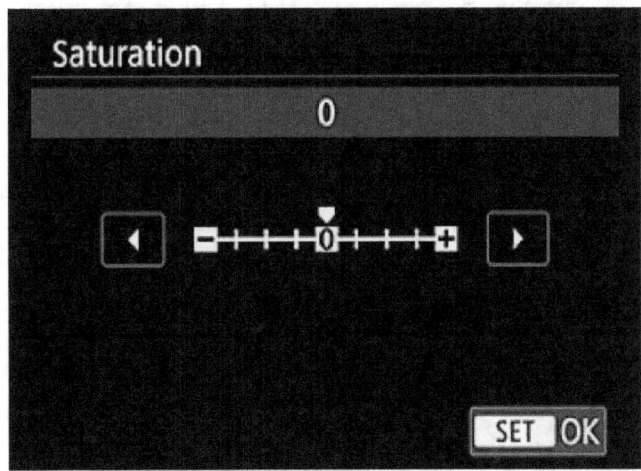

Limiting the Maximum Brightness.

When [HDR shooting (PQ)] is set to [HDR PQ], this option is activated.

- Selecting [Disable] allows for unrestricted brightness levels. It's recommended to view the image on a monitor with a brightness of over 1000 nits for optimal results.
- A brightness level of [1000 nits] is considered ideal.

Time-lapse Movie

A flower bud gradually unfolding into its full beauty is just one of the many subjects that can be captured with time-lapse photography, a technique that has gained popularity beyond wildlife photography. Time-lapse is widely used in movies and TV shows to illustrate the passage of time, such as the sun moving across the sky or the changing seasons. Canon allows you to explore this technique yourself. Here are the key options:

Time-Lapse Movie: Begin by selecting either Enable or Disable to start the setting process.

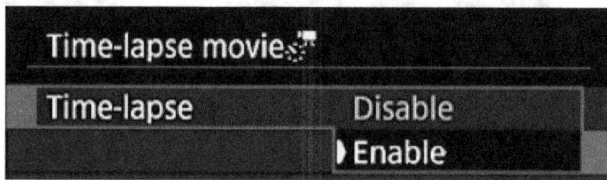

Interval: You can set the duration between each shot, with a maximum interval of 99 hours, 59 minutes, and 59 seconds.

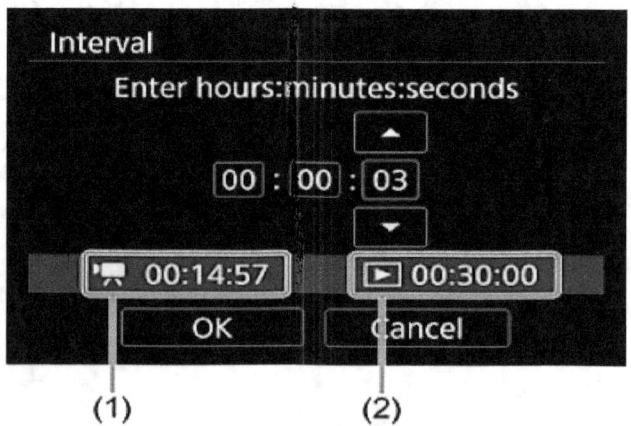

Number of Shots: Select the total number of shots needed for your time-lapse sequence, which can range from 2 to 3,600. At the bottom of the screen, you can get an estimate of how much time has passed since the scene began.

If the duration of the music is highlighted in red, it indicates that either the memory card lacks sufficient space or your settings will result in a file larger than 4 gigabytes, especially if the card isn't formatted in exFAT.

If the playback time is highlighted in red, one of the following conditions applies: As long as you don't format SDXC cards before inserting them, the camera will do it automatically. This issue only affects SDHC cards and those not formatted in the camera. Recording will stop once the memory card is full or the maximum file size is reached.

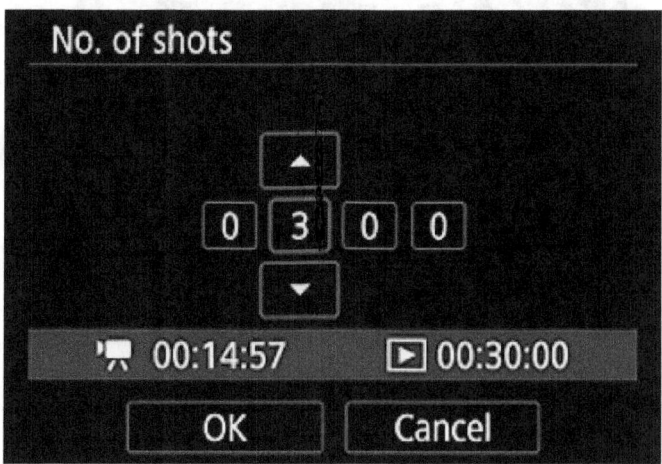

Movie Recording Size: This option displays the various available movie recording sizes, which vary based on quality, frame rate, and compression. The choices you see will depend on the selected [Main Rec. Setting for Format].

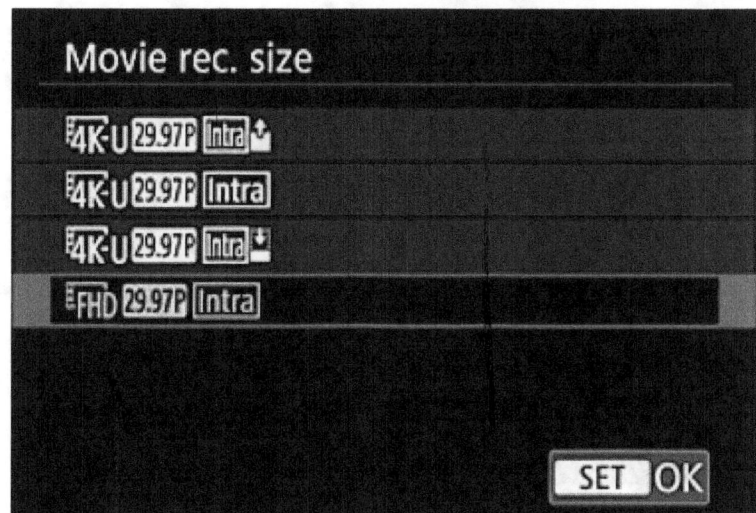

Select [Main Rec.]. Format].

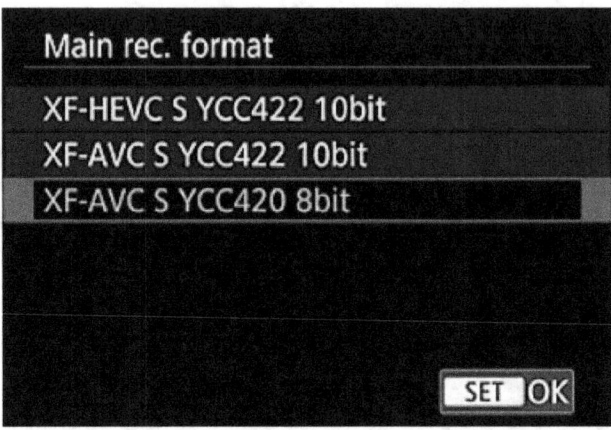

Auto-Exposure Setting: You can choose from the following options:

- **Fixed 1st Frame**: After measuring the exposure for the first frame, that setting will be applied to all subsequent frames. This mode is ideal when you want consistent exposure outdoors, regardless of changing light conditions.
- **Each Frame**: This option allows for individual measurement of each shot in the sequence. For instance, a film that begins at sunrise and concludes at dusk will have the appropriate exposure for each time of day.

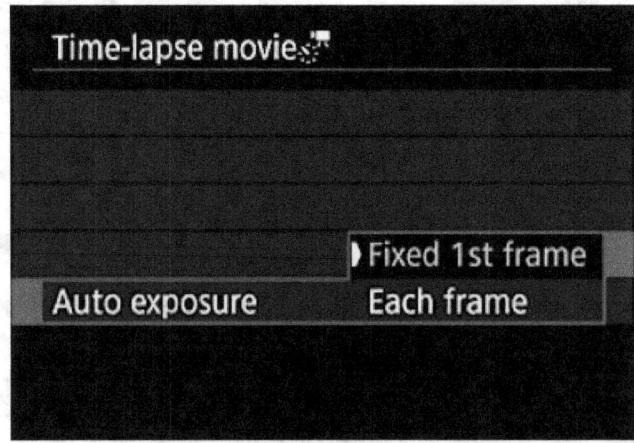

Screen Auto Off: This setting may require some scrolling to access. If you select **Enable**, the screen will dim 10 seconds after you begin shooting, allowing you time to check your exposure and framing before it turns off automatically after 30 minutes. Alternatively, you can choose **Disable** to have the screen turn off by itself after approximately 30 minutes.

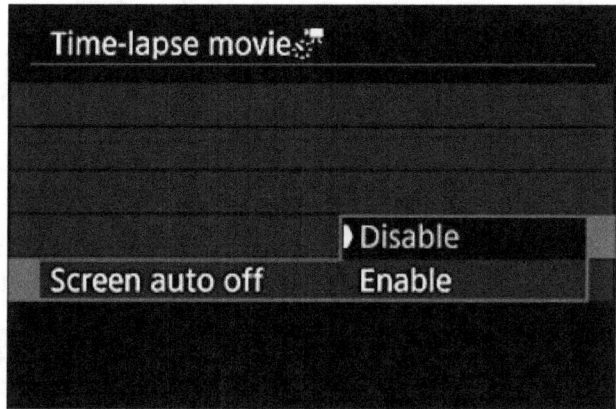

You can enable or disable a beep that sounds for each encounter. Adjust the **Beep As Image Taken** feature to determine whether a sound is emitted when an image is captured (especially when using the silent electronic shutter). You can also modify the volume of the beep.

Movie Self-timer

This feature is helpful as it allows users to delay the start of video recording by either two or ten seconds. With a 10-second delay, you have time to fix your hair, while a 2-second delay gives you just enough time to get ready without worrying too much about your appearance. Either way, you'll have a moment to position yourself in front of the camera.

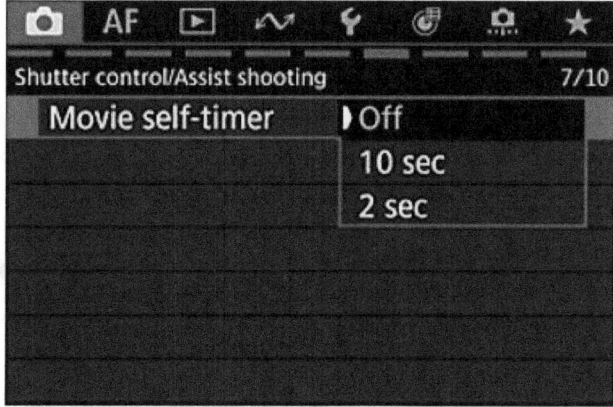

When you press or tap the video button, the camera beeps and displays a countdown of the seconds remaining until recording starts. This gives the camera a moment to stabilize after you've initiated recording with your index finger. It's especially useful if you don't have a remote release.

While some vloggers might find this feature unnecessary, it can still come in handy for spontaneous recordings. Vloggers who choose an R5 Mark II over a smartphone are typically adept at editing, allowing them to seamlessly edit out any awkwardness from their footage.

Tally Lamp

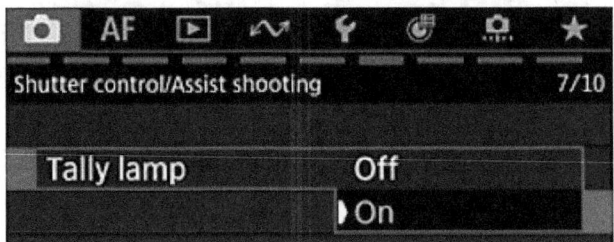

When set to [On], this controls how the tally lamp blinks or lights up.

Lit	Movie recording in progress
Blinking rapidly	• Cannot record movies, due to a low battery level or insufficient card free space • High internal camera temperature, due to hot shooting conditions or extended movie recording
Blinking slowly	Movie recording is now possible for up to 6 min.

Pre-recording Settings

With pre-recording, you can configure your camera to begin recording a few seconds before you manually start it. This initial recording is known as pre-recording, and the camera automatically captures a pre-roll while in standby mode, ensuring you don't miss any important moments.

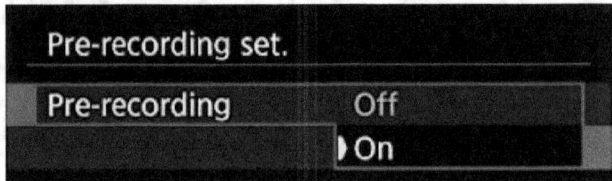

- Press [On].

Select [Recording time]

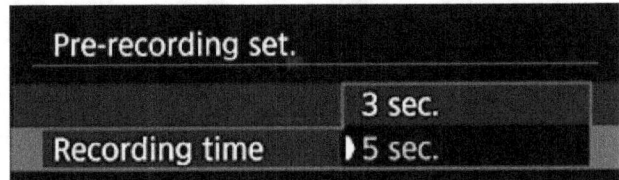

- Choose how long the pre-recording will last before manual recording starts.

Record the Movie.

- Record the movie just like you would with any other footage.
- The pre-recorded segment will be included in the final movie as it is being filmed.

IS (Image Stabilizer Mode)

Thanks to the camera's IS mode and movie digital IS features, shake is minimized during recording. These features effectively stabilize footage even with non-IS lenses. When the Image Stabilizer switch on an IS lens is activated, both the lens and the camera work together to enhance stabilization.

It's recommended to use this feature alongside the optical image stabilization of your lenses. If IS is disabled, the camera will prompt you to enable it. When combining optical and digital stabilization, Canon refers to this as combination IS, and they provide a list of compatible lenses. However, movie IS should not be used with fisheye, tilt/shift (TS-E), or third-party lenses, nor with lenses exceeding a focal length of 800 millimeters.

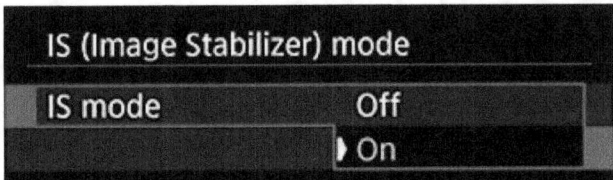

You can adjust the following settings for image stabilization:

IS Mode

- **On, Off**: This option appears only if your lens lacks built-in image stabilization. You can toggle the camera's in-body image stabilization (IBIS) on or off. It's advisable to turn it off when the camera is on a tripod, as IBIS may still introduce unwanted adjustments. However, it's beneficial to keep it on when using smaller devices.

Movie Digital IS

- **Off, On, Enhanced**: This option is available regardless of whether your lens has an image stabilization system.
    - **On**: Activates a slight crop with significant motion correction, providing a more stable image. This setting works best with wide-angle lenses.
    - **Enhanced**: Further corrects existing camera shake, with an additional minor crop. Use this option cautiously, as it may increase noise levels and reduce clarity during playback.
-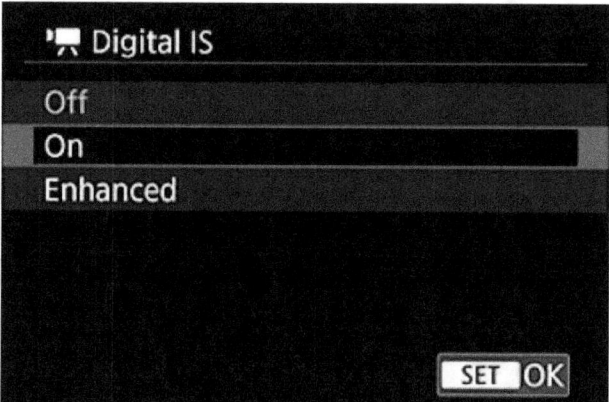

False Color Settings

False Color is a valuable tool for exposure monitoring, especially in video production. Here's a breakdown of how it works:

False Color Overview

- **Purpose**: Converts different exposure levels into colors, providing a clear visual guide to identify areas that are overexposed (too bright) or underexposed (too dark).
- **Usage**: Commonly used by cinematographers to quickly assess exposure without relying on traditional methods like zebra stripes.

Functionality

- **Color Mapping**: Each color corresponds to a specific exposure level, allowing users to gauge which parts of the image may need adjustment.

- **Visual Feedback**: Instead of flashing indicators, the false color display gives a continuous visual representation of exposure across the frame.

Limitations

- **Conflicts with Other Features**: When False Color is activated, several other exposure tools are disabled, including:
    - Zebra Display
    - Auto Lighting Optimizer
    - View Assist for Canon Log
    - Manual Focus Peaking
    - Time-lapse recording

Important Note

- **Color Temperature Changes**: The feature may also adjust the color temperature of the image, which can affect how the scene appears. This is important to consider during filming to maintain the desired aesthetic.

Using False Color can significantly streamline the process of achieving proper exposure, especially for those new to video shooting.

False Color Display

The **Fake Color Index** provides valuable information about the colors displayed in the viewfinder and on the camera screen when using the False Color feature. Here's what you need to know:

Fake Color Index Overview

- **Purpose**: The index serves as a reference guide to interpret the colors on the screen, indicating various exposure levels.
- **Color Associations**: Each color corresponds to specific exposure ranges, helping you quickly identify areas that are properly exposed, overexposed, or underexposed.

Typical Color Mappings

- **Red**: Usually indicates overexposed areas.
- **Yellow**: Suggests areas that are approaching overexposure.
- **Green**: Often represents correctly exposed areas.
- **Blue**: May indicate underexposed regions.

Usage

- **Assessing Exposure**: By consulting the Fake Color Index, you can make informed adjustments to your lighting or camera settings to achieve the desired exposure.
- **Quick Reference**: It's a handy tool for cinematographers and photographers to ensure that key parts of the frame are exposed correctly.

Using the Fake Color Index in conjunction with the False Color feature enhances your ability to monitor and control exposure effectively during filming.

Color	Meaning
Red	White clipping
Yellow	Just below white clipping
Pink	One stop over 18% gray
Green	18% gray
Blue	Just above black clipping
Purple	Black clipping
Neutral color	Brightness other than above

Zebra Settings

The **Zebra Pattern Warnings** feature is a useful tool for monitoring highlights in your shot, helping you prevent overexposure during filming. Here's a breakdown of how it works:

Zebra Pattern Warnings Overview

- **Purpose**: This feature alerts you when highlights exceed a specified brightness level, similar to the flashing blinkies on older digital cameras that indicate overexposed areas in images.
- **Functionality**: By displaying zebra stripes on the areas that are too bright, it provides a visual cue to adjust your exposure settings in real-time.

How to Use

1. **Access the Menu**: Navigate to the Zebra Pattern Warnings setting in your camera's menu.
2. **Select a Pattern**: Choose the desired zebra pattern style.

3. **Set IRE Brightness Level**: Enter an IRE (Institute of Radio Engineers) brightness number ranging from 5 to 100. This number determines the threshold for when the zebra pattern will appear on your display.

Adjusting Exposure

- **Feedback**: Once you see the zebra stripes, it indicates that the corresponding highlights are too bright and at risk of being overexposed.
- **Fine-Tuning**: You can adjust your lighting, aperture, or ISO settings based on the feedback from the zebra patterns, ensuring a well-balanced exposure in your shot.

Using the Zebra Pattern Warnings effectively helps you make informed decisions while shooting, leading to better overall image quality.

Zebra 1 level

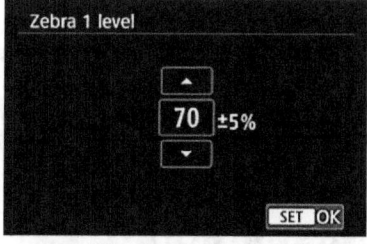

Zebra 2 level

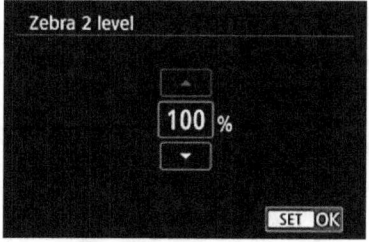

Shooting Information Display

You can customize the on-screen display and viewfinder information while recording video to enhance your shooting experience. Here's how:

Customizing Display Information

1. **Access Display Settings**: Go to the camera's menu and find the section for display or video settings.
2. **Select Info Display Options**: You can choose what information to show, such as:

- **Exposure Settings**: Shutter speed, aperture, ISO.
- **Focus Indicators**: Focus peaking or magnification.
- **Audio Levels**: Metering for audio input levels.
- **Histogram**: For analyzing exposure across the image.
- **Timecode**: To track recording time and sync multiple cameras.

3. **Enable/Disable Elements**: Toggle various elements on or off based on your preferences. For example, you might want a clean display with minimal distractions, or you might want detailed settings visible.
4. **Adjust Layout**: Some cameras allow you to customize the layout or position of the displayed information, enabling you to prioritize what's most important to you.

Benefits

- **Real-Time Feedback**: By tailoring the display, you can have immediate access to critical information without taking your focus away from the shot.
- **Enhanced Workflow**: Knowing exactly what settings are in play allows for quicker adjustments and smoother operation during shoots.

Customizing your display can significantly improve your efficiency and the quality of your video recordings.

Standby: Low Resolution

This feature is designed to optimize performance and manage heat while using the Canon EOS R5 Mark II. Here's a summary of its functions and implications:

Low-Quality Preview Mode

- **Purpose**: To reduce power consumption and heat generation when the camera is idle or in preview mode.
- **Operation**: When activated, the camera displays a lower-quality preview image and refresh rate. This helps keep the sensor and memory card from overheating during extended usage, especially when shooting in 4K.

Benefits

1. **Heat Management**: Reduces the risk of sensor damage from prolonged operation, especially during high-demand tasks like recording high-resolution video.
2. **Extended Shooting Time**: Allows for longer sessions by conserving battery life when the camera is in standby or preview mode.

3. **Quicker Response**: When deactivated, the camera can respond more quickly when transitioning back to active shooting, improving usability.

Limitations

- **Incompatibility**: This setting cannot be used simultaneously with Pre-Recording mode or Digital Zoom.
- **Quality Trade-off**: While in this mode, the preview image is of lower quality, which may not be suitable for critical focus or composition adjustments.

Customization

You can toggle this setting based on your shooting conditions and preferences. If overheating is not a concern for you, or if you prioritize quick responsiveness and better preview quality, you may choose to disable this feature.

Canon Log HDMI Output Range

When using an HDMI connection, you have the option to select the output range for the video data.

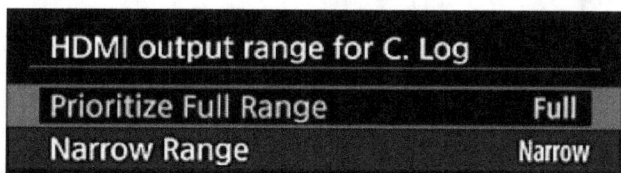

- **Prioritize Full Range**
  Full-range audio should be utilized whenever possible. Keep in mind that the output range will automatically adjust to meet the requirements of the monitor.
- **Narrow Range**
  A narrow output range, or video range, is employed in this case.

Time Code

Professional producers find that the time codes integrated into video files, which adhere to SMPTE (Society of Motion Picture and Television Engineers) standards, are invaluable for editing. Essentially, this time system provides precise markers for hours, minutes, seconds, and frames, enabling accurate synchronization of audio and video frames.

You might recall that a recording at 30 frames per second actually delivers 29.97 frames per second, while a 24 frames per second setting results in 23.976 fps. The process of dropping frames is part of the time coding system that ensures the recorded video's fractional frame rate aligns with real-time playback.

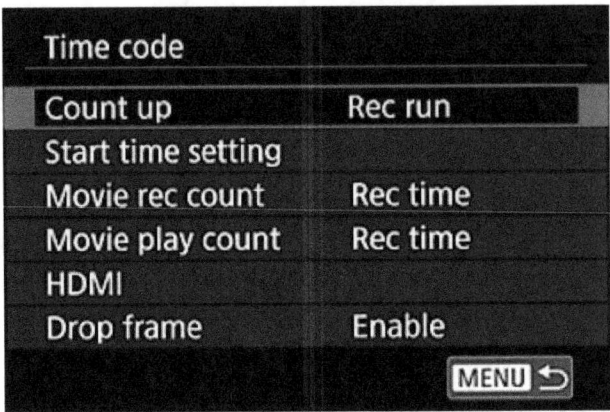

Count Up

You can select between Rec Run and Free Run modes, also known as Time of Day. In Rec Run mode, the time code advances only during recording. In contrast, Free Run mode allows the time code to progress regardless of whether you are capturing clips, making it beneficial for synchronizing footage from multiple cameras at the same event.

Free Run enables you to adjust the appearance of your recorded footage, creating the impression that all clips were filmed simultaneously, even if the cameras were activated at different times. When using Free Run, the time code remains in the video file regardless of edits made, except for high frame rate (HFR) sections.

Start Time Setting

At the start of recording, the frames are set to 0:00, with hours, minutes, and seconds determined by the camera's internal clock. You can manually input the hour, minute, and second, or set the start time to 00:00:00:00.

Movie Rec. Count

This menu option allows you to record video while displaying either the time code or the elapsed time for the current clip on the LCD screen.

Movie Play Count

While playing back video, you can toggle between the time code and actual elapsed time using the same controls.

HDMI

To include the time code in the video output, select "Enable." To omit it, choose "Disable." When the Record Command output is activated, users can synchronize the camera's stop/start function with an external recording device. If this setting is off, the external device will control the recording start and stop.

Drop Frame

When set to a frame rate of 30, for example, you'll actually get 29.97 frames per second. At 60 fps, it results in 59.94 fps, and for HFR, it yields 119.9 fps. Selecting "Enable" allows the camera to occasionally skip certain time code segments in drop-frame mode to minimize discrepancies. You may notice a change of a few seconds after an hour when this feature is not in use.

Other Menu Functions

HDMI Display

If you want to display your output on both the recorder or monitor connected to your device and the camera itself, that's possible.

Camera + External

In this mode, both the camera and the external device show the video simultaneously. However, you won't be able to record to the memory card while in this setting. The HDMI output will display only the video, without any overlays, and can be used for both playback and menu navigation. The camera screen will show the live recording along with any information displayed by pressing the INFO button, but it won't show settings or playback options.

Even if the devices are far apart and connected by a long cable, this mode allows you to monitor the video on both the HDMI device and the camera.

External Only

In this mode, the video, data, menus, and playback images are only visible on the external device, while the camera does not display any of this information.

HDMI RAW Output

When you enable this setting, you can transmit RAW movies to compatible devices via HDMI at resolutions of up to 8K. Once recording begins, the footage will also be saved to card 2 in XF-AVC format, provided that card 2 is installed in the camera.

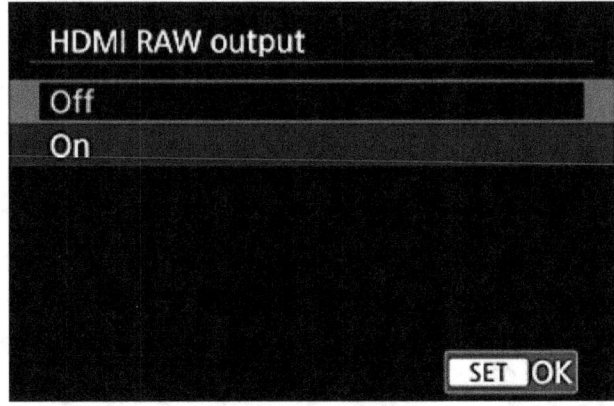

If you set [Rec Command] to [On], you can only use external recorders for recording when card 2 is not connected.

Manual Exposure Settings for Video

The Canon EOS R5 Mark II offers users enhanced control over video recording with its adjustable brightness settings. Here's a detailed look at the manual video brightness settings:

1. Aperture

In custom exposure mode, the aperture is a key setting. It controls the amount of light entering the camera and affects the level of detail in your recordings. Lowering the f-number enlarges the aperture, resulting in a shallower depth of field, which can help isolate a subject and create a cinematic effect. For broader scenes, like landscapes, a higher f-number and smaller aperture will yield a deeper depth of field, keeping more of the image in focus.

2. Shutter Speed

Shutter speed is another critical adjustment in manual exposure mode. It determines how long light hits the camera's sensor. Slower shutter speeds can introduce motion blur, ideal for capturing movement or low-light conditions, while faster shutter speeds are better for freezing action and enhancing detail in dynamic scenes.

3. ISO

The ISO setting indicates the camera's sensitivity to light. Higher ISO levels allow shooting in dim conditions but can introduce more digital noise. Conversely, lower ISO settings provide clearer images but may not be suitable in low light. Achieving the right exposure often involves balancing ISO, aperture, and shutter speed.

4. Exposure Compensation

Exposure compensation allows for adjustments in brightness without altering ISO, shutter speed, or aperture. This feature is useful for fine-tuning exposure; each stop adjustment can allow in four to six times more light, measured in stops.

5. Manual Focus

The EOS R5 Mark II offers manual focus capabilities, allowing users to adjust the lens focus manually. This is particularly beneficial in low light or when achieving a specific depth of field. The focus peaking feature highlights in-focus areas, helping ensure precision in focusing.

6. Zebra Pattern

The zebra pattern overlay indicates areas of the image that are overexposed, making it easier to identify and adjust bright spots to improve overall image quality. Users can customize the zebra pattern to display different exposure levels based on their needs.

7. Histogram

A histogram visually represents the distribution of brightness levels in an image, helping users identify areas that are too bright or too dark. Adjusting the brightness settings becomes easier with this graphical representation, allowing for more precise exposure control.

8. Peaking

The peaking feature enhances image edges using a contrasting color, making it easier to identify focal points. This is especially helpful in low-light situations or when a specific depth of field is desired. Users can customize the peaking color and sensitivity to suit their preferences.

Movie Playback and Editing

Here's a summary of the Canon EOS R5 Mark II's video playback and editing capabilities:

1. Movie Playback Modes

The Canon EOS R5 Mark II offers multiple playback options for videos. Users can watch their footage normally or choose slow motion, fast motion, or frame-by-frame playback. Additionally, a loop playback function allows for repeated viewing of specific segments.

2. Movie Editing

This camera includes various editing tools for trimming, splitting, and mixing video clips. Users can capture still images from their footage either automatically or manually. The video clip mode also allows for recording short videos that can be combined to create longer films.

3. In-Camera Raw Processing

The R5 Mark II allows for in-camera raw editing, enabling users to adjust exposure, white balance, contrast, and more directly on the device. Creative filters and effects can also be applied, making this feature particularly useful for quick edits while on the go.

4. HDMI Output

The camera features an HDMI output for connecting to external displays or recorders, enhancing viewing and editing experiences. It can produce 10-bit 4:2:2 video in Canon Log and HDR PQ modes, providing greater flexibility for post-production work.

5. Wi-Fi and Bluetooth Connectivity

With built-in Wi-Fi and Bluetooth, users can transfer video clips to a computer or smartphone for editing and sharing. The camera can also be controlled via a tablet or smartphone, allowing for adjustments and recording without physical movement.

6. Canon Image Transfer Utility

The free Canon Image Transfer Utility facilitates transferring video footage from the R5 Mark II to a computer for editing and storage. The software provides various organizational and editing features, as well as multiple export options.

7. Canon Digital Photo Professional

This free tool allows users to edit Canon camera raw video. It offers features such as creative filters, color adjustments, and exposure changes, along with the ability to export videos in formats compatible with other editing software.

8. Third-Party Editing Software

While many users appreciate Canon Digital Photo Professional, many prefer third-party editing programs like Adobe Premiere Pro or Final Cut Pro X. These alternatives provide greater creative freedom, control, and access to advanced features and effects.

Chapter 7
The Photo Shooting Menu

The Photo Shooting Menu is a key feature of the Canon EOS R5 Mark II that allows users to adjust various settings related to photography. Here's an overview of some of the most important settings within the Photo Shooting Menu and their impact on your images.

Image Quality

Image Quality is the top option in the photography menu, allowing you to select the format for your stored images. You can choose to capture photos in JPEG, RAW, or both formats. RAW files contain all the data captured by the camera's sensor, giving you greater flexibility for post-editing. In contrast, JPEG files are compressed, which means they occupy less space on your memory card.

Picture Size

Another key option in the Photo Shooting Menu is Picture Size, which allows you to adjust the resolution of your images. The Canon EOS R5 Mark II offers various sizes, ranging from small to large. Larger images capture more detail and are ideal for printing, while smaller images are better suited for online sharing due to their reduced file size.

Picture Style

The Picture Style function allows you to adjust the color and contrast of your photos using a selection of predefined options. In addition to Standard, Portrait, Landscape, Neutral, and Faithful, Canon offers several other styles. You can also create and save your own Picture Style, giving you the flexibility to achieve your desired look for your images.

White Balance

The white balance option allows you to adjust the color temperature of your photos, enhancing their natural appearance. Canon provides various settings, including Auto, Daylight, Shade, Cloudy, Tungsten, Fluorescent, and Flash. Additionally, you can set a custom white balance tailored to the specific lighting conditions of your shooting environment.

Auto Lighting Optimizer

When a scene has high contrast, the Auto Lighting Optimizer tool automatically adjusts the exposure and contrast of your photos. This feature can be particularly useful if the camera's metering system struggles to achieve the correct exposure in challenging lighting conditions.

High ISO NR

When using a high ISO setting, the High ISO NR (Noise Reduction) option adjusts the camera's approach to minimizing noise. This can be particularly beneficial in low-light situations where noise can be a significant issue.

Lens Aberration Correction

Selecting the Lens Aberration Correction option automatically addresses issues like lens distortion, chromatic aberration, and vignetting in your photos. This feature enhances image quality overall and reduces the need for extensive post-processing adjustments.

Long Exposure Noise Reduction

The Long Exposure Noise Reduction option helps minimize noise in your photos during long exposures. This feature is particularly useful when you need to use a slower shutter speed to achieve a specific aesthetic.

High ISO Speed Noise Reduction

Using the High ISO Speed Noise Reduction setting can significantly reduce noise in your images when shooting at a high ISO. This feature is especially helpful for achieving well-exposed photos in low-light conditions when you need to increase the ISO.

Multiple Exposure

The Multiple Exposure preset allows you to combine two or more images into a single photograph directly in the camera. This capability enables creative individuals to produce unique and original compositions that would be challenging to capture in a single frame.

HDR Mode

The HDR (High Dynamic Range) Mode setting allows you to combine multiple exposures into one image with an expanded dynamic range. This feature is particularly useful for capturing detail in areas with extreme lighting conditions, ensuring you retain information from both dark and bright parts of the scene.

Interval Timer

By selecting the interval timer option, you can capture a series of images at predetermined intervals. This feature allows you to create time-lapse videos or compile a collection of photos for further editing.

Time-Lapse Movie

You can create time-lapse videos directly from the camera using the Time-Lapse Movie feature. This function offers a fun and creative way to capture the passage of time.

Image Quality

This option is located first in the Shooting 1 menu, where you can manage all settings related to image quality when saving files. When selecting a quality setting, you have several options:

Resolution: The quality of your photos is determined by the total number of pixels in an image. For example, the Medium setting offers 3984 x 2656 pixels (11MP), while the Large/RAW/C-RAW option provides 6000 x 4000 pixels (24MP). Smaller options include Small 1 at 2976 x 1984 pixels (5.9MP) and Small 2 at 2400 x 1600 pixels (3.8MP).

HEIF/JPEG Compression: To reduce the size of your photo files and allow for more storage on your memory card, the camera employs compression. By lowering the source image size, you create smaller file sizes. You can choose between Fine and Normal compression, with the understanding that Normal compression may result in lower quality. Icons help differentiate the two: quarter-circle indicators represent Fine compression (smoother images), while stair-like indicators signify Normal compression (jaggier images). Note that the Small 2 (S2) file option uses Fine quality but lacks a specific icon.

File Format: You can opt to save your images as uncompressed RAW files or as JPEG/HEIF files, which take up about half the space on your memory card. Many photographers prefer to keep both a RAW file and a JPEG/HEIF version, allowing them to preserve the original RAW file while also having a more manageable format for editing. This is important since JPEGs and HEIFs are lossy formats, whereas RAW files retain all image data, making them easier to work with later. If a file includes both a JPG extension (indicating it's from a Canon camera) and a CR3 extension (indicating a Canon RAW file), it signifies that two versions of the same image are saved.

To adjust the settings, access the Image Quality option and press the SET button to select the setting that best meets your needs. The screen will display a selection menu similar to the example below. (If you've selected HDR recording in the Shooting 2 menu, HEIF will appear at the bottom of the list instead of JPEG.)

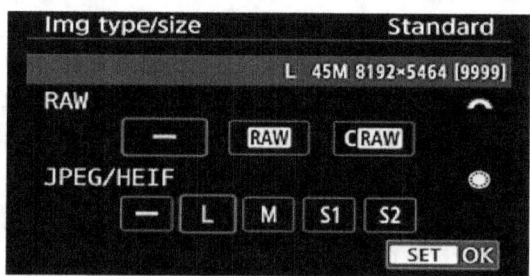

By rotating the Main dial, you can select from the options of (no RAW), RAW, or C RAW. To toggle between JPEG and HEIF, simply turn the QCD-1 in the desired direction. You can also choose from the previously mentioned sizes: Large, Medium, or Small, with either Fine or Normal compression (indicated by smooth and stepped icons), as well as Small 2 (with Fine compression). The currently selected option will be highlighted with a red circle. If you choose both RAW and JPEG/HEIF, the output file will be JPEG/HEIF Fine. Remember to select an option and then press the SET button to confirm your choice.

Cropping/Aspect Ratio

You can crop photos directly on your device. For recording high-definition or ultra-high-definition video, you can select an aspect ratio of 1:1 (square), 4:3, or 16:9. Additionally, there's an option for a 1.6X APS-C crop with a 3:2 ratio that corresponds with the full setting, where the sensor frame measures 36 mm x 24 mm. You also have the option to display the shooting area within the frame. You can choose to hide it, showing only the current crop or aspect ratio, or enable blue lines to outline the area.

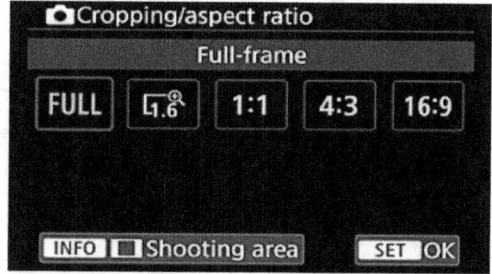

The R5 Mark II utilizes a 1.6x crop factor to support APS-C format RF-S lenses, as well as APS-C format EF-S lenses when using an EF/EF-S mount adapter. This crop factor enhances the reach of RF and EF lenses, producing images that measure 3744 by 2496 pixels, resulting in 9.3 megapixels. If you attach an RF-S or EF-S lens, the 1.6x crop will be automatically selected, limiting your options to this aspect ratio.

Since the aspect ratio for APS-C images matches that of full-frame images, using an RF-S or EF-S lens or selecting the 1.6x crop will enlarge the image to fill the screen. You'll see a 1.6x indicator within the frame. To change the aspect ratio, press the INFO button and choose either Masked or Outlined for the Shooting Area display.

In Masked mode, the screen displays only the portion of the image that was captured. In Outlined mode, the entire frame is visible, along with a blue line marking the captured area. This option is useful if you want to see parts of your subject outside the recording area.

When playing back a RAW image, you will see lines indicating the cropped area. During a slideshow, only the captured portion will be displayed. If you select a crop while shooting in RAW format, the image will be saved at the highest quality of 6000 x 400 pixels. However, when you playback the RAW image, the crop lines will indicate the boundaries of the captured image.

Expo.comp./AEB: 0 –

Here's how to set up exposure bracketing or make exposure adjustments. However, since you can quickly adjust these settings using the large rotary dial on the back of the camera, it's more efficient to use that instead of navigating through the menu.

ISO speed settings

- **ISO Speed:** My favorite feature is the Auto ISO function, as it effectively adjusts the shutter speed for varying lighting conditions.
- **ISO Speed Range:** By adjusting the ISO, the range from 100 to H determines the visibility of your images. I keep my ISO setting at 100-H to maintain the full range.
- **Auto Range:** The range of 100–12800 is particularly useful when using the Auto ISO setting. I typically set the EOS R5 II's maximum ISO to 12800, as I find the noise levels become unacceptable beyond that point.
- **Min. Shutter Speed:** When set to Auto, the camera adjusts the shutter speed according to the reciprocal rule, which can help keep your shots steady. However, if you tend to have shaky hands, the Auto setting may not suffice. You can move the slider towards Faster on the top dial to double the shutter speed, which can help eliminate blurriness in your images.

Anti-Flicker Shooting

Many amateur sports photographers often wonder why they encounter issues like banding, uneven exposure, or noticeable color shifts in certain stadiums or gyms. These problems are usually caused by the type of artificial lighting used in those venues.

The phenomenon occurs because some artificial lights flicker at a rate that is imperceptible to the human eye but can be captured by the camera. When this setting is activated, the camera measures the flicker frequency of the light source (optimal for 100 to 120 cycles per second) and captures images at the precise moment when the flicker has the least impact on image quality. However, this feature cannot be used for recording videos or during live viewing.

Anti-flicker shoot: Disable

This feature is excellent for capturing sports or events under artificial lighting, as it helps ensure your images are evenly exposed from top to bottom. Shooting indoors can be challenging, but once you activate this setting, the camera will delay the shutter to synchronize with the light frequency, resulting in better-exposed shots.

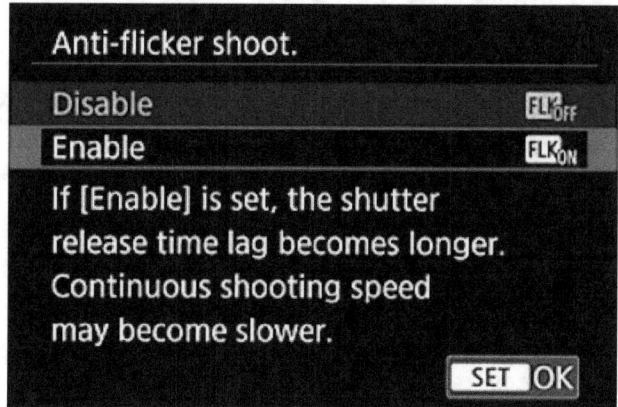

You may experience a slight delay in the shutter release as the camera waits for the optimal moment to capture the shot. While this can slow down your shooting pace, it's essential for recording fast-paced sports or events, allowing you to capture fleeting moments that might otherwise be missed. When shooting in P or Av mode, the shutter speed may adjust between shots to ensure proper exposure, which can lead to varying results. To maintain a consistent shutter speed, consider using either TV or M mode.

Once this feature is enabled, you can manually detect flicker by pressing the INFO button, followed by the Q button, and selecting Anti-Flicker Shooting from the Quick Control menu. This allows you to check for flicker detection by the camera.

Keep in mind that Anti-Flicker is disabled in Basic Zone modes and may not perform well in certain situations, such as when using wireless flash in a dimly lit room or one with bright lights. Canon recommends taking a few test shots to ensure the feature operates effectively in the specific lighting conditions you encounter.

High-Frequency Anti-Flicker Shooting

You may not have noticed this phenomenon because you've grown accustomed to the bright, flashing lights of modern society. In 60 Hertz (Hz) circuits, traditional incandescent bulbs flicker at a rate of 100 to 120 cycles per second, with only about a 10 percent change in brightness. This typically isn't enough to interfere with your photos.

The Anti-Flicker Shooting feature works well with various types of artificial lighting, even those that can cause banding due to significant intensity changes. However, some newer lighting technologies, like advanced LED bulbs, may flicker at much higher rates and lower intensities, requiring more sophisticated solutions.

By adjusting the shutter speed to align with the flicker cycles of these light sources, this feature can reduce or eliminate banding effects in your images. If you're shooting in environments with high-frequency flickering lights, this feature allows you to capture photos at shutter speeds that minimize the visibility of flicker.

Recommended Tv Setting

The camera will display the appropriate shutter speed for shooting in environments with high-frequency flickering light sources, capable of detecting flicker rates between 50 and 8193.7 Hz. You can then use the recommended shutter speed for your shots.

1. **Select Your Shutter Speed:** Choose the shutter speed you wish to use. The camera will suggest a shutter speed that aligns well with the flickering frequency of the light source.
2. **Click on [Recommend TV set]:** After making your selection, click OK to confirm the recommended setting.

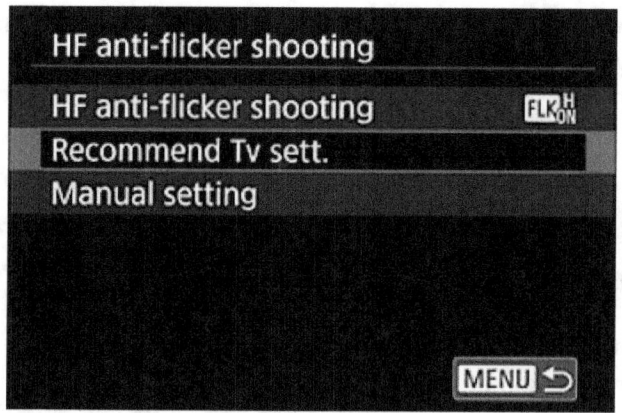

3. **Adjust the Shutter Speed:**
    - Press [Yes] to switch to the recommended shutter speed.
    - The [Manual setup] screen will appear once you select [Yes (go to TV settings)].

For Manual Setting:

- **Select the Shooting Mode:** Set the Mode dial to either M (Manual) or Tv (Shutter Priority) to choose your desired camera settings.
- **Choose the Shutter Speed:** Select the shutter speed that best suits your needs for the shot.

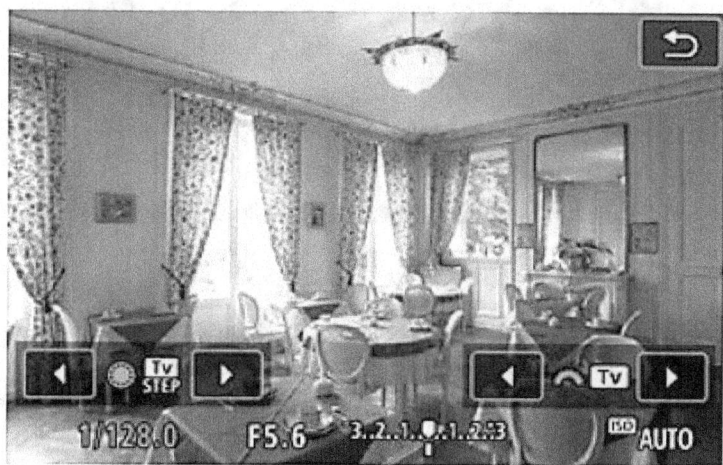

- **Choose the Manual Setting:** The first option on the setup screen will display the shutter speed closest to your desired setting. The camera can detect flickering within a frequency range of 50 Hz to 2011 Hz.

- **View the Scene:** In addition to assessing the overall scene, examine various parts of the image for any visible banding.
- **Adjust the Shutter Speed:** You can fine-tune the shutter speed until the banding disappears by simultaneously turning the QCD-1 and Main dials.
- **QCD-1:** This dial allows you to select the optimal shutter speed. Turning it counterclockwise will increase the speed (e.g., 2X to 3X to 4X), while turning it clockwise will decrease the speed (e.g., 1/2X, 1/3X, 1/4X).
- **Main Dial:** Slowly adjusting the Main dial to the right or left will help make the bands in your image less noticeable.
- **If Banding Persists:** You can either use automatic detection or rotate the camera 90 degrees. Keep in mind that when this function is activated, switching from HDR Mode to Dynamic Range Mode is not possible. Canon recommends setting Custom Function 2: Same Exposure for New Aperture to ISO Speed to maintain consistent exposure, ensuring that only the aperture changes while the shutter speed remains fixed. When this function is active, the fastest flash sync speed available is 1/181.0 seconds, and a manual safety shift will only adjust the aperture, keeping the shutter speed constant.

Flash Function Settings

External Speedlite control	
Flash firing	Enable
E-TTL balance	Standard
E-TTL II meter.	Eval (FacePrty)
Contin flash ctrl	E-TTL each shot
Sync speed priority	OFF
Slow synchro	1/250-1/60 sec.
Clear settings	MENU

Flash Firing

This feature allows you to toggle the flash light on or off. Once you connect the flash to the camera and turn it on, selecting the Enable option will activate it properly. If you choose the Disable option, the AF-assist beam will continue to function, but the flash itself will not fire.

For those who enjoy shooting in low light but still require assistance with autofocus, considering the second option might be beneficial.

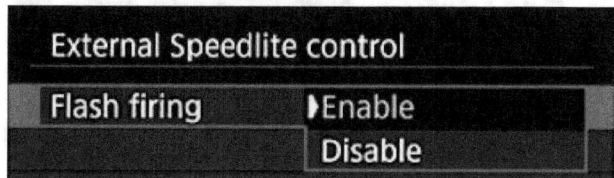

E-TTL Balance

This feature provides greater control over how the flash and natural light combine to affect exposure. The default setting is Standard, but you have the option to select another mode. In the Standard setting, the Speedlite and existing light are given equal importance.

If you opt for Ambience-priority mode, the flash will serve only as a fill light to brighten shadows, allowing the natural light to remain prominent. Without this mode, the flash can dominate and overshadow any existing ambient light.

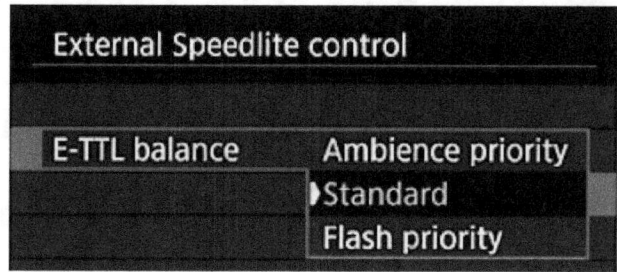

When you switch the setting to Flash priority, the Speedlite will act as the primary light source, illuminating both the subject and the background of your image. This mode is particularly effective in low-light conditions where there is minimal ambient light available.

E-TTL II Metering

When using the electronic flash exposure meter, you can choose between Evaluative (Matrix) and Average metering modes. Evaluative metering is typically the preferred option, as it analyzes the scene to determine the best exposure. In contrast, Average metering assesses the entire scene for flash exposure, making it a suitable choice if you want to gauge exposure across the whole image.

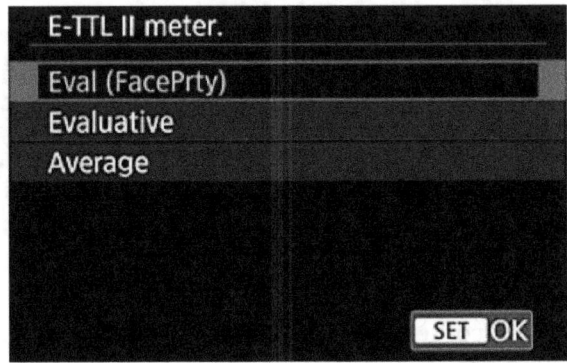

Another option available is Evaluative (Face-priority) metering. This setting prioritizes exposure based on the faces detected in the scene. Because this process takes a bit longer, you may experience slightly slower continuous shooting rates in this mode. However, the most important factor to consider when selecting a shooting speed for continuous shots is likely the flash's recycle time.

Continuous Flash Control

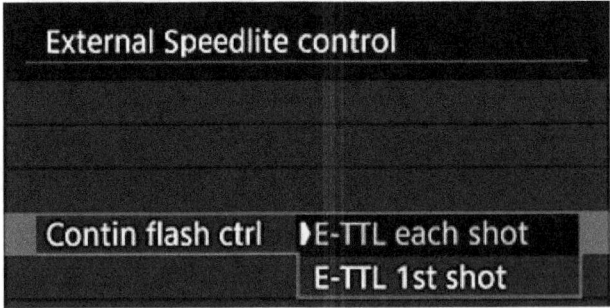

This setting also affects how a Speedlight operates when taking multiple shots in succession. If you select E-TTL Each Shot, the camera will evaluate the scene's brightness just before capturing each shot in a series. On the other hand, if you choose E-TTL 1st Shot, the exposure settings from the first image will be applied to all subsequent shots.

This mode is ideal for shooting at the fastest continuous speed, especially when the composition remains unchanged between shots. However, if the subject moves, the optimal exposure may shift, which could result in the initial settings not being suitable for later images.

Sync Speed Priority

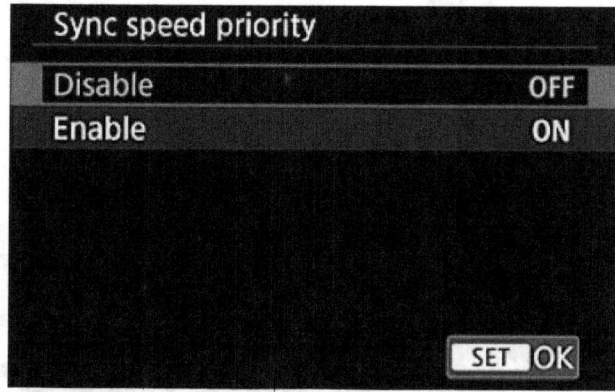

You can achieve a sync speed that exceeds the standard rate when using flash photography.

- This is available if E-TTL II flash metering is selected in Flash mode.
- When this feature is activated, the flash sync rates may vary based on the combination of different camera settings.

Camera Setting		Flash Sync Speed (Fastest)
Shutter mode	Cropping/aspect ratio	
Elec. 1st-curtain	FULL	1/320 sec.
	1.6*	1/400 sec.
Electronic ES	FULL	1/200 sec.
	1.6*	1/320 sec.

* Equivalent to APS-C size

Note:

- This feature is compatible with a Speedlite 580EX II or later when Manual flash is selected in Flash mode.
- If the Flash mode is set to Manual and the fastest flash sync speed is used, the flash units may not fire at the preset output level.
- This setting does not affect Mechanical shutter mode.
- The following Speedlites support Sync speed priority:
    - Speedlite 430EX III, 470EX-AI, 600EX II-RT, EL-5, EL-10, and EL-1
    - Macro Ring Lite MR14-EX II / Macro Twin Lite MT-26EX-RT

- When Sync speed priority is enabled, there may be instances where the exposure is not optimal.
- If the receiver Speedlites have a positive exposure compensation value while shooting wirelessly via radio transmission, Sync speed priority may not achieve the correct exposure.

Slow Synchro

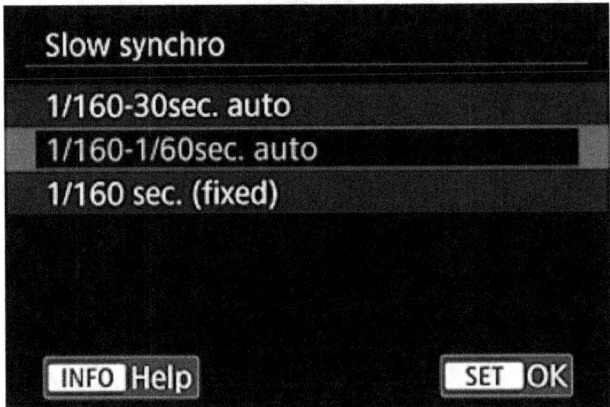

You can select the flash sync speed while the camera is in Av (Aperture-priority) or P (Program) exposure mode. Here are your options:

- **1/*-30 sec. auto:** The shutter speed will be automatically determined within a range to match the brightness, allowing for fast sync speeds as well.

Shutter mode	Cropping/aspect ratio	Shutter Speed
Mechanical	FULL	1/200–30 sec.
Mechanical	1.6*	1/250–30 sec.
Elec. 1st-curtain	FULL	1/250–30 sec.
Elec. 1st-curtain	1.6*	1/320–30 sec.
Electronic	FULL	1/160–30 sec.
Electronic	1.6*	1/250–30 sec.

- **1/*-1/60 sec. auto:** This setting prevents the camera from automatically selecting a slow shutter speed in low-light situations, helping to reduce camera shake and blur. While the flash will illuminate the subject, be aware that the background may appear darker.
- *1/ sec. (fixed):* This option maintains a constant shutter speed, providing better control against subject blur and camera shake compared to the 1/*-1/60 sec. auto setting. However, in low-light conditions, the background will likely be darker than it would be with the auto option.

Shutter mode	Cropping/aspect ratio	Shutter Speed
Mechanical	FULL	1/200 sec.
	1.6*	1/250 sec.
Elec. 1st-curtain	FULL	1/250 sec.
	1.6*	1/320 sec.
Electronic	FULL	1/160 sec.
	1.6*	1/250 sec.

In most cases, you need to select the f-stop to be locked in when using flash in aperture-priority mode. The camera will then adjust the exposure by varying the power of the electronic flash. In program mode, the camera automatically determines the aperture number. Since the flash provides the main exposure, the shutter speed has a more significant impact on the secondary exposure, which depends on the amount of ambient light present in the scene.

Flash Function Settings

What appears on the screen, where it is displayed, and the available options can vary based on the Speedlite model, its Custom Function settings, the flash mode selected, and other influencing factors.

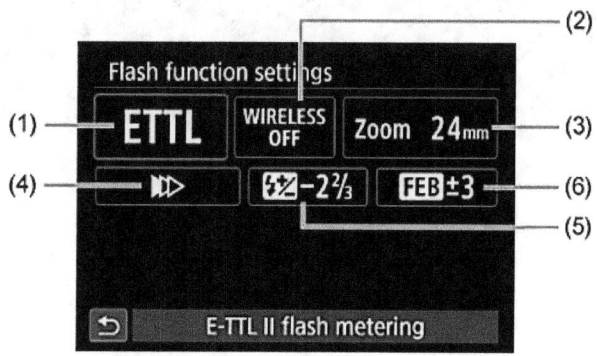

In E-TTL Flash mode, you can choose from various flash exposure options, including manual, multi-exposure (repeating), and automatic (E-TTL II). The automatic option helps conserve battery life while allowing continuous shooting with the flash activated, as both ISO speed and flash output are increased by one stop.

Wireless Functions: You can utilize radio or optical wireless communication to set up multiple flash units for wireless illumination when taking pictures.

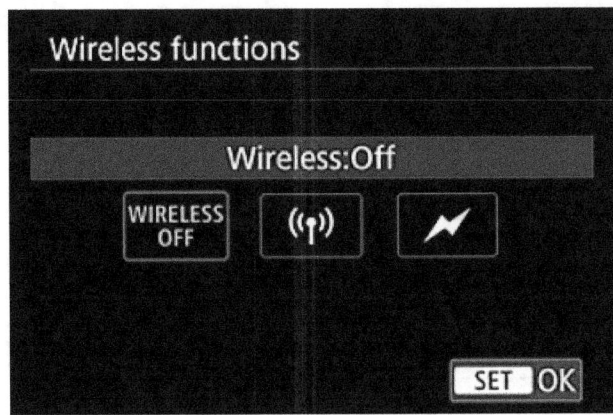

Zoom: You can select a flash zoom setting to adjust the coverage area of compatible Speedlites. This allows you to tailor the flash output to match your shooting conditions.

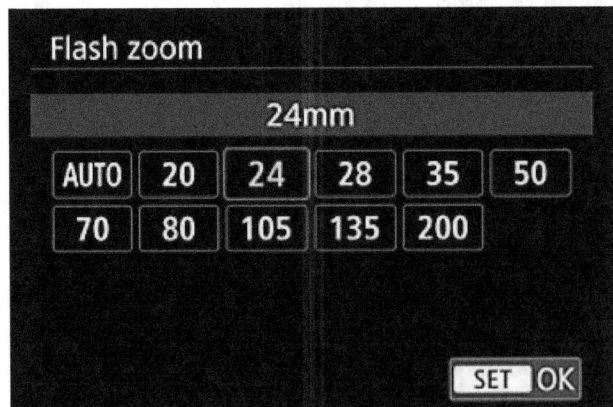

Shutter Sync

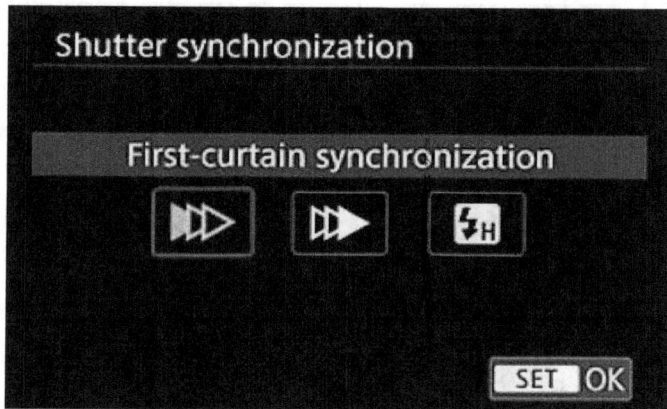

If you select first-curtain sync, the pre-flash will fire just before the shutter opens, setting the exposure. Once the shutter is fully open, the main flash will activate. This default setting combines the pre-flash and main flash into a single burst.

You can also opt for second-curtain sync, where the main flash fires just before the shutter closes, following the pre-flash. This allows for sharp images at the beginning and end of the exposure, creating a motion trail effect for moving subjects. This type of flash exposure differs significantly from that of some other cameras with second-curtain sync.

- **Default Setting:** First-curtain synchronization is the default, ensuring the flash activates as soon as shooting begins.
- **Motion Trails:** Use second-curtain sync with slow shutter speeds to capture motion trails, such as those created by passing cars.
- **High-Speed Synchronization:** By setting the shutter speed to High-speed sync, you can achieve flash exposures at speeds faster than the usual maximum sync speed (1/250th or 1/200th of a second). This is particularly useful for outdoor shots during the day with a wide aperture to create a blurred background.

To use high-speed sync, ensure you have a compatible external Speedlite connected and select the option through the External Flash Function Setting menu.

Flash Exposure Compensation.

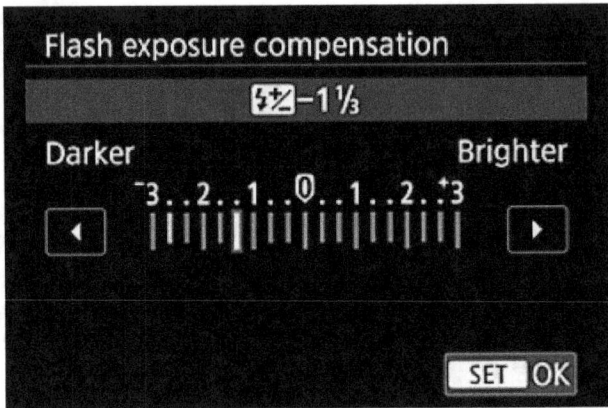

You can adjust the flash exposure through the menu instead of using the ISO/Flash exposure adjustment button. If you enter a value using both methods, the menu value will take precedence. To use this option, press the SET button to select it, then use the QCD-1 to set the flash EV correction to your desired level. A blue light indicator will help you quickly return to the previous EV setting if needed. Once you've confirmed your adjustment by pressing SET again, you can exit the menu by pressing the screen.

Flash Exposure Bracketing

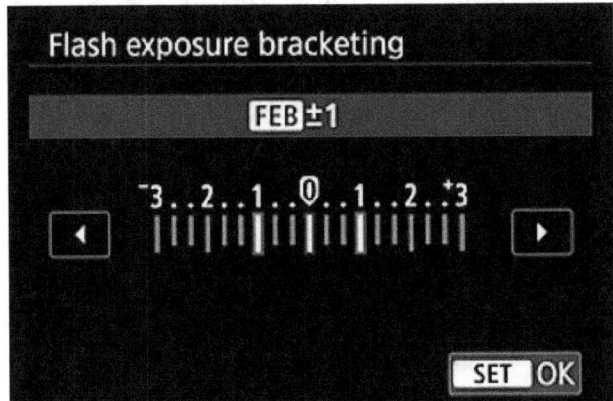

When using bracketing with a compatible electronic flash, these options allow you to adjust the output of your flash unit, giving you greater flexibility in your shots.

Flash Custom Function Settings

With many of Canon's external Speedlites, you can configure specific functions, allowing you to adjust settings such as flash metering mode and flash bracketing sequences. Advanced features may include modeling light/flash (if available), utilizing external power sources (if connected), and managing the operations of any slave units linked to the external flash.

This menu option allows you to modify the Custom Functions of an external flash directly from your camera's menu. The available functions vary by model; for instance, high-end models like the Speedlite 600EX-RT offer a wider range of options. In contrast, the Speedlite 320EX has four Custom Functions:

1. Auto Power Off
2. Quick Flash with Continuous Shot
3. Slave Auto Power Off Timer
4. Slave Auto Power Off Cancel

Clear Settings

This option allows you to reset both your Custom Functions and your external flash to their original default settings, undoing any modifications you've made. However, this reset does not apply to the C.Fn-00 Distance Indicator Display (if supported by your flash), which will remain unchanged until you adjust it manually. To modify or reset the Personal Functions (P.Fn) of a flash, you need to access the settings directly on the Speedlite, as this cannot be done through the camera.

Metering Mode

This option offers a menu-based method for selecting the desired metering mode. If you prefer, you can assign this function to a user-defined key for easier access, as it is primarily located in this menu.

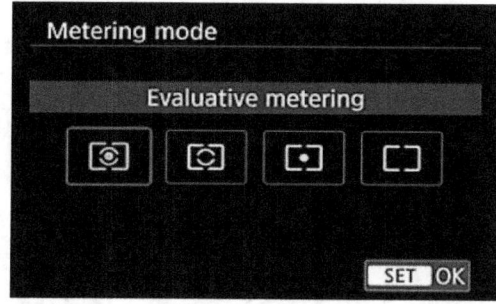

Evaluative Metering

What It Does:
Evaluative metering is the default metering mode for the camera. It analyzes the subject, background, and overall scene to adjust exposure in real-time. This mode performs effectively in various situations, including those with glare or uneven lighting.

When to Use It:
Evaluative metering is ideal for everyday photography and diverse lighting conditions. The camera makes smart exposure decisions based on the scene, making it suitable for portraits, events, and landscapes alike.

Partial Metering

What It Does:
Partial metering is useful when there's a significant contrast in lighting between your subject and the background. This often occurs when the subject is backlit or surrounded by brighter areas. The camera meters a small portion of the frame, focusing on the area around the subject to minimize the influence of the background on exposure.

When to Use It:
This mode is effective when your subject is distinctly different from its background. It helps ensure the subject is properly exposed while preventing overexposure or underexposure caused by surrounding light.

Spot Metering

What It Does:
Spot metering allows the camera to measure light in a very small, specific area of the frame, typically at the center. This ensures that the exposure is based solely on this tiny section, rather than the entire image.

When to Use It:
This mode is ideal for precise exposure control, especially when photographing subjects with vibrant colors or when you want to ensure that a specific part of the image is correctly exposed. It's particularly useful for close-ups, portraits, or in low-light situations, where capturing fine details is essential.

Center-Weighted Average Metering

What It Does:
Center-weighted average metering evaluates the entire scene for exposure but gives greater emphasis to the central portion of the frame. Rather than performing complex analyses, it focuses primarily on what's in front of the camera, particularly in the middle.

When to Use It:
This mode is effective for portraits and other compositions where the subject is centered. It's beneficial when you want more control over the brightness of the subject while maintaining even lighting across the image, making it a good choice for various general photography situations.

Practical Tips for Using Metering Modes:

- **Evaluative Metering:** Ideal for general photography, this method assesses the entire scene to determine exposure, making it suitable for various lighting conditions.
- **Partial and Spot Metering:** Best for high-contrast situations, these modes focus on ensuring that a specific subject is correctly exposed, minimizing the influence of the background.
- **Center-Weighted Average Metering:** This approach prioritizes the central area of the frame, ensuring that subjects placed in the middle receive proper exposure while considering the surrounding background.

Choosing the appropriate metering mode for your Canon EOS R5 Mark II will help you achieve well-exposed images across different lighting scenarios.

AE for Priority Subjects During AF

When using the Canon EOS R5 Mark II, you can adjust the metering to prioritize exposure based on detected subjects, especially when using the autofocus (AF) system. Here's how it works:

Metering for Detected Individuals

- **AF Detection:** The camera can identify and track individuals within the frame using its advanced autofocus system. This allows it to adjust metering based on the detected subjects.
- **Preset Subject Detection:** You can set a specific subject for the camera to prioritize. This ensures that the exposure is optimized for the detected individual's face or body, which is particularly useful in portraits or when subjects are moving.

How to Use This Feature

1. **Select AF Mode:** Choose an AF mode that supports subject detection, such as Face Detection or Eye Detection.
2. **Access Metering Settings:** Go into the camera's menu and find the metering options.
3. **Enable Subject-Based Metering:** Look for an option to prioritize metering based on the detected subject. This may involve setting it to Evaluative metering with a focus on the detected area.
4. **Take Photos:** The camera will automatically adjust the exposure based on the lighting conditions affecting the detected subject, ensuring accurate exposure even in challenging lighting situations.

This feature enhances your ability to capture well-exposed images of individuals, particularly in dynamic environments where lighting can change rapidly.

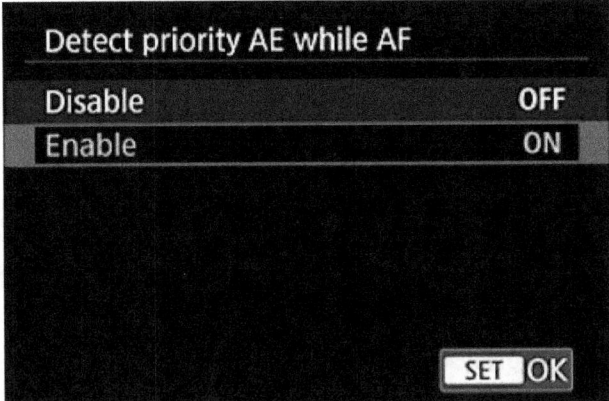

Metering Options for Detected Subjects

Enable

- **Functionality:** When this option is enabled, the camera uses the specific AF point or region where the subject was detected as the basis for metering.
- **Benefit:** This allows for more accurate exposure adjustments, particularly when your subject is in a challenging lighting situation (like backlighting), ensuring they are properly exposed.

Disable

- **Functionality:** When disabled, the camera measures exposure across the entire frame, treating all areas equally.

- **Benefit:** This can be useful in situations where you want a more general exposure, such as landscapes or when the lighting is even across the scene.

How to Set This Up

1. **Access the Menu:** Go to the camera's settings menu.
2. **Find Metering Settings:** Look for the metering options related to AF detection.
3. **Choose Enable or Disable:** Select your preferred setting based on your shooting scenario.

Using these options effectively can help you achieve optimal exposure tailored to your subject and environment.

Picture Style

Picture Styles Overview

Picture Styles allow you to customize how your photos are rendered, enhancing specific features for different shooting scenarios. Here's a breakdown of what you can adjust and the available styles:

Key Adjustments

- **Sharpness:** Control the clarity and detail in your images.
- **Contrast:** Adjust the difference between the light and dark areas, influencing the overall dynamic range.
- **Color Saturation:** Change the richness and intensity of colors in full-color photos.
- **Skin Tone Adjustment:** Specifically for portraiture, this helps ensure natural-looking skin tones.

For black-and-white photos, while sharpness and contrast can still be modified, you can add:

- **Tonal Overlays:** Options to tint your monochrome images with sepia, blue, purple, or green tones.
- **Filter Effects:** Simulate the effects of physical filters used in traditional photography.

Available Picture Styles

1. **Standard:** A balanced style suitable for general photography.
2. **Portrait:** Optimized for skin tones and softer contrasts, ideal for people.
3. **Landscape:** Enhances blues and greens, perfect for nature shots.
4. **Fine Detail:** Increases sharpness and contrast for intricate details.
5. **Neutral:** Offers a more subdued color palette, good for post-processing.

6. **Faithful:** Aimed at reproducing colors as close to reality as possible, useful for product photography.
7. **Monochrome:** Tailored for black-and-white photography, with options for filters and color tones.
8. **Auto:** Automatically selects a style based on the scene.
9. **User Def. 1, 2, 3:** Customizable styles for specific needs, such as sports or architecture.

Customizing Your Style

To change or select a Picture Style:

1. **Access the Menu:** Navigate to the Picture Style settings in your camera menu.
2. **Select a Style:** Choose from the established options or modify a User Defined style to suit your needs.
3. **Adjust Parameters:** Fine-tune sharpness, contrast, saturation, and any specific adjustments for monochrome styles.

Using Picture Styles effectively can significantly enhance the visual impact of your photography!

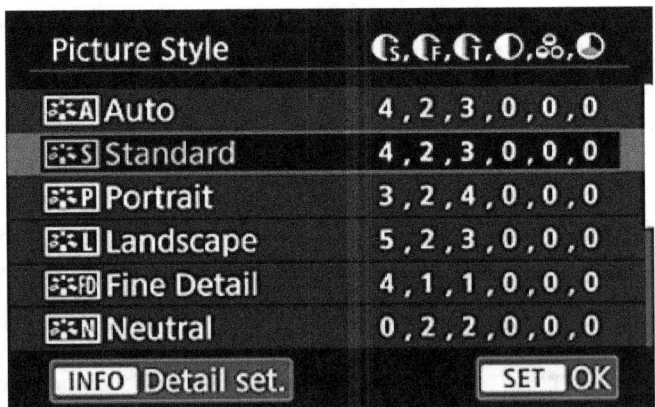

Picture Styles offer a wide range of options for photographers. Canon has improved the Auto setting, preset color Picture Styles, and the single black-and-white option to better cater to the needs of most users. You can still customize any of these default styles to achieve your desired look. Furthermore, you can create entirely new styles using User Definition files based on the three original styles.

If you're aiming for vibrant, colorful images reminiscent of Velvia film or the works of Pete Turner, you can develop a bold style. Conversely, for a softer, more charming atmosphere, opt for gentler colors with lower brightness and contrast. Shooting outdoors on overcast days can also help reduce contrast in brighter conditions.

The graphic at the top of the page displays the current settings for each option, from left to right: Strength (S), Fineness (F), and Threshold (T). The Contrast icon appears as a half-black, half-white circle, the Saturation icon is a triangle with three inner circles, and the Color Tone icon is a divided circle. The Filter Effect is depicted by overlapping circles, while the Toning Effect is represented by a paintbrush icon. You can explore these settings further within the Monochrome Picture Style.

Here's a breakdown of the settings:

- **Sharpness**: This refers to the clarity of your image, affecting how defined edges appear. Adjusting sharpness doesn't follow a strict guideline; for instance, adding slight softness can help reduce moiré effects by using an "anti-alias" filter that blurs the image slightly. Canon's default sharpening settings minimize detail loss while softening moiré interference.

Increasing sharpness—whether in editing or through a Picture Style—can lead to moiré patterns and undesirable halos around overly sharp edges, so proceed cautiously. You have control over three aspects:

1. **Strength**: This ranges from 0 (minimal outline focus) to 7 (high outline focus). Excessive sharpness can introduce haze and highlight details unnecessarily.
2. **Fineness**: This scale goes from 1 (enhancing fine lines) to 5 (emphasizing larger, rougher lines). Use lower values for intricate textures and higher ones in portraiture to soften facial features.
3. **Threshold**: This setting adjusts the contrast between sharpened edges and their surroundings, with values from 1 to 5. A lower number can enhance sharpening even with less contrast, while higher values sharpen edges that already have a distinct brightness difference, sometimes resulting in a poster-like effect.
4. **Contrast**: Adjusting this parameter alters the tonal range from dark to light, with settings between -4 (lower contrast) and +4 (higher contrast). Low contrast can flatten an image, while high contrast may enhance tones but risk losing detail in highlights and shadows.
5. **Saturation**: This indicates color intensity, ranging from -4 (high saturation) to +4 (low saturation). For instance, more saturated reds appear deeper, while lower saturation shifts reds toward lighter, pinkish hues. Excessive brightness can lead to "clipping," where details are lost, which can be monitored through RGB histograms.
6. **Color Tone**: Values between 0 and +4 can adjust skin tones toward yellow or red, while values between 0 and -4 will shift them toward orange.
7. **Filter Effect (Monochrome only)**: This does not add color to black-and-white images; instead, it alters grayscale tones to simulate the effect of a color filter.
8. **Toning Effect (Monochrome only)**: This adds a color overlay to black-and-white images, creating a sepia, blue, purple, or green tint, while keeping the tones monochrome.

The preset Picture Styles include:

- **Auto**: Adjusts color settings for vibrant outdoor scenes.
- **Standard**: Automatically applies enhanced sharpness and features for general photography.
- **Portrait**: Increases brightness for richer colors, particularly suitable for capturing children and women, while softening skin tones.
- **Landscape**: Enhances sharpness and color saturation, especially for blues and greens, making landscape images pop.
- **Fine Detail**: Prioritizes detail through contrast and sharpening, potentially introducing visual noise.
- **Neutral**: Offers less saturation and contrast, ideal for less vibrant images.
- **Faithful**: Strives for accurate color representation, mirroring human vision.
- **Monochrome**: Exclusively captures black-and-white images. If shooting in JPEG, colors are removed. However, shooting in JPEG+RAW retains color information in RAW files for later editing. The camera displays the images in black and white, but the RAW files still hold the original color data for potential use in editing.

Tip: You can edit your photos using the Monochrome Picture Style even if working solely with RAW files. The camera recognizes the RAW file as black and white, applying the style immediately upon opening it in an editing program, while still retaining the color information for further adjustments.

Symbols

Icons for Contrast, Strength, Fineness, and Threshold related to Sharpness can be seen on the screen where you select your Picture Style. The displayed numbers indicate the current settings for these specific options within the chosen Picture Style.

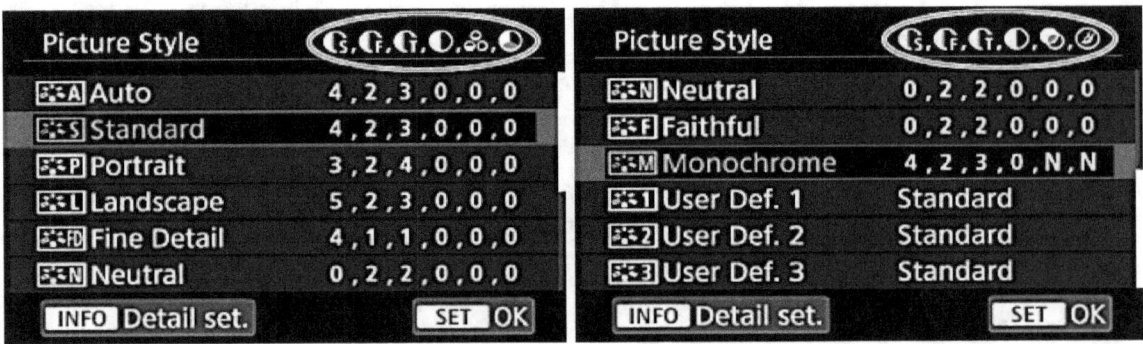

		Sharpness	
			Strength
			Fineness
			Threshold
		Contrast	
		Saturation	
		Color tone	
		Filter effect (Monochrome)	
		Toning effect (Monochrome)	

Settings and Effects

		Sharpness		
		Strength	0: Weak outline emphasis	7: Strong outline emphasis
		Fineness*1	1: Fine	5: Grainy
		Threshold*2	1: Low	5: High
	Contrast		−4: Low contrast	+4: High contrast
	Saturation		−4: Low saturation	+4: High saturation
	Color tone		−4: Reddish skin tone	+4: Yellowish skin tone

- This setting indicates the thinness of edges that can be enhanced; as the number decreases, it allows for finer details to be sharpened.
- The contrast threshold determines the level of enhancement between the edges and the surrounding areas. When the contrast difference is minimal, it's crucial for the shape to stand out, but a lower number may also make noise more noticeable.

Monochrome Adjustment

Filter effect

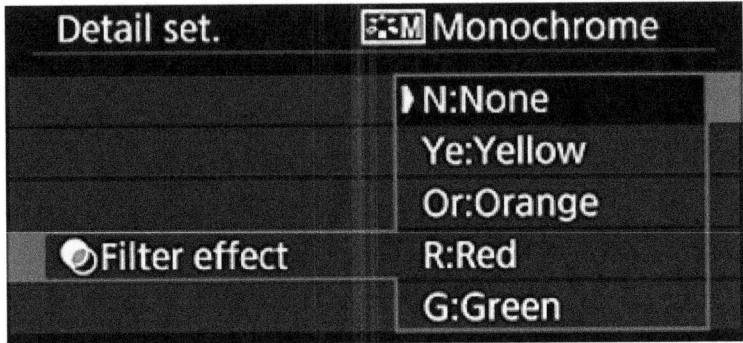

Applying a filter effect to a black-and-white image can enhance the visibility of features like white clouds, green trees, and other elements, making them stand out more distinctly.

Selecting Picture Styles

Canon has streamlined the process of selecting a Picture Style by separating the selection and modification steps to prevent accidental changes to existing styles. You can choose from your available Picture Styles using the following methods:

- **Picture Styles Menu**: Press and hold the QCD-1 button, then navigate down the styles list until your desired style is highlighted. Press the SET button to confirm your choice.
- **Quick Control Screen**: Access the Picture Styles tab by moving to the right column and holding the Q button. Once the icon is selected, you can turn the dial or use the directional buttons to choose your preferred style. Press the SET button to confirm your selection.

Defining Picture Styles

Understanding and modifying your Picture Style options is straightforward. The menu screen displays numbers that indicate the current values for each Picture Style choice. While some camera retailers may use vague terms like "sharp," "extra sharp," "vivid," or "more vivid," the Picture Styles menu allows you to adjust the preset styles or create your own. Here's how to do it:

1. **Select the Style**: Choose the Picture Style you want to modify and click the Edit button.
2. **Access Detail Set Menu**: Press the INFO button to open the Detail Set menu. The next screen will show either the six color styles or the three User Defined color styles. You can

scroll down to find additional options for Sharpness and Contrast, along with settings for Saturation and Color Tone. In the Monochrome panel, these are replaced by Toning Effects and Filter Effects, though the layout remains the same.
3. **Choose a Setting to Change**: Select a setting to modify using the QCD-1. If you click "Default Set" at the bottom, the values will revert to their previously saved settings.
4. **Confirm Changes**: Press SET to apply the changes to the highlighted parameter.
5. **Adjust Values**: Use the QCD-1 to move the triangle to the desired value. The scale will still show the old number with a gray triangle, making it easy to revert to the previous setting if needed.
6. **Exit Menu**: After pressing the MENU button three times, you will return to the previous screen. Pressing SET will keep the current settings.

If you change a default setting in a Picture Style, it will be highlighted in blue, making it easy to track any modifications you've made. This feature ensures you won't forget changes, as they are saved and visible in the Picture Style menu.

Customizing the Monochrome Picture Style differs slightly, as you'll find options for Filter Effect and Toning Effect instead of Saturation and Color Tone. Remember, once you capture a JPEG image in black and white, you cannot revert it to full color. You can choose from options like None, Orange, Yellow, Red, or Green for Filter Effects, and None, Blue, Purple, Green, or Sepia for Toning Effects. You can still adjust Contrast and Sharpness settings after selecting a different Picture Style.

Adjusting Styles with the Picture Style Editor

The Picture Style Editor (PSE) included with your camera is compatible with both Windows and Mac computers, allowing you to manage Picture Styles on your computer. This tool lets you modify existing styles like Standard, Landscape, and Faithful, as well as create your own.

You can adjust various aspects of an image, including contrast, sharpness, color intensity, and color tone. Once you've made your changes, you can save the file as a PF2 file, which can then be transferred to your camera or used in Digital Photo Professional to adjust a RAW image during the transfer.

Here's how to create and load your Picture Style:

1. **Open the Picture Style Editor**: Note that this is different from Photoshop Elements, which also uses the abbreviation PSE.
2. **Load a RAW Image**: Open Photoshop Elements and import a RAW CR3 image that you want to use as a reference. You can do this via the File menu or by dragging a file directly into the editor's main window.

3. **Select a Base Style**: Choose a default style other than Standard as your starting point. It's beneficial to pick a base style that closely resembles your desired look since your new style will inherit characteristics from it. Adjusting an existing style is generally easier than creating one from scratch.
4. **Compare Styles**: View your old and new styles side by side to evaluate them. Three buttons in the lower left corner of the window let you toggle between vertical and horizontal comparisons.
5. **Access Advanced Settings**: Click the Advanced button in the Tool Palette to open the Advanced Picture Style Settings box on the left. These settings mirror what you can adjust on the camera. Don't forget to click OK when you're finished.
6. **Make Thoughtful Adjustments**: If you're familiar with advanced photo editing tools in software like Photoshop or Digital Photo Professional, explore additional options for adjusting color, tonal range, and curves. These tools offer more extensive modifications than the camera's Picture Styles, making them worth learning.
7. **Save Your Style**: When you're satisfied with your edits, select "Save Picture Style File" from the File menu. This will save your new style as a PF2 file on your hard drive. Be sure to fill in the title and copyright details when prompted. If you check "Disable Subsequent Editing," the style will be locked and cannot be altered again.

If you want to keep your changes private and don't plan to edit the style further, you can opt for "Disable Subsequent Editing." However, note that this will prevent any future modifications. If you might want to make adjustments later, save a second copy of your unique Picture Style without checking that box.

Uploading a Picture Style to the Camera

To apply your new Picture Style to one of your three User Defined slots, follow these straightforward steps:

1. **Turn on Your Camera**: Start your camera and open the EOS Utility. Select "Camera Settings/Remote Shooting" from the splash screen. Ensure your camera is connected to your computer and ready for shooting.
2. **Select the Shooting Menu**: Look for the Shooting menu on the control panel, identifiable by a white camera icon on a red background, which will appear about halfway down your computer screen.
3. **Open the Register Picture Style Box**: Click on the appropriate box to bring up the Register Picture Style window.
4. **Choose a User Def Slot**: Select one of the three User Def tabs (User Def 1, User Def 2, or User Def 3). Each tab will display the currently assigned Picture Style.
5. **Load Your Saved Picture Style**: Picture Styles saved locally or downloaded will be tagged with a PF2 suffix. Click on the desired style, then click the Open button.

6. **Confirm Registration**: The Registering Picture Style File box will appear again. Press the OK button to confirm. The camera will then register the selected Picture Style in the User Def slot you chose. The menu will now display the name of the selected Picture Style instead of "User Def."

Color Space

By selecting this menu option, you can choose between two different color spaces, also known as color gamuts, while in one of the Creative Zone modes. The first color space is Adobe RGB, developed by Adobe Systems in 1998. The second is sRGB, which is recognized as the standard RGB color space. Each of these color gamuts offers a distinct range of colors for your photography.

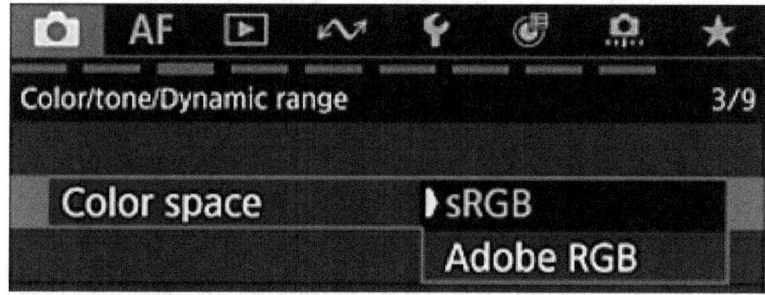

When you take a JPEG or HEIF photo in P, Tv, Av, or M exposure modes, the Color Space option is immediately applicable. In Scene Intelligent Auto mode, all JPEG and HEIF images will automatically use the sRGB color space, while RAW images contain information for both Adobe RGB and sRGB. If you don't change the settings during import, your image editor will default to sRGB for Scene Intelligent Auto or Creative Auto images.

It's worth noting that cameras can't capture all the colors visible to the human eye due to limitations in sensors, filters, and the way colors are displayed on screens and printed. The inks used in printing also can't replicate every visible color accurately. Consequently, the colors recorded by your camera, displayed on screens, and printed can differ significantly.

RAW images provide a wider color range than JPEGs. For instance, converting a 14-bit RAW file to an 8-bit image allows for 16.8 million colors, whereas a 14-bit RAW can encompass up to 281 trillion colors. A color space defines the range of colors a device can capture or display, whether it's a camera, monitor, or printer.

ProPhoto RGB, indicated by a yellow triangle, is gaining popularity among professional photographers as many printing labs can accommodate it. Although you cannot save photos in ProPhoto directly, Adobe Camera RAW allows conversion of RAW files to a 16-bit ProPhoto format, offering extensive processing options.

Different color spaces like Adobe RGB and ProPhoto RGB enable a broader range of colors, making them suitable for professional and commercial printing. When using advanced editing software like Adobe Photoshop, it's crucial to ensure the software is set to the correct color space.

While both sRGB and Adobe RGB can represent the same number of colors, sRGB distributes those colors more evenly across a narrower spectrum, making it ideal for web and general use. If you're planning to print photos on standard inkjet printers, it's best to use the sRGB color space, as it aligns closely with typical printer output.

Choosing the right color space alone won't resolve all color issues, as each stage of the image process can affect color representation. To achieve consistent results, you should learn about color management and calibration tools. A reliable method for calibrating your monitor is essential, as display colors can shift over time or due to ambient light changes.

For calibration, I use Datacolor's SpyderX Pro software, which measures and adjusts my monitors regularly, ensuring they reflect accurate colors based on the surrounding light conditions.

Clarity

You can enhance an image's clarity by adjusting the contrast of its main tones rather than affecting the entire picture. Increasing clarity sharpens the image by making the differences between midtones more pronounced, while decreasing it makes the image appear softer. It's important to note that clarity adjustments differ from sharpness; clarity focuses on midtones, whereas sharpness enhances the overall contrast between light and dark areas.

This adjustment can be made directly in your camera or in editing software like Photoshop. When you increase clarity, you'll notice that the contrast between midtones is amplified, which can help details stand out more and reduce the appearance of digital noise. The clarity slider typically ranges from -4 to +4, with 0 being the default setting.

Before applying significant adjustments, it's advisable to experiment with the clarity tool to see how it affects your images, as the camera may not fully display these quality settings. Keep in mind that high contrast areas may have their brightness or darkness altered near the edges when you adjust clarity, especially if they lack many midtones. This is something to watch for to maintain the desired look of your photos.

Highlight Tone Priority

You can recover highlights that are clipped or overly bright.

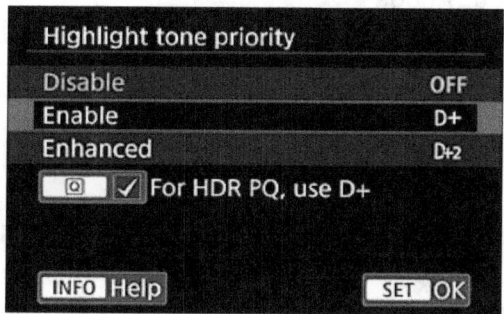

- **Enable:** Clicking this option improves the shading in the outlines, creating a smoother transition from gray to color.
- **Enhanced:** When shooting in specific conditions, this option further reduces overexposed highlights compared to Enable.

White Balance

You can set your white balance manually by entering a specific color temperature in the Custom menu if you're not satisfied with the default settings or any of the six presets (Daylight, Shade, Cloudy, Tungsten, White Fluorescent, or Flash). This option is available even if your camera has an automatic adjustment feature.

The interface resembles the one shown on the left in the image below when you select White Balance from the Quick Control screen. By choosing the K option on the Main scale, you can specify a color temperature anywhere between 2,500 and 10,000 degrees Kelvin.

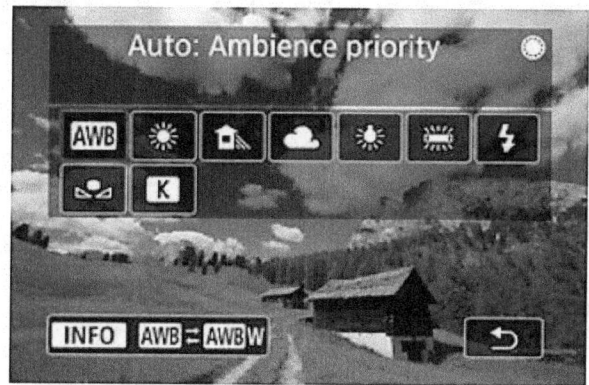

If you don't have a color temperature meter, knowing the color temperatures for the preset options can help you make adjustments. Here's a breakdown of the color temperatures for each setting:

- **Auto (AWB)**: 3,000K to 7,000K
    - **Ambience-priority**: Keeps colors bright under tungsten lighting.
    - **White-priority**: Maintains neutral whites under tungsten lighting. Make sure this choice is activated.
- **Daylight**: 5,200K
- **Shade**: 7,000K
- **Cloudy**: 6,000K
- **Tungsten**: 3,200K
- **White Fluorescent**: 4,000K
- **Flash**: Automatically set
- **Custom**: 2,000K–10,000K
- **Color Temperature**: 2,500K–10,000K (settable in 100K increments)

These values can help you select a suitable color temperature for your specific lighting conditions!

(Approx.)

Display	Mode	Color Temperature (K: Kelvin)
AWB	Auto: Ambience priority	3000–7000
AWBW	Auto: White priority	
☀	Daylight	5200
⛰	Shade	7000
☁	Cloudy, twilight, sunset	6000
💡	Tungsten light	3200
🗏	White fluorescent light	4000
⚡	When using Flash	Automatically set*
☻1	Custom	2000–10000
K	Color temperature	2500–10000

Choosing the right white balance is crucial for accurate color representation in your photos. While the preset options (like Daylight, Shade, etc.) may not always be perfect, they often provide a decent starting point. Here are some key points to consider:

1. **Presets and Auto**: The presets are usually close enough for most situations, but they can be slightly off depending on the lighting conditions. Auto white balance (AWB) can also work well, as the human eye can adjust to various lighting conditions.
2. **Shooting in RAW**: If you frequently find that the color balance isn't to your liking, shooting in RAW is a great option. RAW files retain more data, allowing you to adjust the white balance easily in post-processing without sacrificing image quality.
3. **Custom White Balance**: For situations where precision is critical, consider using a custom white balance. This involves measuring the color temperature of your specific lighting conditions, ensuring your images reflect true colors.

By using these strategies, you can achieve more accurate and pleasing colors in your photography!

White Balance Shift/Bracketing

With the white balance shift tool, you can change the color bias of the white balance along the magenta/green or blue/amber scale. When you change the color balance of your picture, you can make it a little more blue or yellow, a little more purple or green, or a mix of the two. You could also shoot several photo graphs one after the other, each with a slightly different color balance that is skewed in the way you choose.

Taking a look at the picture below will help you picture the process better. There is no bias at the point where lines BA and MG meet in the middle. Remember that from math class in high school? When you use the arrow keys to move the point, you can put it anywhere on the line. To find the point, you can use where the blue/amber and magenta/green lines are. The number of shifts will be shown in the box to the right of the line that says **SHIFT**.

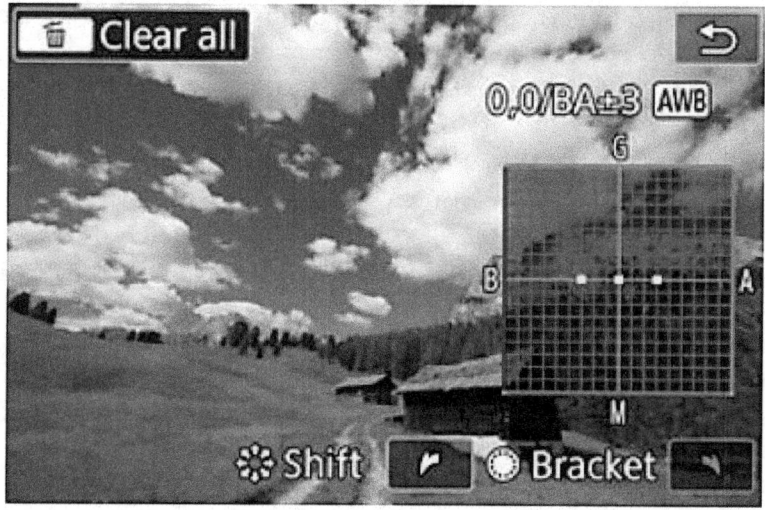

Changing the white balance and adjusting its range through bracketing are indeed distinct processes. Here's a breakdown of how white balance bracketing works:

1. **Understanding Bracketing**: Just like exposure bracketing, white balance bracketing allows you to capture multiple versions of the same scene with different color balances. This is especially useful when you're uncertain about the optimal white balance setting.
2. **Bracketing with JPEG/HEIF**: You can use this bracketing method in modes that support JPEG or HEIF images. It won't work with RAW files since RAW captures already hold the necessary data for adjusting white balance in post-processing.
3. **Adjusting the Bracket**: When you access the WB SHIFT/BKT option, you can adjust:
    - **Vertical Distance**: By turning the QCD-1 left, you can space the three different white balance settings further apart.
    - **Color Range**: Turning it right changes the blue/amber shift, affecting how warm or cool the images will appear.
4. **Visual Indicators**: As you adjust these settings, the three dots representing the different white balance options will change color, allowing you to see how your adjustments will affect the images.
5. **Color Perception**: In bright conditions, it can be challenging to assess your current settings on the LCD. It's important to pay attention to the color shifts—whether you want your image to lean more towards green, pink, blue, or yellow.

Using this bracketing method can help ensure you capture the best color rendition for various lighting scenarios!

Lens Aberration Correction

When you select Shooting 5 from the menu, the first option allows you to enable lens corrections directly in your camera, which can help address some common lens flaws. Here are the three primary corrections you can make if your lens has correction data:

1. **Distortion Correction**: This setting helps reduce barrel or pincushion distortion, which can occur with certain lenses. It ensures straight lines in your image remain straight, particularly in wide-angle shots.
2. **Chromatic Aberration Correction**: This option reduces color fringing that can occur along high-contrast edges in your images. It helps to minimize the unwanted color edges that may appear, especially in images taken with wide apertures or at the edges of the frame.
3. **Vignetting Correction**: This setting adjusts for light fall-off at the corners of your images, which is common in many lenses. It brightens the corners to match the center of the image, creating a more even exposure throughout.

By enabling these corrections, you can improve your images right in the camera, saving time on post-processing later!

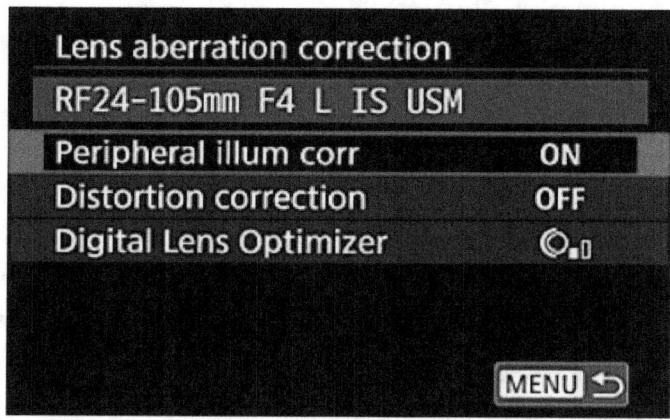

Here's a concise overview of the various lens correction features available in your camera:

Peripheral Illumination Correction

- **Function**: Fixes vignetting, which causes dark corners in images.
- **Caution**: In certain shooting conditions, noise may appear at the edges. Higher ISO settings may reduce the time for adjustments.
- **Note**: Corrections may not be as extensive as those done in Digital Photo Professional.

Distortion Correction

- **Function**: Addresses image distortion (warping).
- **Caution**: This may slightly alter the angle of view, potentially cropping the image and reducing clarity.
- **Note**: Can be applied to videos when using RF or RF-S lenses.

Focus Breathing Correction

- **Function**: Minimizes angle of view changes during video recording if focus points shift.
- **Note**: This feature activates when Distortion Correction is set to Enable.

Digital Lens Optimizer

- **Function**: Corrects issues from lens optics, including sharpness loss from diffraction and low-pass filters.
- **Note**: If adjustment data for Peripheral illumination is missing, add lens info using EOS Utility.

Chromatic Aberration Correction

- **Function**: Reduces color fringing around high-contrast edges.
- **Note**: This feature won't activate if the Digital Lens Optimizer is set to Standard or High.

Diffraction Correction

- **Function**: Enhances sharpness lost due to diffraction effects.
- **Note**: Only active if Digital Lens Optimizer is not set to Standard or High. It allows adjustments even when the lens is fully open.

Cautions

- **JPEG/HEIF Limitation**: Lens distortion cannot be corrected in already captured JPEG or HEIF images.
- **Non-Canon Lenses**: If using third-party lenses, set corrections to Disable unless correction data is specifically available.
- **Edge Viewing**: Zooming in on image edges may reveal artifacts not accounted for in corrections.
- **Distance Reporting**: Lenses that do not report distance may have less effective corrections, except for diffraction.

These features can significantly enhance your image quality by addressing common lens-related issues directly in-camera!

Long Exposure Noise Reduction

Here's a streamlined overview of noise reduction settings for long exposures and how they affect your photography:

Noise Reduction Settings

1. **Function**: This setting allows you to manage noise during long exposures, which can manifest as colored particles or graininess in your images.
2. **Visual Noise**: Similar to grain in high-speed film, digital noise is generally undesirable, though it can be used creatively. It resembles background noise that obscures the main signal in audio, making the desired tones less clear.
3. **ISO and Noise**:
    - **Higher ISO**: Raising the ISO sensitivity increases noise because each pixel gathers fewer photons, making it more likely to register random noise along with actual light.

- **Common Settings**: ISO 800 and 1600 typically maintain acceptable noise levels. ISO 3200 can also be effective, thanks to advancements in camera processing.
4. **Longer Exposures**:
   - **Photon Accumulation**: Longer exposure times allow more light to reach the sensor, but they can also introduce noise due to sensor heat and random fluctuations in photosites.
   - **Noise Introduction**: Extended exposure can lead to misrecording of light due to heat, which may be interpreted as additional light.
5. **Adjustment Options**:
   - **Enable/Disable Noise Reduction**: You can choose to let the camera manage noise reduction automatically or manually set your preferences.
   - **Noise Level Adjustment**: You can change the noise reduction level to suit your shooting conditions.

Key Considerations

- **Impact of Settings**: While increasing ISO or exposure time can enhance sensitivity and light capture, it also increases the potential for noise.
- **Balancing Act**: Find the right balance between ISO, exposure time, and noise reduction settings to achieve clear, high-quality images.

Using these settings thoughtfully can help you minimize noise in your long exposure photos and enhance overall image quality!

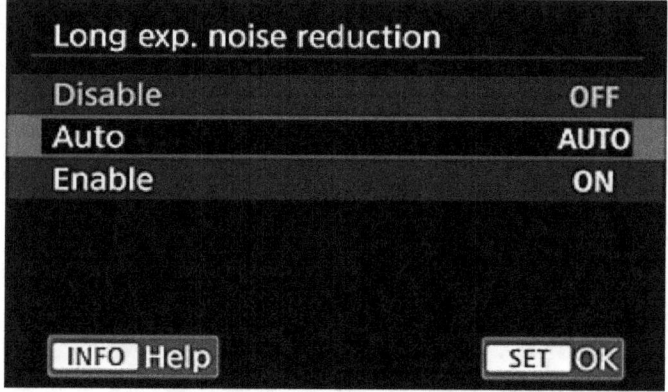

Here's a concise summary of the noise reduction options for long exposures:

Noise Reduction Settings for Long Exposures

1. **Off/Disable**:
   - **Function**: Turns off long exposure noise reduction.

- o **Usage**: Ideal for maximizing detail, especially in static scenes, as it allows for faster shooting without the wait for noise reduction processing.
- o **Consideration**: Higher noise may be present, but it can be manageable at lower ISO settings (e.g., ISO 100) during long exposures. Suitable for capturing smooth water effects using neutral density filters.

2. **Auto**:
   - o **Function**: Automatically applies noise reduction for exposures lasting one second or more.
   - o **Process**: Takes a second exposure (dark frame) to compare against the original, removing noise before saving the final image.
   - o **Consideration**: Effective for reducing noise in longer exposures without manual adjustments.

3. **On/Enable**:
   - o **Function**: Applies noise reduction to all exposures longer than one second using the dark-frame reduction method.
   - o **Usage**: Beneficial for high ISO settings where noise is more pronounced.
   - o **Consideration**: This setting can slow down shooting as each photo will require additional time for noise reduction processing. Live View mode will show a blank screen during this process.

Key Tips:

- **Shooting Limitations**: While noise reduction is active, you may be limited in how many shots you can take consecutively, especially in Live View mode.
- **Ideal Conditions**: Choose your setting based on the shooting environment and the desired balance between detail and noise control.

Understanding these options allows you to make informed choices based on your shooting conditions and artistic intentions!

High ISO Speed Noise Reduction

Here's a breakdown of the noise reduction options related to ISO settings:

ISO Noise Reduction Settings

1. **Standard**:
   - o **Function**: Default setting for noise reduction.
   - o **Effect**: Balances noise reduction and detail preservation. Most images will look good without significant loss of information.

2. **Low**:
    - **Function**: Applies less aggressive noise reduction.
    - **Effect**: Retains more image detail, suitable for situations where some noise is acceptable. Good for maintaining sharpness in detailed images.
3. **High**:
    - **Function**: Maximizes noise reduction.
    - **Effect**: Significantly reduces noise, especially useful at high ISO settings. However, this can lead to loss of finer details and a smoother appearance, which may not be ideal for all subjects.

Considerations:

- **ISO Impact**: Higher ISO settings naturally introduce more noise, particularly in darker areas of the image. Adjusting the noise reduction can help manage this.
- **Processing Time**: Selecting a higher noise reduction setting can extend processing time, reducing the number of continuous shots you can take. This is important to consider during fast-paced shooting situations.
- **Use Cases**: Choose the setting based on your shooting context and desired outcome. For example, use **Low** for detailed subjects, **High** for low-light environments where noise is prominent, and **Standard** for a balanced approach.

These settings help you tailor noise management to your specific shooting conditions and artistic vision!

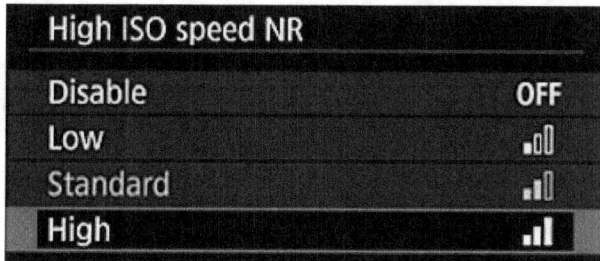

Here's a summary of the noise reduction options, focusing on their key features and when to use them:

Noise Reduction Options

1. **Disable**:
    - **Description**: No noise reduction applied.
    - **Effect**: Maintains maximum detail but allows for the highest level of noise in images.

2. **Low**:
    - **Description**: Minimal noise reduction.
    - **Effect**: Preserves small details, but images may appear grainier. Suitable for capturing texture.
3. **Standard**:
    - **Description**: Balanced noise reduction.
    - **Effect**: More aggressive in shadow areas with low ISO; less effective in mid-tones at high ISO. Good for general use.
4. **High**:
    - **Description**: Aggressive noise reduction.
    - **Effect**: Reduces noise significantly but can lead to a mushy appearance, losing visual clarity. Not ideal for detailed subjects.
5. **Multi Shot Noise Reduction**:
    - **Description**: Takes four images and combines them using dark-frame subtraction.
    - **Effect**: Produces a cleaner image than the High setting, particularly effective for stationary subjects.
    - **Requirements**: Use a tripod, ensure the subject is still, and set Picture Quality to RAW, RAW+JPEG/HEIF, or Dual Pixel RAW. Flash, live view, and certain bracketing modes disable this option.

Tips for Use:

- **Choose Disable** if you want maximum detail and are okay with noise.
- **Select Low** for textured shots where you want to preserve detail but can tolerate some grain.
- **Use Standard** for everyday shooting, balancing clarity and noise control.
- **Opt for High** in very noisy conditions, but be mindful of potential loss in image quality.
- **Employ Multi Shot NR** for the best results in stable shooting conditions, especially in low light.

These settings help you customize noise control based on your shooting environment and desired image quality!

Dust Delete Data

You can capture an image of any dust or debris on your camera by selecting this option from the menu. Digital Photo Professional includes software that can quickly identify and eliminate dust spots in your images. It utilizes information about the dust's location to efficiently clean it.

Regularly taking a Dust Delete Data photo is essential as it serves as your final defense against sensor dust. When you select this menu item, the time and date of your last adjustment will be displayed.

To use the Dust Delete Data feature, select it, ensure the OK button is highlighted, and then press the SET button. The camera's self-cleaning process will initiate by applying UHF waves to the low-pass filter above the sensor.

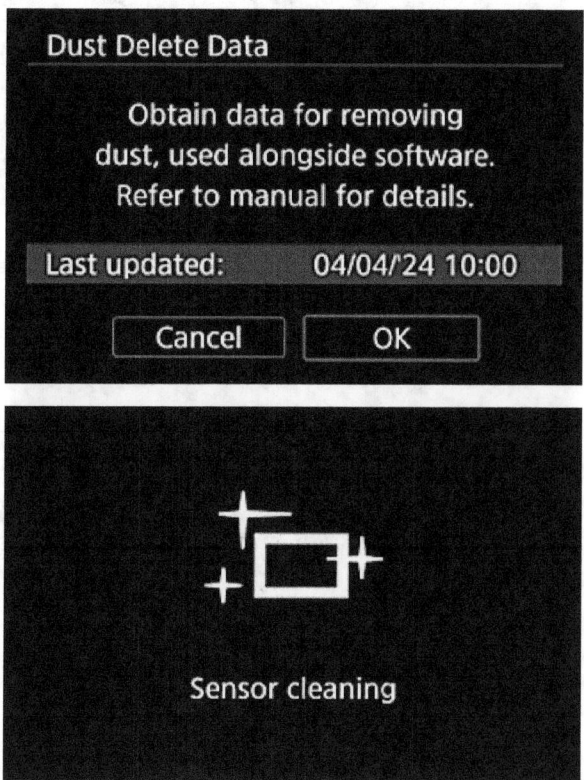

After the picture sensor has completed its self-cleaning, a message will appear on the screen. You'll hear a sound during the cleaning process, but no photo will be captured. Once it's done, the display will prompt you to press the shutter button. Point the camera at a solid white card, and switch the lens to manual focus. Then, rotate the focus ring to the right until it indicates "infinity."

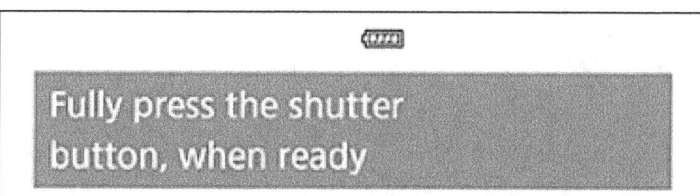

When you take the shot from a distance of 20 to 30 cm (about 0.7 to 1 ft), the screen should display a fresh piece of white paper or another plain white object. You can still capture the data even if there's no memory card in the camera, as the image won't be saved.

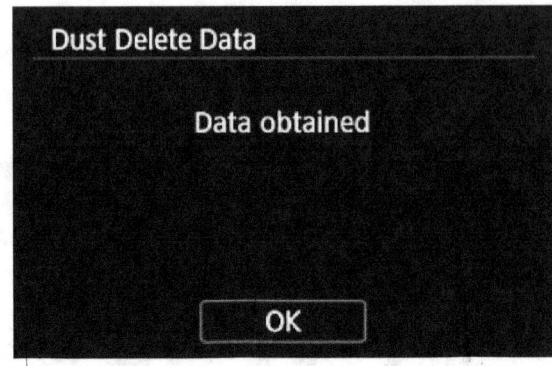

As soon as the photo is taken, the camera will process the Dust Delete Data. If it successfully detects the data, a warning message will appear. Conversely, if it cannot locate the information, an error message will be displayed.

Dust Delete Data Appending

From this point onward, all photos will have the Dust Delete Data incorporated. It's best to capture the Dust Delete Data just before taking your shot. The Digital Photo Professional Instruction Manual offers guidance on how to effectively remove dust spots using Digital Photo Professional by EOS.

Adding Dust Delete Data does not alter the file size of your images.

Caution:

- If the cropping aspect ratio is set to 1.6x or you are using RF-S or EF-S lenses, you will not be able to obtain Dust Delete Data.
- Dust Delete Data cannot be added when [Distortion correction] is enabled.
- If the subject has a pattern or design, Digital Photo Professional (EOS software) may mistakenly recognize it as dust data, which can reduce the accuracy of dust removal.

Multiple Exposure

With this feature, you can combine up to nine different photos into a single image, eliminating the need for an image editor like Photoshop. It's a fun way to reminisce about the days when you could create complex images directly in the camera.

Before digital cameras, creating collages from multiple photos was a popular and exciting activity. Nowadays, many opt to take several pictures and merge them using editing software like Photoshop. However, Canon's multiple exposure function allows for creative planning and even happy accidents. The camera's RAW data can be used to seamlessly blend two or more shots, resulting in better integration than if you struggled with Photoshop.

Canon has simplified this feature by removing the need to adjust the menu for each additional shot in a set. You can configure it once and leave it, perfect for taking multiple photos in one go—just remember to turn it off when you're finished!

Keep in mind that in low light, high dynamic range, or movie mode, you can only capture one image at a time. Before you start with multi-exposure, you'll need to adjust your camera settings. Disabling the multi-exposure option is quick, and you can easily switch between the two "On" settings. This master control lets you choose between different multiple shot types while retaining your other settings.

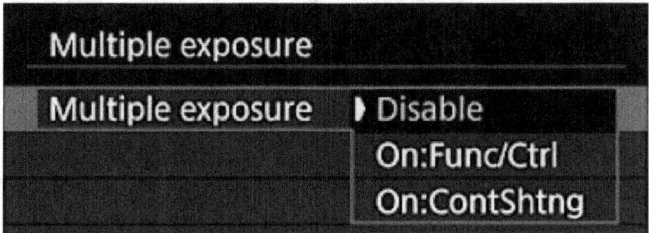

Multiple Exposure Options

- **Disable:** This option turns off the multiple exposure feature.
- **On: Func/Ctrl:** In Function and Control-priority mode, you can adjust camera settings between shots. Each set of photos is taken immediately, allowing you to review the results and make adjustments, such as altering brightness. This mode is ideal for experimenting with compositions when the subject is relatively still. However, keep in mind that the camera tends to shoot slowly, making it less suitable for fast-moving scenes.

During shooting in Function or Control-priority modes, you can check exposure levels, alignment, and other details by pressing the Playback button. If a photo doesn't meet your expectations, tap the Trash button to access four options:

- **Undo Last Image:** Removes the current image, allowing you to view the next one.
- **Save and Exit:** Saves all photos taken but halts shooting. If you select "All Images" from the Save Source Images menu, both the single exposure and the composite image will be saved. Choosing to save only the modified image will keep just the composite.
- **Exit Without Saving:** Stops the multiple exposure session without saving any photos.
- **Return to Previous Screen:** Allows you to go back to the last screen you were on.
- **On: ContShtng:** In Continuous Shooting-priority mode, the camera operates in continuous mode. This is particularly useful for capturing multiple exposures during live ballet or dance performances. While you can't review or play back images, or use tools to undo

shots during this mode, it enables you to document every movement as it unfolds. Note that due to the rapid shooting, only the final composite image will be saved on your memory card.

Multiple Exposure Control

You can customize how the shots are combined using the Multiple Exposure Control tool. Here are your options:

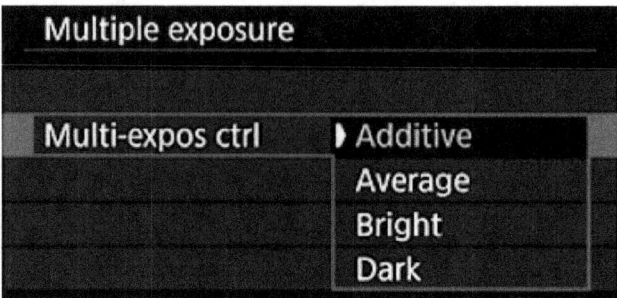

You can select how the images are combined using the Multiple Exposure Control tool, with the following options:

- **Additive:** In this mode, all shots in the set will have full exposure. For example, if the background is black and the subject moves without overlapping, it will appear as if two separate photos have merged into one. You can adjust the exposure for each shot by setting the exposure adjustment. Generally, you should adjust by one stop for two shots, 1.5 EV for three shots, and 2 EV for four shots. For a more realistic overlap, you can manually calculate the necessary negative exposure adjustment.
- **Average:** This option automatically applies the correct amount of negative exposure adjustment based on the number of shots combined. If you take multiple photos of the same scene, the background will receive the same light level as if you had captured just one image.
- **Bright:** This method uses complex techniques to align the first image with subsequent photos. It emphasizes the brighter pixels where the images overlap. The underlying concept is similar to the "lighten" layer blending found in Photoshop and other editing tools.
- **Dark:** This option operates like the Bright mode, but it gives greater importance to the darker pixels. The effects of Bright and Dark modes may not be fully understood until you experiment with both. Choosing one over the other often comes down to personal preference.

Number of Exposures

In each multiple-exposure set, you can select between two to nine different images. Simply choose an option, press the SET button, and then turn the QCD-1 dial to determine the number of shots. When you're first experimenting with this tool, I recommend starting with three settings. With practice, you'll become adept at knowing when to capture images that require multiple exposures to create a cohesive final picture.

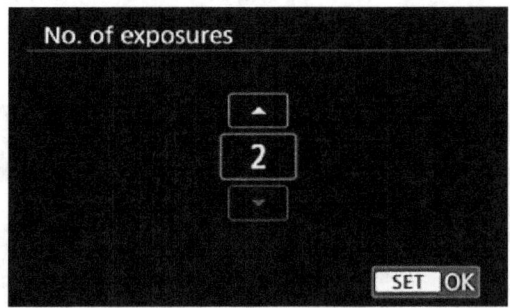

Save Source Images

Multiple exposure shots must be taken one at a time and combined before the final image can be saved. This method prevents sensor overload and data loss, allowing the camera to seamlessly merge the images using exposure correction and other pixel techniques. This process differs from movie multiple exposures, where all images are captured on the same photosensitive frame, layering each new shot on top of the previous ones.

When saving your images, if you choose **All Images**, all captured photos will be preserved for future use. If you opt for **Result Only**, only the composite image will be saved. Each approach has its advantages and disadvantages. Merging images manually may yield better results than the camera's automatic processing, and it allows you to easily access the standout shot without wading through the other mixed photos. However, saving **All Images** will consume more time and memory card space.

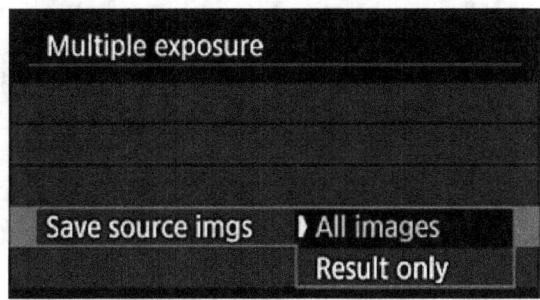

Continue Multiple Exposure

You can choose between **1 Shot Only** or **Continuously**. If you only want to take a single set of multiple exposures, select **1 Shot Only**. After capturing your shots, you can turn off Multiple Exposure and return to normal shooting.

If you prefer not to stop and navigate back to the menu after each shot to re-enable the feature, select the **Continuously** option. This allows you to keep shooting without interruption after taking multiple exposures.

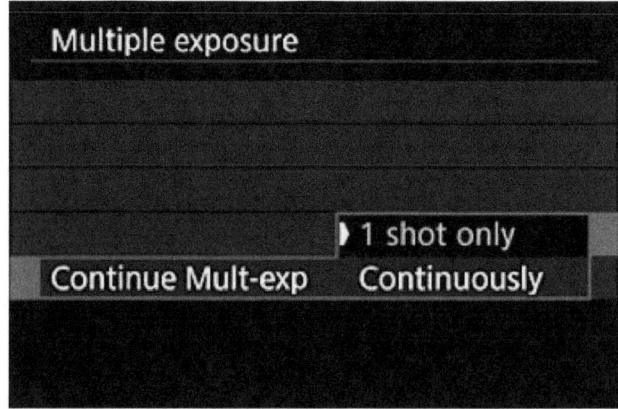

Focus Bracketing

Using the camera's focus bracketing feature, you can capture a series of images with gradual changes in focus between each shot. This allows you to move from the closest point of focus to the area that needs to be the sharpest. You can select between 2 and 999 shots for this process.

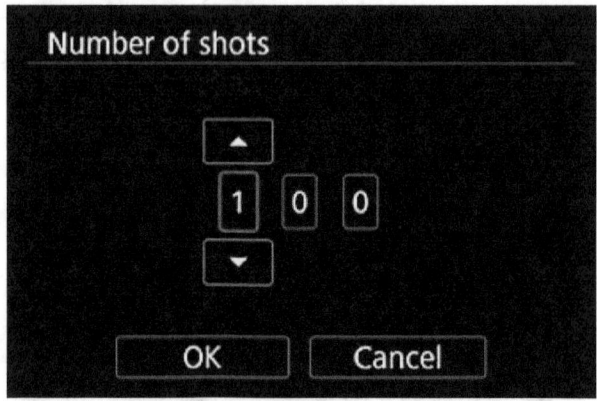

In this step, you can adjust the **Focus Increment**, which determines how much the focus shifts between shots. This value is instantly updated to match the starting point when the first photo is taken.

Using a larger aperture allows the focus to cover a wider range with the same number of shots and focus steps. Once you've finished your adjustments, press the SET button to confirm your settings.

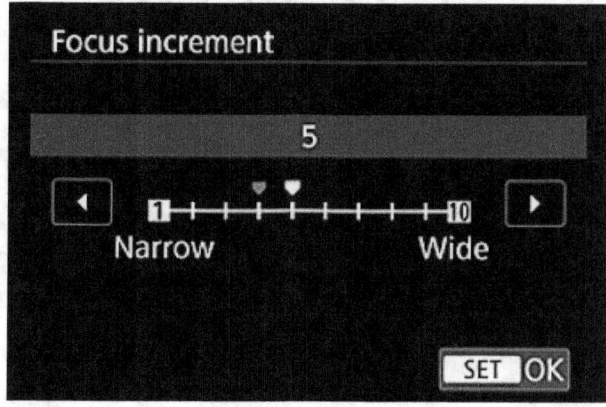

- **Enable:** When you select this option, the camera will adjust based on the difference between the displayed aperture value and the actual effective f-number, which varies with the focus position. This setting accounts for changes in lighting while focus bracketing.
- **Disable:** If you prefer not to correct for variations in brightness during focus bracketing, choose this option. Note that this setting should not be used to enhance depth in photos that you've already edited in applications like DPP.

Set [Depth composite]

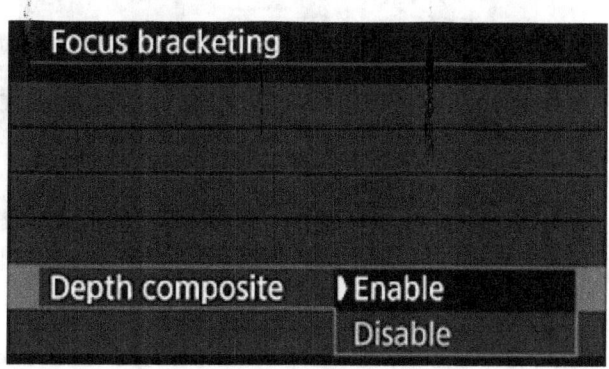

- **Enable:** Press this option to allow the camera to perform depth compositing. Both the original source shots and the final image with added depth will be saved.
- **Disable:** Select this option to turn off in-camera depth compositing. In this mode, only the shots taken will be saved, without any additional depth processing.

Set [Crop depth comp.]

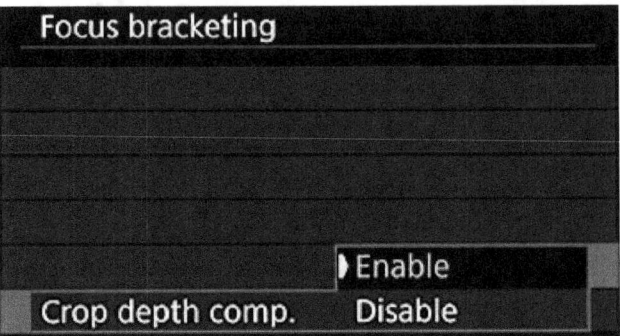

- **Enable:** Choose this option to crop images before compositing. This will eliminate any photos that don't align properly due to angle issues, ensuring better compositing.
- **Disable:** If you prefer not to crop the images, select this option. In this case, areas in the saved images that lack a suitable view will be marked with a black line. You can then modify or crop the images as needed.

Set [Flash interval]

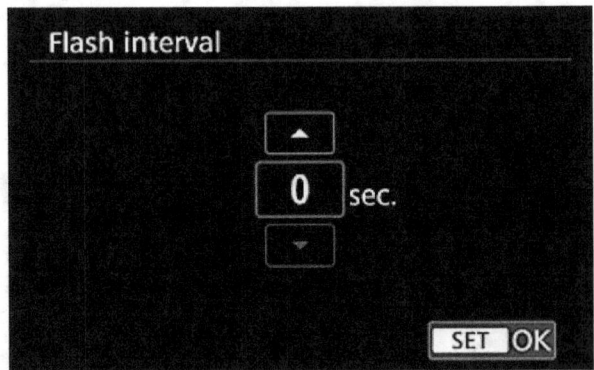

- Focus bracketing is compatible with both Canon Speedlites and non-Canon flash units that connect via the sync port.
- If this setting is at 0, the camera will start shooting as soon as the Speedlites are fully charged. Be sure to check the instructions for the Speedlite that came with your camera

for safety tips on continuous shooting. If you're using multiple compatible Speedlites for wireless flash photography, you might want to extend the wait time.
- For non-Canon flash units, set an appropriate interval between charges to determine how long the flash lasts and how long it takes to recharge.

Take the picture

- To save your pictures in a new folder, press the designated button and confirm by selecting OK.
- To set the focus, position the camera at the closest end of your desired range, then press the button down.
- After capturing an image, release the camera button.
- The camera will continue shooting, gradually shifting the focus towards the horizon.
- Once the focus range reaches the set distance or the selected number of shots is complete, shooting will stop.
- To manually stop shooting at any time, simply press the camera button down again.

Interval Timer

You can set exposure times of up to 99 hours, 59 minutes, and 59 seconds with this feature. By pressing the INFO button, a screen will appear that allows you to adjust the number of shots and the interval between them.

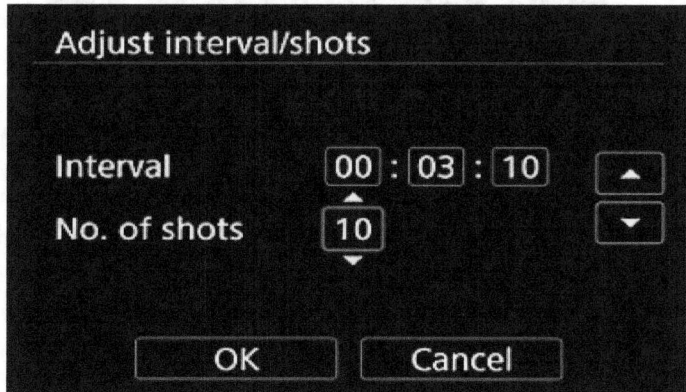

Silent Shutter Function

By enabling this setting, you can take photos discreetly, minimizing sounds and visual cues that indicate you're capturing images. When using the electronic shutter, the focusing beep, touchscreen sound, and self-timer alerts are all muted. The flash will not fire, the self-timer light won't blink, and the tracking assist beam will be turned off.

Long-duration noise reduction is disabled, allowing you to turn off the camera while keeping the shutter open. You can still listen to audio through headphones while recording video, as the headphone output remains active. With minimal activity, the only sounds you're likely to hear will be your breathing and the lens motor focusing.

Shutter Mode

If you opt not to use the mechanical shutter on your camera, you can take photos silently. Alternatively, you can select a third mode, which utilizes an electric first-curtain shutter to initiate the shot while the mechanical shutter is used to finish it. This approach resembles traditional camera operation.

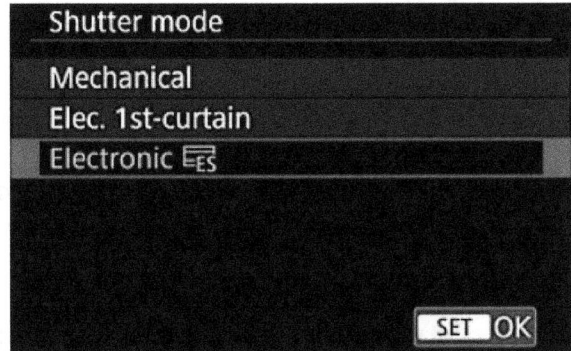

Mechanical Shutter

In the mechanical shutter mode, a motorized first curtain pulls back to expose the sensor, which is the standard operation. This curtain remains open until a second curtain is drawn back by a motor. Often referred to as "traditional mode," this method creates a gap in the middle of the sensor when using shutter speeds between 1/200th and 1/8000th of a second. During this time, only a small portion of the sensor is exposed, which can result in a delay of thirty seconds to one-hundredth of a second between the first and second curtains. When using a mechanical shutter, the flash sync speed is limited to a maximum of 1/200 of a second. To maximize dynamic range, it's recommended to use a camera with moving components.

Electronic 1st-Curtain Shutter

In this mode, if the exposure time is extended, the mechanical shutter could bounce, potentially resulting in less sharp images. This setting prevents that issue. The actual first curtain is lowered, and after the shutter opens, the sensor is automatically cleared, simulating a manual first curtain.

The exposure lasts until the second curtain drops automatically, typically occurring between 30 seconds and 1/250 of a second. In this mode, the electric flash sync speed is also set to 1/250 of a second.

Electronic Shutter

This setting allows for automatic start and stop of exposure, with a maximum exposure time of 1/8000 of a second in Tv and M modes, and up to 1/1600 of a second in Fv, P, or Av modes. In continuous shooting mode, the camera can capture 20 images per second, resulting in a white frame indicator. However, there are some limitations associated with this mode:

- To eliminate all sounds from the camera, go to the Setup 3 screen and turn off the Beep option. The camera will still beep when using the electronic shutter method to indicate a photo has been taken.
- The electronic flash and automatic exposure bracketing cannot be used with this mode, as the flash burst is typically louder than the electronic shutter.
- With a rolling shutter, recording an entire frame can take longer, potentially leading to banding artifacts, especially in scenes where the light source is difficult to identify. Fast-moving subjects may appear distorted, as the part of the subject captured first may have moved by the time the camera records the rest.
- The electronic shutter changes from 14-bit to 12-bit readout, which decreases dynamic range and can complicate tone retrieval in dark shadow areas, particularly in scenes with ISO settings above 400. Lower ISO settings and/or keeping the automatic camera feature active will yield better results.

Release Shutter Without Card

Users can enable the **Release Shutter Without a Card** feature, allowing them to take photos even without an SD card in the camera. When activated, the camera will continue to capture images, but they won't be saved immediately. Instead, the photos will be stored in the camera's temporary memory until a memory card is inserted, at which point they will be saved to the card.

This feature can be particularly useful in situations where you need to take a quick shot but don't have a memory card on hand, or if your current card is full. For example, if you're outside shooting and your memory card begins to fill up, this option lets you keep taking photos without pausing to switch cards.

It's important to remember that images taken while this feature is active will not be permanently saved if a memory card is not connected. The temporary memory can fill up quickly, and you won't be able to take more pictures until you insert a new memory card or delete some existing images. If you continue to shoot without a card, the available memory will be exhausted.

Touch Shutter

This feature allows you to take a picture by simply touching the touchscreen on the back of the camera. It's particularly useful for photographers who want to capture images quickly without adjusting settings or pressing the shutter button manually.

High-Speed Display

When shooting in high-speed continuous drive mode and using a shutter mode other than the electronic shutter, you'll see a high-speed display that alternates between each shot and the live view.

Metering Timer

You can adjust the duration of the metering timer, which determines how long the AE lock or exposure number display remains active after performing an action, such as pressing the shutter button halfway.

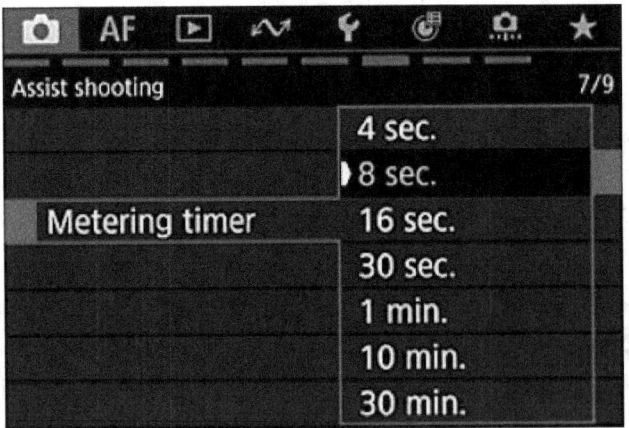

Display Simulation

When you select **Shooting 9** from the menu, the first option allows you to decide how the live view image is displayed. You can choose whether the live view reflects the same brightness level as the final image or if it displays a brighter picture (based on the Screen Brightness setting from the Setup 4 menu), which can be helpful in well-lit environments. You can select from the following options:

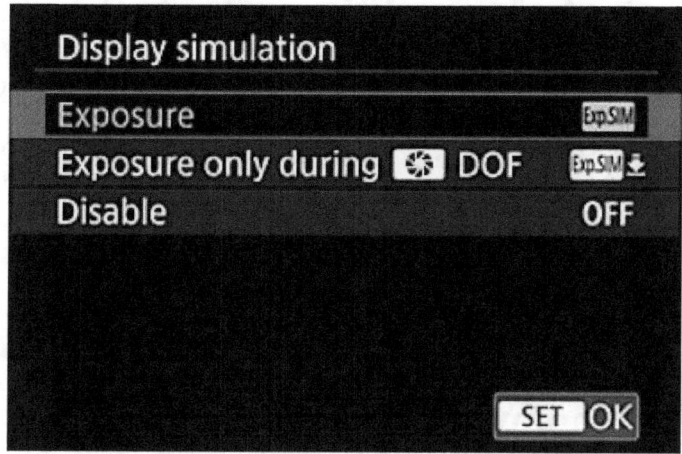

- **Exposure + Depth-of-Field**: This option displays a live view image that reflects the actual brightness of the scene based on your current exposure settings and any adjustments you've made. It provides a real-time representation of how these settings affect the exposure and shows the true depth of field for the selected angle.
- **Exposure**: This setting alters the brightness of the live view to match the actual exposure, even if the exposure is already fixed. However, depth of field information will not be displayed. This option is ideal if you want to observe how lighting impacts the image without considering what is in focus.
- **Exposure Only During DOF Preview**: Initially, the live view displays at the camera's default brightness. When you press the designated depth-of-field preview button, the display adjusts to reflect your exposure settings. This is useful for checking exposure while shooting.

Using these options allows you to effectively plan your shots on a bright screen while assessing how brightness and depth of field will influence the final image. Personally, I find this setting the most helpful for capturing the right shot.

Optical Viewfinder Simulated View Assist

If you long for the experience of using an optical viewfinder, this function can bring you back to that sensation. Recently, electronic viewfinders (EVFs) in mirrorless cameras have become as clear and easy to see as the large, bright optical viewfinders found in both digital and film SLR cameras. The Canon EOS R5 Mark II features an organic light-emitting diode (OLED) viewfinder that performs exceptionally well in low light.

This feature was first introduced with the higher-end EOS R3. When activated, it adjusts the overall brightness of the scene in the EVF, as long as no significant exposure compensation has been applied, providing a preview similar to that of a traditional optical viewfinder.

With this setting enabled, Display Simulation will be turned off, and the tone curve will be modified to create a softer look. This adjustment makes the scene's blacks and whites appear lighter compared to the midtones. If the OVF simulation is not used, the EVF output will switch to JPEG format, which has a tone curve resembling an S-shape, resulting in higher contrast and reduced dynamic range. While this feature exists, I don't use it frequently, as I prefer to see images that closely resemble the final JPEGs I'll be producing.

To achieve an optical viewfinder-like appearance, you need to enable OVF simulation. Keep in mind that this modeling won't work on the EVF or LCD if you're viewing the output on an external monitor connected via HDMI.

Blackout-Free Display

This display option eliminates the blackout that occurs at the start of continuous shooting, making it easier to capture moving subjects.

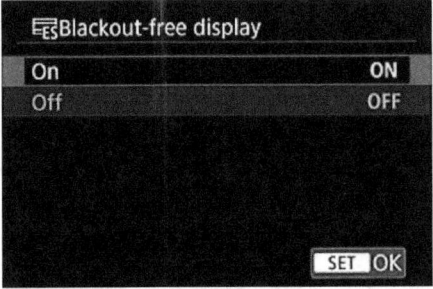

Shooting Information Display

You can customize the information displayed while taking a picture at various levels. While capturing images, you'll see different details on the lens or the camera's LCD screen. However, having too much information repeatedly can be overwhelming and difficult to interpret.

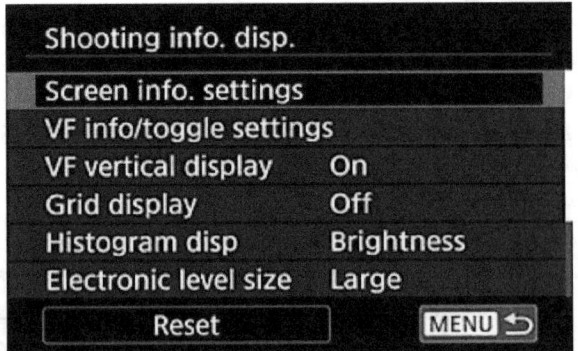

Here's a breakdown of the display settings available:

Screen Information Settings

- **INFO Button**: Pressing this button reveals five different types of information on the LCD screen.

Viewfinder Information/Toggle Settings

- **Camera Views**: You can choose to show or hide three different views in the viewfinder.

VF Vertical Display

- **Vertical Mode**: When enabled, the display shows different information when the camera is held upright.

Grid Display

- **Grid Options**: Select from a 3x3, 6x4, or a 3x3 grid with diagonal lines. You can also choose to turn off grid lines on both the LCD screen and the camera.

Histogram Display

- **Histogram Options**: Choose between two types:
    1. **RGB Live Histogram**: Displays all three primary colors.
    2. **Brightness Live Histogram**: Shows overall brightness.

Display Size

- **Size Options**: Choose between Large and Small display sizes.

Lens Information Display

- **Focus Distance Display**: This can be set to show focus distance only in manual focus mode or not at all.
- **Unit Settings**: Change the focus distance display to either meters or feet.
- **Focal Length Display**: Option to display the current focal length or not.
- **SA Variable Amount**: Adjusts the amount of spherical aberration correction for compatible lenses, such as the RF 100mm f/2.8 Macro.

Reset

- **Reset Settings**: This option restores the above settings to their default values.

Reverse Display

You can capture a mirror image by pointing the camera screen towards the person you're photographing.

Viewfinder Display Format

Even if you can't remove all obstacles, you can still see past them. There are two types of screens to choose from for your view. On Display 1, additional information appears above the frame, while your image is visible in the viewfinder. A black bar at the bottom of the screen displays some of this information.

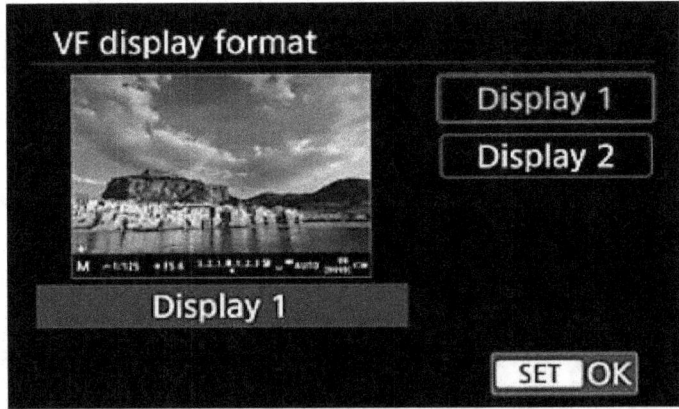

If you select Display 2, you'll see black bars on the left, right, and above the frame. There won't be a picture frame on top of these black bars; instead, additional details will be displayed within them. Pressing the INFO button will toggle between the various information screens you configured in the Shooting Information Display settings.

Display Performance

This setting influences the screen's power consumption and how easily it displays fast-moving objects. I always opt for the Smooth setting since I don't worry about conserving power and never run low on battery.

Chapter 8
EOS R5 MARK II Custom Settings

To customize the Canon EOS R5 to suit your shooting style, you can use the Custom Functions Menu. This menu allows you to adjust various settings, including autofocus and brightness, among others. You can modify how the camera focuses, measures light, and what each button does.

The Custom Functions Menu provides options to tailor the camera's performance to your specific needs. Whether you're shooting sports, portraits, or landscapes, you can configure the camera to optimize it for those scenarios. This menu offers a range of adjustments, enabling you to make each shooting experience unique.

Tab Menus: Custom Functions

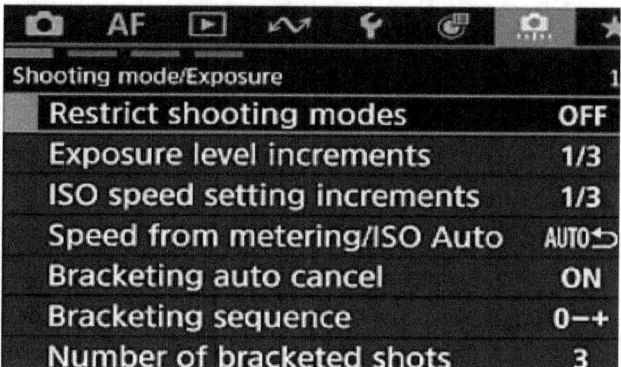

Restrict Shooting Modes

The MODE button allows you to select your desired shooting mode. You can choose from Fv, P, Av, M, Tv, BULB, or the custom modes C1/C2/C3. Once you've made your selection, press SET to confirm, and then hit OK to save your changes.

Exposure Level Increments

You can adjust the camera settings, such as shutter speed, aperture value, exposure compensation, AEB, and flash exposure compensation, in increments of 1/2 stop. Here are the options available:

- **1/3**: 1/3-stop
- **1/2**: 1/2-stop

ISO Speed Setting Increments

You can adjust the ISO speed setting in full stop increments. The options available are:

- **1/3**: 1/3-stop
- **1/1**: 1-stop

Speed from Metering/ISO Auto

While the metering timer is active, you can adjust the ISO speed if the camera modifies it during the metering process, or for ISO Auto operation in P/Tv/Av/M/B modes.

- AUTO↩: Restore Auto after metering
- AUTO⇘: Retain speed after metering

Bracketing Auto Cancel

You can disable AEB and white balance bracketing when the power switch is off.

- **ON**: Enable
- **OFF**: Disable

Bracketing Sequence

You can adjust the settings for AEB and white balance bracketing as needed.

- **0–+**: 0, -, +
- **–0+**: -, 0, +
- **+0–**: +, 0, -

AEB	White Balance Bracketing	
	B/A Direction	M/G Direction
0: Standard exposure	0: Standard white balance	0: Standard white balance
–: Underexposure	–: Blue bias	–: Magenta bias
+: Overexposure	+: Amber bias	+: Green bias

Number of Bracketed Shots

With white balance and AEB, you can specify the number of shots to be taken. When the bracketing order is set to 0, -, +, the table below indicates the shots that will be captured.

- **3: 3 shots**
- **2: 2 shots**
- **5: 5 shots**
- **7: 7 shots**

(1-stop/step increments)

	1st Shot	2nd Shot	3rd Shot	4th Shot	5th Shot	6th Shot	7th Shot
3: 3 shots	Standard (0)	−1	+1				
2: 2 shots	Standard (0)	±1					
5: 5 shots	Standard (0)	−2	−1	+1	+2		
7: 7 shots	Standard (0)	−3	−2	−1	+1	+2	+3

Safety Shift

If the lighting on the subject changes and the autoexposure range cannot achieve the standard exposure, the camera will adjust the manually selected settings to reach the standard exposure. The aperture and shutter speed settings you choose will apply in both Tv and Av modes. You can use ISO speed in modes P, Tv, or Av.

- **OFF**: Disable
- **Tv/Av**: Shutter speed/Aperture
- **ISO**: ISO speed

Same Expo. for New Aperture

You can switch lenses, add an extension, or use a zoom lens with a variable maximum aperture. If you do, the largest aperture value may decrease and the smallest f-number may increase when shooting in M mode (manual exposure) with manually set ISO instead of ISO Auto. This function adjusts the ISO speed or shutter speed (Tv value) immediately to maintain the same exposure level as before (1), (2), or (3), preventing underexposure.

Once you press the ISO speed/Shutter speed button, the ISO speed will change instantly within the specified range. If the ISO speed adjustment results in an exposure change, the shutter speed (Tv number) will also be adjusted immediately.

- **OFF**: Disable
- **ISO**: ISO speed
- **ISO/Tv**: ISO speed/Shutter speed
- **Tv**: Shutter speed

AE Lock Meter. Mode after Focus

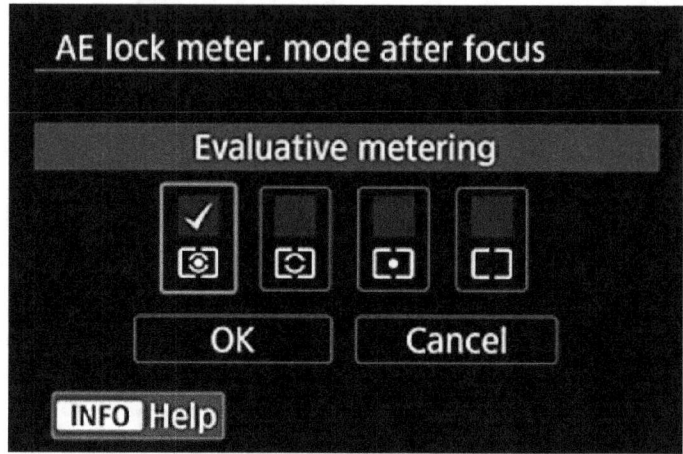

Once the subject is in focus using One-Shot AF, you can lock the exposure (AE lock) for any metering mode. The exposure will remain locked as long as you hold the shutter button halfway down. To set up AE lock, select the sensing modes you wish to use and press OK to save your changes.

Set Shutter Speed Range

You can select from various shutter speeds for each shutter setting. In Fv, Tv, or M mode, you can specify a range for the shutter speed. When in P, Av, or Fv mode with the shutter speed set to AUTO, the speed will be determined by the range you select. This adjustment does not apply when recording a movie. Press OK to save your changes.

Mech Shutter/Elec 1st-curtain

- **Lowest speed**: You can set the lowest shutter speed from 30 seconds to 1/4000 seconds.
- **Highest speed**: The highest shutter speed can be set between 1/8000 seconds and 15 seconds.

Electronic

- **Lowest speed**: The slowest shutter speed can be set from 30 seconds to 8000 seconds.
- **Highest speed**: The highest shutter speed can be set between 1/16000 seconds and 15 seconds.

Set Aperture Range

You can select the aperture value range. In Fv, Av, M, or B mode, you can manually set the aperture number within any desired range. In Fv, P, or Tv mode, you can set the aperture to AUTO, which will keep it within the range you specify. Press OK to save your changes.

- **Max. aperture**: You can set this from f/1.0 to f/64.
- **Min. aperture**: You can set this from f/1.4 to f/91.

AE Microadjustment

Caution
Here's how to adjust the standard exposure level, which can be useful if autoexposure results in photos that are too dark or too light.

- **OFF**: Disable
- **ON**: Enable

Press the button and select Enable to access the adjustment screen. You can modify the auto exposure by ±1 stop, which is equivalent to 1/8 of a stop. Moving the adjustment to the right will reduce underexposure, while moving it to the left will increase overexposure.

FE Micro Adjustment

The flash can emit varying amounts of light, which is useful if the main subjects in auto-flash photos appear too dark or too bright without flash exposure adjustments.

- **OFF**: Disable
- **ON**: Enable

To make adjustments, press the Q button and select Enable. You can modify the brightness of a standard flash by ±1 stop, equivalent to 1/8 of a stop. If the main subjects are receiving too much light, move the setting to the left. If they are too dark, adjust it to the right.

Limit Continuous Shot Count.

You can configure the maximum burst size for continuous shooting. The camera will stop capturing images after reaching the set number of shots while you hold down the shutter button. You can choose a burst size ranging from 2 to 99 shots. Pressing the DELETE button will reset the setting to Disable.

When Disable is selected, the camera will continue shooting until the maximum burst size displayed in the viewfinder is reached.

Add Cropping Information

You can arrange your photos as if using a medium or large-format camera (such as 6x6 cm or 4x5 inch) by adding scaling information that displays vertical lines for the selected aspect ratio at the time of shooting. The camera does not crop the image before saving it to the card; instead, it includes aspect ratio information, allowing you to crop the images later in Digital Photo Professional (EOS software).

When editing your photos on a computer with Digital Photo Professional, cropping to your chosen size is straightforward.

- **OFF**: Disable
- **6:6**: Aspect ratio 6:6
- **3:4**: Aspect ratio 3:4
- **4:5**: Aspect ratio 4:5
- **6:7**: Aspect ratio 6:7
- **5:6**: Aspect ratio 10:12
- **5:7**: Aspect ratio 5:7

Av Setting Without Lens

You can choose whether to allow changes to the aperture number even when a lens is not attached.

- **OFF**: Disable
- **ON**: Enable

With this setting enabled, you can adjust the aperture without needing to connect a lens, making it convenient when you're prepared to shoot and already have a specific aperture value in mind.

Default Erase Option

You can select the default option in the erase menu that appears when you press the Erase button while reviewing photos. When you press the SET button, you can quickly delete images, provided you don't press Cancel.

🗑: [Cancel] selected

🗑: [Erase] selected

RAW: [EraseRAW] selected

J/H: [Erase non-RAW] selected

Release Shutter w/o Lens

You can choose whether to allow taking pictures or movies without a lens attached.

- **OFF**: Disable
- **ON**: Enable

Retract Lens On Power Off.

If desired, you can set gear-type STM lenses, such as the RF35mm F1.8 Macro IS STM, to retract automatically when the camera is turned off.

- **ON**: Enable
- **OFF**: Disable

Add IPTC Information

You can add IPTC (International Press Telecommunications Council) information to JPEG, HEIF, or RAW photos while shooting by using the EOS software. This feature aids in managing files and other tasks that require IPTC support.

For detailed instructions on adding IPTC information and the types of data you can include, refer to the EOS Utility Instruction Manual.

- **OFF**: Disable
- **ON**: Enable

Custom Function C. Fn 5

Clear all Custom Functions (C.Fn)
Select [ ] to reset all custom functions. Pressing the C.Fn key will clear all Custom Function settings, except for the settings related to customized buttons and knobs.

Chapter 9
Image Review and Playback

This menu allows you to customize how the Canon EOS R5 Mark II views and manages photos and movies after capture. From here, you can watch movies and review images stored on your memory card, as well as delete or lock them. You can rate photos, create movies, and enable automatic photo rotation.

Additionally, you can access shooting information, zoom in on photos for detailed inspection, and make basic or artistic adjustments like cropping in the Playback Menu. Having all these features accessible from the camera simplifies the organization and review of your work.

Playback Menu

You can select how to display, review, copy, and print the photos you've taken from the seven blue-coded Playback options located on the back of the camera. Most of these options don't come with preset settings, but a few do, such as Image Jump with Main Slider (10 pictures), Magnification (2X), and HDMI Control (Disable). Since many of these are functions rather than settings, there aren't many fixed values available. You can choose from the following options:

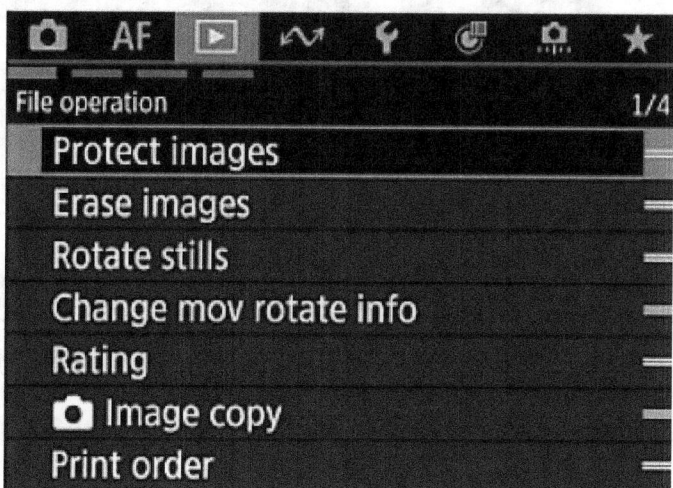

Protect Images

The Protect Images feature allows you to lock certain photos on your memory card, preventing accidental deletion or overwriting. This is an effective way to safeguard important images, such as wedding or family photos, ensuring they remain intact even if the memory card is removed or fails.

In the Playback 1 menu, which consists of seven options, the Protect feature is the first. You can mark a photo as secure to avoid accidental deletion, which can be done by pressing the Erase button or selecting Erase Images from the Playback menu.

To access Protect, go to the Quick Control menu under Playback, or press the MENU button and select Protect from the Playback 1 menu to safeguard one or more photos.

The default screen presents the following options:

- **Select Images**: Scroll through a grid of thumbnails to choose which photos to protect from the current card.
- **Select Range**: Highlight the first and last photo, pressing SET to select a range.
- **All Images in Folder**: Select all photos within a folder. If there are multiple folders, a list will appear for selection; press the SET button to choose the highlighted folder.
- **Unprotect All Images in Folder**: Choose a folder to remove protection from all its images.
- **All Images on Card**: Protect every photo on the card.
- **Unprotect All Images on Card**: Remove protection from all photos stored on the card.
-

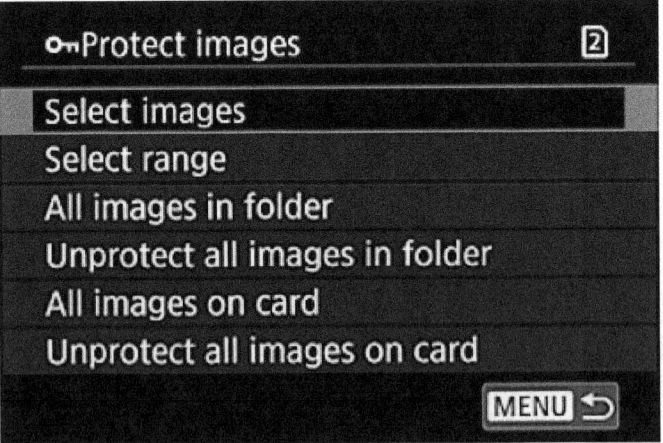

Erase Images

- When you choose this option from the menu, you can select from the following actions: Select and Erase Images, Select Range, All Images in Folder, or All Images on Card. The first three options allow you to choose specific photos to delete from the card, while the fourth option enables you to delete all images at once. Note that photos that have already been saved will not be deleted.

- In contrast, the Format function is generally quicker and provides more comprehensive options. This function shares some similarities with the Protect Images feature. If no Image Search Conditions are specified, the following screen will appear, allowing you to:

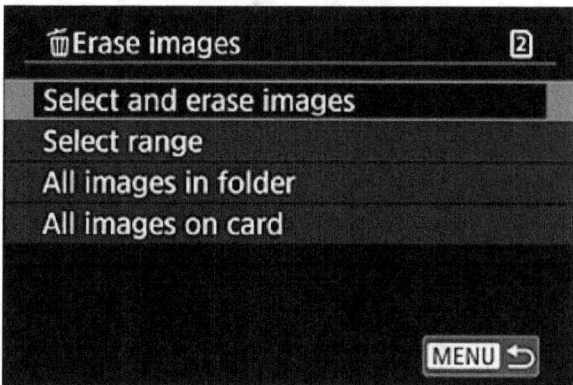

Select and Erase Images

To navigate through your photos on the card, use the left and right arrow keys. You can remove a checkmark or delete a photo by pressing the SET button. After making your selections, press the Q button to bring up a confirmation box. You can then click Cancel or OK and press SET to complete the process.

Select Range

This option functions similarly to the Select and Erase Images choice. First, choose the Select Range option and select the first photo in the series. Press SET to mark it, then select the last photo you want to delete and press SET again. Confirm your choice by pressing the Q key to ensure you want to remove the selected images.

All Images in Folder

You'll see a list of folders on your memory card. After pressing SET, a message will ask for confirmation to delete all images in the selected folder, noting that protected images will remain untouched.

All Images on Card

When you select this option, you'll need to confirm your choice. Picking All Images on Card will delete every photo stored on the card, except for those that are protected. While the images will be erased, the memory card itself will remain intact.

Additional Options after Setting Image Search Conditions in Playback 5 Menu

- **Select and Erase Images**: Browse a short list of photos already on the card and select any you wish to delete.
- **Select Range**: Choose images that span the entire card.
- **All Found Images**: If no protected photos were saved, you can delete all images that match the search criteria set in the Image Search Conditions.

Note: Deleting photos using the Erase function will not free up space in the camera's internal memory. To reclaim space on your memory card after saving your photos to a computer or another drive, you'll need to format the card. This process erases all images on the card, allowing it to store new data.

Rotate Stills

In the Setup 1 menu, you can select the Auto Rotate option to configure the camera to automatically rotate photos taken in portrait orientation. You can also manually rotate a photo during playback using this menu. To rotate still images, navigate to the Playback 1 menu and select this option.

Then, use the QCD-1 to scroll through the photos on your card until you find the one you want to rotate. Press the SET button to rotate the image 90 degrees to the left. If you press the SET button again, the image will rotate 270 degrees. Remember, you can also navigate through photos in the menu that appears when you press the Q button while viewing.

Change Movie Rotate Info

If you've recorded videos on your phone, you know you can adjust their orientation while filming. This feature allows you to change the orientation of videos captured with your camera, so they can be viewed in either portrait or landscape mode on other platforms.

Keep in mind that this setting only affects how your videos are displayed on devices like phones; on the camera's screen, videos will always appear in their original side-by-side format. To enable this option, go to the Setup 1 screen and select "Add Movie Rotate Info."

Then, from the Playback 1 menu, choose this option. Use the QCD-1 to scroll through and select the movie you want to watch.

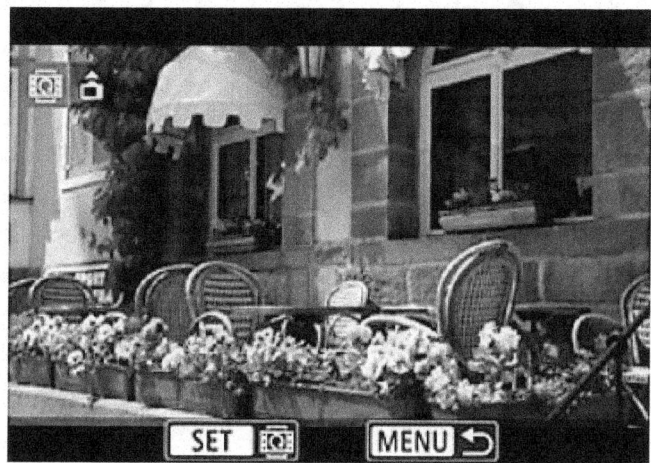

When you play the video again, an icon will appear in the upper left corner of the screen, featuring an arrow that indicates the orientation of the movie frame displayed at the top. The arrow will always point to the top of the frame. Pressing the SET button will rotate the icon to the right and then to the left.

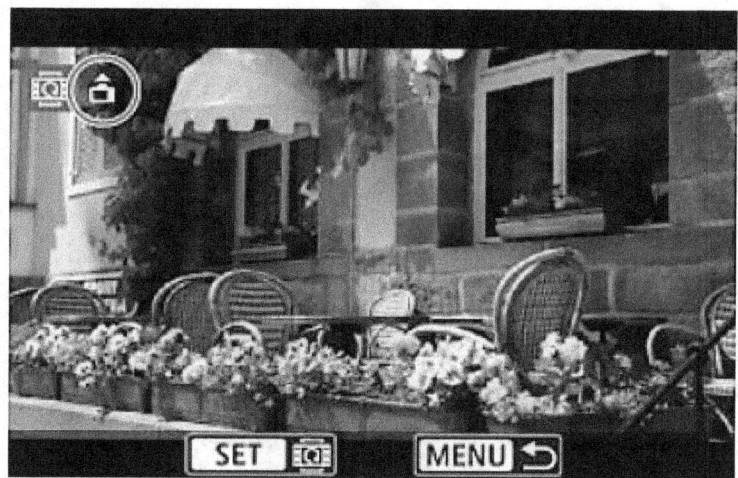

Rating

While a song plays, you can press the RATE button multiple times to assign a rating to your photos or videos. This is useful for evaluating quality or organizing content based on a numerical system. You can disable this scoring feature if needed, but it allows for ratings from one to five stars.

With Picture Jump, you can filter to see only the images that match your rating criteria. For example, at a track meet, you might rate jump events one star, run events two stars, throw events three stars, and so on. This way, you can easily access specific groups of shots later.

You can also customize how you assign ratings to suit various events. For instance, at a wedding, you could categorize photos of the bride and groom, their parents, guests, and staff. In school photos, you might rate first graders differently from second graders and so on.

This tool offers broader functionality than you might initially realize. In Digital Photo Professional, you can use these ratings to select photos for slideshows or to help curate your selection.

There are three ways to rate a photo or video:

1. **RATE Button**: Pressing this button multiple times allows you to assign any number of stars, or none at all. This works only if the Rate Button Function setting is set to Rate in the Playback 6 menu. You can also choose not to assign a rating. If you adjust the Rate Button Function settings, you can set a minimum rating threshold, such as not allowing scores below three stars.
2. **Quick Control Menu**: While in Playback mode, press the Q button to bring up the Quick Control menu, where you can also rate your images. The rating option is located in the left column, next to the third image from the top.
3. **Menu Entry**: To use the Ratings menu, follow these steps:
    1. Access the menu and select Rating.
    2. Choose from Select Images, Select Range, All Images in Folder, or All Images on Card to specify which pictures you want to rate.

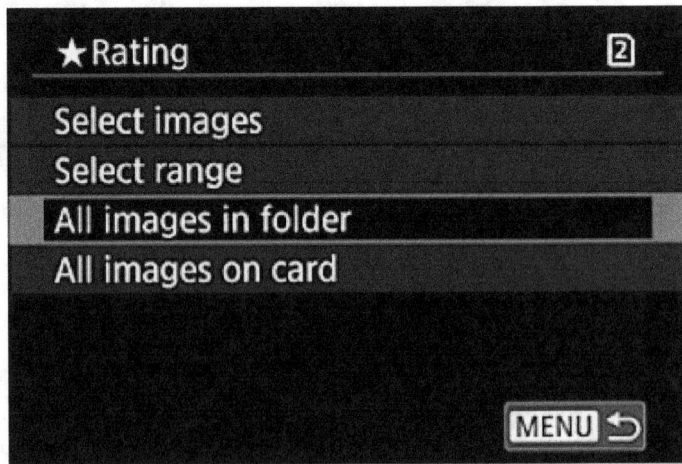

- When you find the movie or picture you want to rate, press SET. You can also select multiple images, all images in a folder, or all images on the card.

- To assign a rating from one to five stars or to remove a star, use the QCD-1 now. You can rate as many images as you like.
- Once you're finished, press MENU to exit.

Image Copy

The great advantage of cameras with dual memory card slots is the ability to use both cards simultaneously without needing to switch them out. This feature is particularly useful for backing up files on two cards, which is convenient when you're away from your computer, such as while traveling. Here are some of the things I do:

- **Shoot to Two Cards Simultaneously**: This allows you to back up your images in real time, ensuring you have a copy in case the primary card is lost or damaged. It's best to use cards with similar storage capacities. Go to the Record Functions + Card/Folder Settings in the Setup 1 menu and select Record to Multiple. This lets you save to both cards at once.
- **Make a Copy**: You can transfer images from one memory card to another using the Image Copy tool. It's best to use only one card for shooting to avoid slowing down the camera. At the end of your shooting session, you can make a copy on the second card, ensuring that you capture all the important moments in your life. You can copy any number of images, from one to all, through this menu.
- **Make Copies for Distribution**: If you frequently need to share images, having multiple memory cards can simplify and expedite the process.

To copy images from one memory card to another when both are in use, follow these steps:

1. Select Image Copy from the Playback 1 menu. The screen will display which card will be the source and show how much space is available on the destination card.

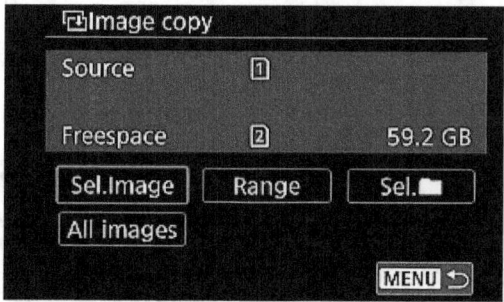

- On the first screen, you can choose from All Images, Range, Select Folder, or Select Image. Selecting Image allows you to pick just one photo. Press the SET button to confirm your choice.

- If you choose Select Image, Select Range, or Select Folder, a screen will appear displaying the files on the source card. Navigate to the desired folder by pressing the SET button. Note that if you select All Images, you won't need to complete steps 3 and 4.

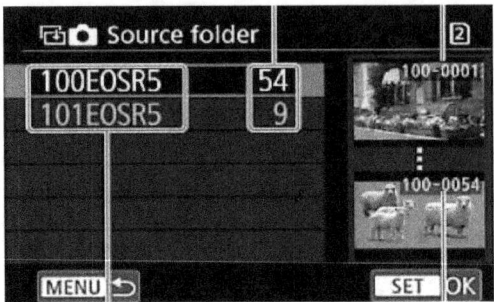

4. If you go to the File menu and select Select Image or Range, you can choose which photos to copy. If you click Select Folder, you can skip Step 4. Remember, you can only copy images from one source at a time.

- **Individual Images**: Browse through the pictures and press the SET button to mark the ones you want to copy. Once you've selected your images, press the Q button to continue.
- **Range of Images**: This option creates a list of images for you to browse. Press SET on the first image in the range, then use the multi-controller joystick to navigate to the last image you want to include and press SET again. Confirm your selection by pressing Q, and then press Q again to proceed.

5. The next screen displays the folders on the different memory cards. To select a folder, press SET. If you want to create a new folder with a custom name, press Create Folder. You can also rename an existing folder using the Canon text-entry interface.
6. After selecting the source images and the destination folder, a confirmation screen will appear. You can choose to proceed by pressing SET or cancel the operation. If the target folder already contains an image with the same file number, you can either skip the transfer of that picture or stop the entire process. The file names will remain the same and will not change.

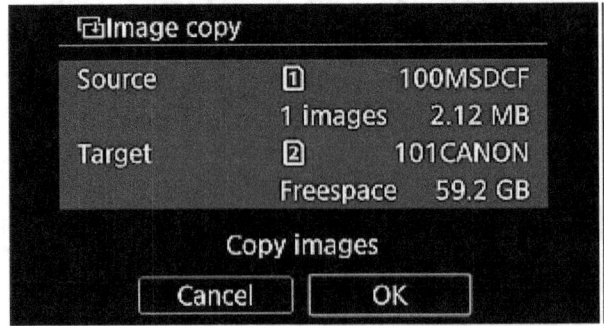

Memory cards come with varying speeds, so the time it takes to copy images will depend on the number of photos you're transferring. To exit the menu, press the SET button when you see the confirmation screen.

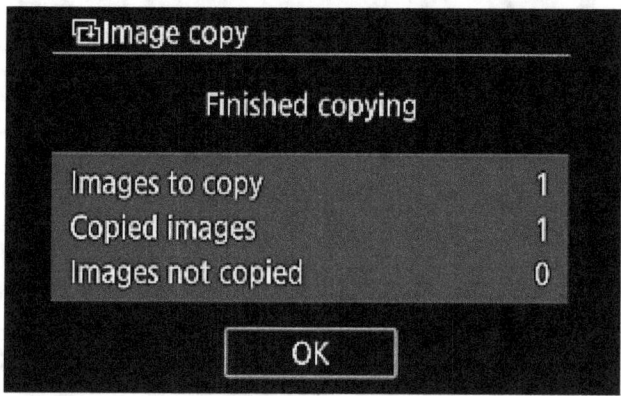

Print Order

The Playback 2 page features two options, one of which is related to DPOF (Digital Print Order Format). This file format allows you to specify which photos on your memory card to print and the quantity of each. If you have a printer that reads memory cards, you can use this feature. Additionally, photo labs can read your memory card to fulfill your print requests.

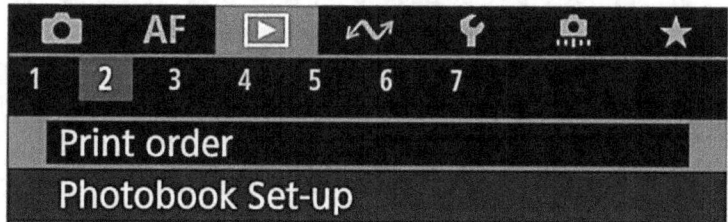

Once you've selected the photos for DPOF printing, you can either print them at home or take your memory card to a digital lab that can read the print order and produce the copies you want. Note that you can't order prints of RAW files. To place a DPOF print order, follow these steps:

1. Select "Print Order" and press the Setup button.
2. The screen for placing a Print Order will appear. Use the arrow keys to highlight "Setup," then press the SET button.

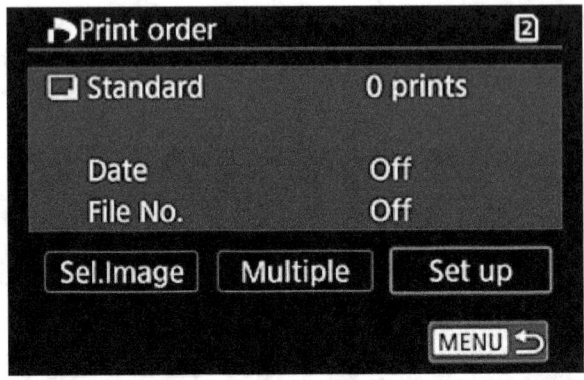

- For the Print Type, you can choose between Standard, Index/Thumbnails, or Both. You can also decide whether to include the Date or File Number on the printouts, but keep in mind that you can only choose one of these options at a time. The same print type will apply to all selected images. To return to the Print Order screen, press the MENU button.
- You can choose between "Sel. Image" (selecting individual photos) or "Multiple."
- For "Sel. Image," use the navigation tools to browse through your photos, and press the SET button to select which ones to print. You can view images as thumbnails by pressing the Thumbnail/Zoom In button and return to single-image view by pressing the Magnify/Zoom Out button.
- For "Multiple," you can select a range of images, mark all items in a folder, delete items in a folder, mark all items on the card, or delete all items on the card. To select a range or group, press the SET button. To go back to the print order screen, press the MENU button.
- If you choose to select individual photos, you can specify between one to ninety-nine copies of the same image. Once an image is selected, use the up and down buttons to set the number of copies. For index images, you can only choose whether to include them; the number of copies cannot be adjusted. Press the SET button to confirm your selections. To return to the Print Order screen when finished, press the MENU button.
- If your camera is connected to a PictBridge printer, a new option called "Print" will appear on the Print Order page. Before you start printing, you may need to adjust the Paper Settings. Another way to exit the Print Order page is by pressing the picture release button on your camera. Ensure both the printer and camera are turned off before removing the memory card and inserting it into the printer, store booth, or digital minilab that supports PictBridge.

RAW Processing

- After selecting "Select Images" or "Select Range," navigate through your RAW files using the QCD-1. You can press the SET button to choose a specific image or a range of images you want to convert.

- Once you've selected the images, the screen will prompt you to confirm your choices. If you're converting a range, ensure that you have marked the correct images before proceeding.
- After confirming your selection, you can choose the output format for your converted files—either JPEG or HEIF. The camera will process the selected RAW files and create new images in your chosen format, while leaving the original RAW files untouched.
- Once the conversion is complete, the camera will display a summary of the process. You can then view your newly created JPEG or HEIF files in the Playback mode, while the original RAW files remain available for future editing.
- To exit the menu, simply press the MENU button or navigate back to the Playback 3 page to continue using other features.

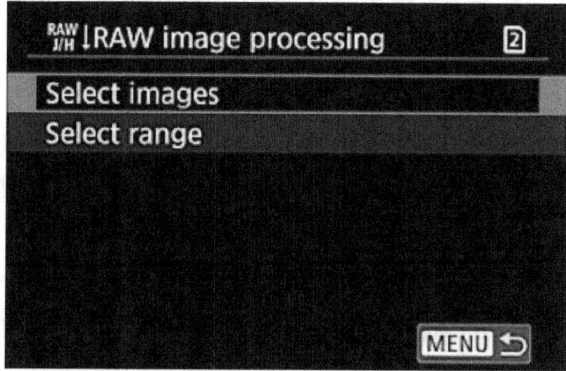

- After pressing the Q button, you'll see options for processing the selected image. You can choose to convert it to JPEG or HEIF.
- Confirm your choice by pressing the SET button. The camera will then process the image and create a new file in the selected format.
- Once the conversion is complete, you'll receive a notification on the screen. You can view the newly created file in the Playback mode while the original RAW file remains intact.
- To exit the menu, press the MENU button or navigate back to the Playback 3 page to continue with other options.

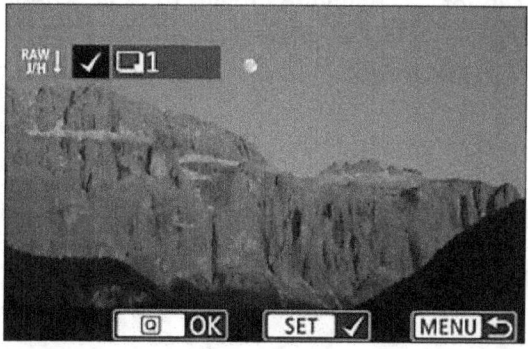

- Once you've selected the images to process, you can confirm your choice by pressing the SET button.
- The camera will begin processing the selected RAW files based on your settings. You'll see a progress indicator while the JPEG or HEIF files are being created.
- After processing, the camera will notify you that the new files have been saved successfully. You can then choose to view the processed images or return to the Playback menu.
- If you want to process more images, repeat the steps as needed. You can also return to the main menu or turn off the camera when you're finished.
- To ensure your settings are applied consistently, you can save any custom settings as a preset for future use. Check the camera's menu for options related to saving presets.
- Finally, remember that the original RAW files remain unchanged, allowing you to reprocess them later if desired.

In-Camera Upscaling

When using the upscaling feature on your JPEG or HEIF files, keep the following in mind:

Upscaling Process:

1. **Double the Pixels**: You can double the pixel count in both horizontal and vertical dimensions, effectively quadrupling the total pixel count.
2. **Applicable Files**: This feature is available for JPEGs or HEIFs captured at size L.

Important Considerations:

- **Processing Time**: The upscaling process can take a considerable amount of time, so be patient.
- **Shooting Restrictions**: You won't be able to take new photos until the upscaling process is complete.
- **Limitations**:
    - Upscaling cannot be applied to images that have been cropped or have an aspect ratio set to anything other than Full-frame.
    - RAW files and images taken with other camera models (not the EOS R5 Mark II) are not eligible.
    - Photos that have already been enlarged, cropped, or modified through editing software also cannot be upscaled.

Quality Considerations:

- Be aware that the results of upscaling may not always meet expectations. The quality of the final image can vary based on the original file's resolution and content.

By keeping these points in mind, you can effectively use the upscaling feature while understanding its limitations and processing requirements.

Resize

To resize images using your camera, follow these steps:

Resizing Images

1. **Access Playback Menu**: Select the resize option from the Playback menu.
2. **Navigate Through Photos**: Use the touch screen or arrow keys to scroll through the images. Only images that can be resized (large, medium, or small JPEG/HEIF) will be displayed. Note that some formats, like Small 2 or RAW images, cannot be resized.
3. **Select an Image**: Press the SET button to choose a photo you want to resize.
4. **Choose Size**: A pop-up will appear with resizing options:
    - **Medium (M)**: 3984 x 2656 pixels (11 megapixels)
    - **Small 1 (S1)**: 2976 x 1984 pixels (3.8 megapixels)
    - **Small 2 (S2)**: 2400 x 1600 pixels (3.8 megapixels)
5. **Confirm Your Choice**: Use the QCD-1 dial to select the desired size, then confirm your selection.

By following these steps, you can easily resize images to fit your needs while keeping quality in mind.

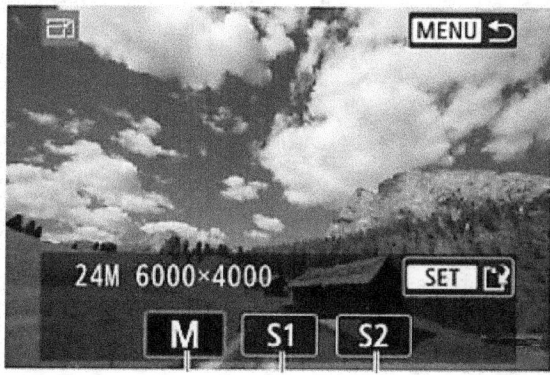

- You can't enlarge a picture beyond its current size; for example, you cannot save a Medium-sized image as a Large one.
- To save the image as a new file, click SET, then confirm your selection by clicking OK on the following screen. If you prefer not to create a new copy, you can click Cancel to exit the app. The image will remain unchanged from the previous version.
- Similar to other Playback menus, the Quick Control menu that appears when you press the Q button allows you to adjust the size of any picture.

Cropping

Simply select a picture and press the SET button to use it. Choose the image you want to crop with the QCD-1. After selecting your picture, press SET to view the screen.

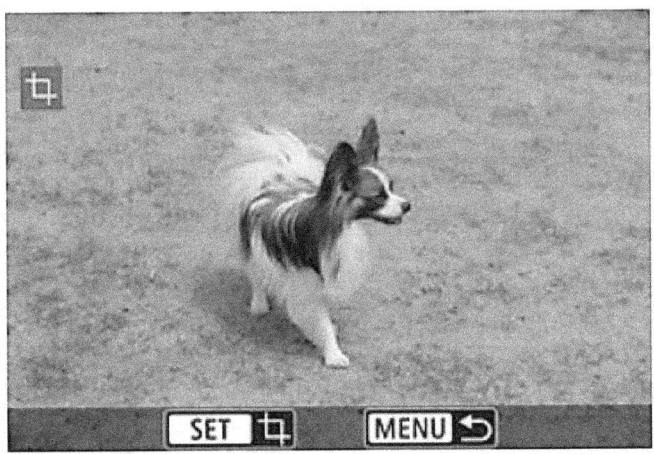

On the cropping screen, you can use several tools:

Select Adjustment: The top row features function buttons for making changes. Turn the QCD-1 to highlight any of the following options:

- **Change Crop View:** Adjust the size of the crop. Select this option, then use the QCD-2 to enlarge or reduce the green cutting frame. You can also move the frame around the image using the multi-controller joystick.
- **Straighten the Image:** Correct any tilt. When you select this option and press SET, a grid will overlay your picture. You can adjust the tilt by up to 10 degrees. The QCD-1 will gradually change direction as you turn it. For finer adjustments (0.5 degrees at a time), tap the lines on the top row of the monitor. The grid will help align your image. To finalize your adjustment, press SET.

- **Change Aspect Ratio:** You can cycle through aspect ratios for the cutting frame, including 3:2, 16:9, 4:3, 1:1, 2:3, 9:16, and 3:4, by repeatedly pressing SET while this option is selected.

To save your edited image as a new file, select this option, press SET, and then press SET again. Your original picture will be preserved in full.

Slide Show

The SlideShow feature allows you to view movies or images consecutively without needing to switch between them manually, making it more enjoyable and efficient. To use this feature, simply select Slide Show from the Playback menu. During playback, you can pause the slideshow by pressing the SET button, which lets you examine a picture more closely. Additionally, you can press the INFO button to adjust the amount of information displayed for each image. Both buttons are located on the top panel. For instance, if you want to evaluate the exposure of several pictures, you might want to view both the images and their corresponding histograms.

Here's how to prepare your slideshow:

1. When you enter Slide Show mode, all pictures on the card will be automatically selected. If this is your preference, proceed to step three. If you want to choose specific images, go to step two.
2. You can filter the images displayed in your slideshow based on various criteria, such as Rating, Date, Folder, Protected status, and File Type (RAW, RAW+JPEG, JPEG, or Movie).
3. To start configuring the slideshow, press the Setup button.

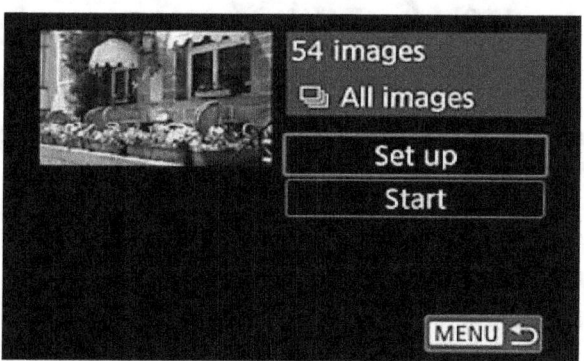

To create a screen showing a list of playback times, select Display Time and press the SET button. You can set different play times for each picture: options include 1, 2, 3, 5, 10, or 20 seconds. Press the SET button again to confirm your selection.

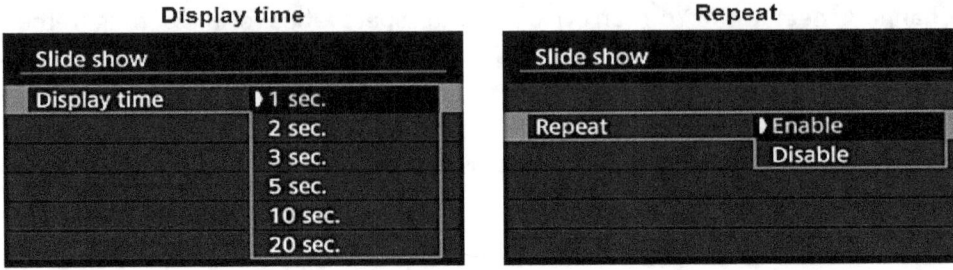

- To enable the slideshow to repeat continuously, press the SET button and the Enable button simultaneously.
- To exit the Setup, press and hold the MENU button.
- Select Start and press the SET button to begin the slideshow. If you want to end the show you just set up, press the MENU button instead. Keep in mind that the size of the picture file will affect how long each slide is displayed.
- To play the slideshow again, press the SET button. Pressing the INFO button will show you different information screens for still images. The camera will not turn off automatically after a period of inactivity; playback will continue. You can adjust the volume of the videos using the Main dial. As the movie plays or pauses, you can navigate to the next slide by turning the QCD-1, where these settings are located.

VR Preview

When you use lenses compatible with the EOS VR System, you can preview how VR content will appear on VR displays directly on the camera screen.

Setting Image Search Conditions

You can select which images to display based on the keywords you used for your search. Once you've set the search terms, you can only play back and view the images that match those criteria. After reviewing a picture, you have the option to protect it, rate it, play a slideshow, delete it, and perform other actions.

Resuming from Previous Playback

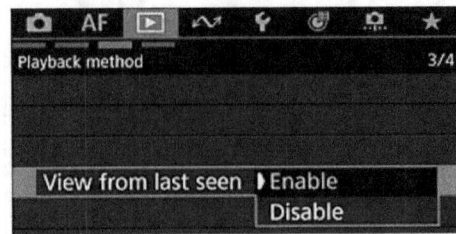

- **Enable:** If you haven't just finished shooting, playback will begin with the last picture shown if this option is turned on.
- **Disable:** The last picture you took is played back when you turn the camera back on.

View from Last Seen

This feature dictates how playback behaves when you restart and browse through your images. If enabled, playback will start with the most recently viewed picture during your review. However, if playback is turned off, the most recent photo taken by the camera will be displayed.

Since I frequently take photos, I usually keep this setting off to immediately see my latest pictures. However, if you were reviewing a large number of photos—perhaps while cropping or resizing—you might prefer to return to the last picture you were focusing on.

Magnification (Approximate)

This parameter allows you to select both the starting point and the initial magnification for the zoomed view during playback. To determine the best starting magnification for your lens, consider how often you closely examine your photos. You can choose from the following magnification options:

- **Magnification Levels:** You can select from three options:
    - **2X, 4X, 8X, or 10X (centered on the frame):** Choosing any of these will display the first zoomed view at that level, centered in the frame.
    - **Actual Size (from a selected point):** If the picture is auto-focused, it will center on that focus point. If manually focused, it will be near the edge, with the focus point at 100% zoom.
    - **Same as Last Magnification (centered):** This will retain the magnification level you used previously and center it in the image.
- **Magnified Position:** This sets where the picture will first be zoomed in. You can choose to start from the Center or the Focus Point.
- **Maintain Position:** While you can move around within the image, this feature prevents you from losing your place in the frame. It allows you to compare the same part of an image—like a person's face—across multiple photos taken in succession.

Blur/Out-of-Focus Image Detection

This feature can automatically detect if a JPEG/HEIF photo is blurry or out of focus, primarily by analyzing faces in the images. You can establish a specific threshold for blurriness or focus loss, and the system will sort, save, or rate all photos according to that criterion.

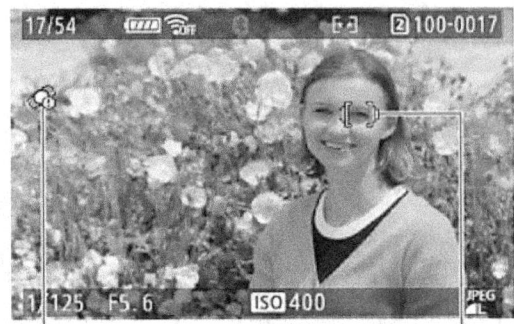

Displaying the Highlight Alert

You can configure the video screen to highlight overexposed areas by making them blink. For improved results, try setting the exposure compensation to a negative value and then re-evaluate. This adjustment will provide better detail in the flashing areas, ensuring they are displayed accurately.

Playback Information Display

Pressing the INFO button during playback allows you to cycle through three display options: a clean screen with no information, a screen showing basic details, and a more detailed screen featuring multiple data panels related to shooting information. This feature lets you customize which screen appears when you press the INFO button.

To add or remove displays, follow these steps:

1. Access the menu. A screen will appear, showing a checkbox next to each option. There are ten options available for the R5 Mark II.
2. Select the panels you want to display with the INFO button and press the SET button to check them. To hide a display, choose the option with a checkmark next to it and press the SET button again. Remember, you can still view unchecked panels by scrolling down on the Shooting Information page using the multi-controller.

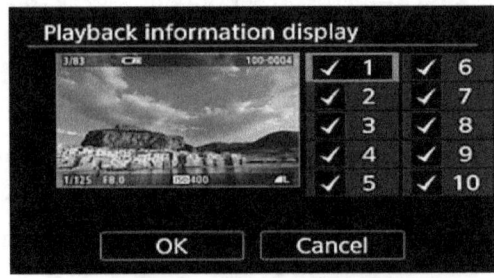

- You can select multiple options. The No Information screen will only appear during playback if none of the other options are selected.
- In the lower-left corner of the Playback Information Display screen, highlight OK and press the SET button to complete the setup.
- When the Shooting Information screen is displayed during playback, use the multi-controller joystick to navigate between the available options. To view the Shooting Information screen, simply press the INFO button.

AF Point Disp.

If you select the Enable option, the AF point(s) used for focusing will be highlighted in red. This is particularly useful if automated AF point selection was employed, as it will draw your attention to multiple focus areas.

Playback Grid

While the video plays, you can choose to turn off the grid entirely or overlay a grid in options such as 3x3, 6x4, or 3x3 with diagonal lines. To access these settings, go to the Shooting 9 menu and select Shooting Information Display. This will allow you to see the same grid options while you're shooting.

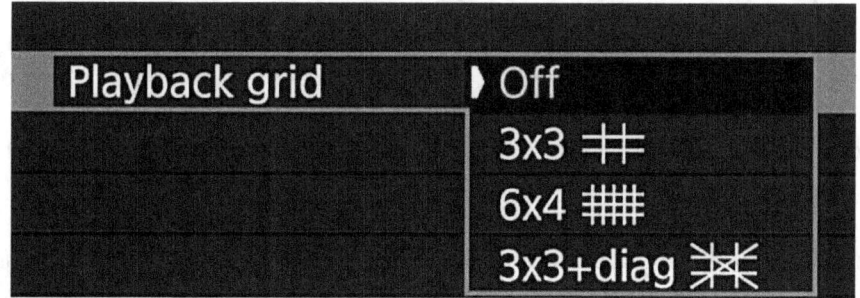

Movie Play Count

This setting allows you to choose whether to display the Time Code, which serves as an exact positioning marker, or the movie's recording and playback time (also referred to as Rec Time) on the screen. You can adjust the Movie Play Count option in either the Movie Shooting menu or this menu, and changes will take effect immediately across both. Additionally, the Movie Shooting menus offer more options for Time Codes.

Conclusion

The Canon EOS R5 Mark II is a remarkable leap forward in the evolution of mirrorless cameras, offering a host of cutting-edge features that cater to both professional photographers and enthusiasts alike. Building on the strengths of its predecessor, the R5 Mark II introduces game-changing advancements in virtually every aspect of performance, making it a versatile powerhouse in the world of imaging.

One of the most exciting upgrades is its groundbreaking pre-capture shooting feature, which allows photographers to capture key moments even before the shutter is pressed, enhancing the chances of getting that perfect shot. This is complemented by the advanced Eye Control AF, a revolutionary autofocus system that offers unprecedented precision and responsiveness, especially when tracking fast-moving subjects or focusing on minute details. The result is an intuitive, faster, and more accurate shooting experience, perfect for photographers who demand both speed and precision.

For hybrid shooters, the R5 Mark II delivers seamless transitions between still photography and video modes, making it ideal for those who need to effortlessly switch between disciplines without missing a beat. Its improved image stabilization also ensures crisp, stable shots, even in challenging handheld conditions, expanding creative possibilities and opening the door to a variety of shooting styles and environments.

Battery life has also seen a significant upgrade, allowing for longer shooting sessions without the constant worry of recharging—an essential feature for those long shoots or travel photography. Additionally, the camera's robust weatherproofing makes it a reliable choice for outdoor adventures or shooting in harsh conditions, offering peace of mind even in unpredictable environments.

Another standout feature is the customizability of the R5 Mark II, allowing photographers to tailor the camera's settings to their unique shooting style. From button layouts to personalized menus, this flexibility enhances workflow and ensures that every photographer can make the most of their gear, whether shooting fast-paced action, intricate portraits, or expansive landscapes.

With its exceptional performance across a broad range of shooting scenarios, from sports and wildlife to portraiture and fine art photography, the Canon EOS R5 Mark II stands out as a versatile and effective tool for creative expression. Its combination of speed, accuracy, and image quality makes it an excellent choice for anyone eager to expand their skills and push the boundaries of their photography. Whether you're a seasoned professional or an ambitious amateur, the R5 Mark II empowers you to capture stunning, high-quality images with ease and confidence, elevating your creative vision to new heights.

In conclusion, the Canon EOS R5 Mark II is not just a camera—it's an investment in creativity, innovation, and versatility. Whether you're documenting fast-moving action, crafting beautiful portraits, or exploring new video possibilities, this camera is a powerful ally for photographers of all levels, offering everything you need to capture life's moments in extraordinary detail.

www.ingramcontent.com/pod-product-compliance
Lightning Source LLC
Chambersburg PA
CBHW062319220526
45469CB00008B/2566